Creating Chinese Urbanism

'The rapid redevelopment of Chinese cities, along with the vast expansion of geographic and social mobility, have almost completely erased the collectivist urban neighbourhoods typical of the Mao era. In this deeply researched book, Fulong Wu vividly documents the varieties of newly emergent urban communities and provides a conceptual framework for understanding a new and distinctive Chinese urbanism.'

Andrew G. Walder, author of *China Under Mao*

'Fulong Wu grapples with the complexities and contradictions of social change in urban China – state-centred but creating new opportunities for individualism, disrupting traditional village and neighbourhood social relations but generating new forms of association. He shows the relevance but also the limited reach of general models like market transition, postcolonialism, and neoliberalism. Like an ethnographer, his approach is to understand social relations at the ground level, working upwards from that vantage point to understand the ongoing Chinese urban revolution on its own terms.'

John R. Logan, Professor of Sociology, Brown University

'This book provides a novel, insightful and inspirational interpretation of the emerging state-society-space relationship in China where an urban revolution is taking place at a scale and speed unparalleled in the world. Theoretically informed and empirically grounded, the book takes us to embark upon a fascinating journey travelling from Chinese workplace (*danwei*) to neighbourhoods, urban communities, and urban villages so as to unveil a phenomenal and restless landscape of greater urbanism and state-centred governance. A path-breaking contribution to the burgeoning literature on global urbanism in general and China's new urban social geography in particular.'

George C.S. Lin, Chair Professor of Geography, University of Hong Kong

'In this masterful study of residential neighbourhoods across regions, generations and classes in China today, Wu successfully convinces us that China's contemporary socio-political transformation is ultimately an urban transformation. This book is one of the most illuminating reads in the last decade on Chinese urbanism.'

You-tien Hsing, Professor of Geography and Director of Global Studies, UC Berkeley

'As observers continue to grapple with the significance of China's urban revolution, this book offers an innovative conceptual framework for thinking about the meanings of this revolution from the perspective of urban neighbourhoods with different housing forms. Richly illustrated, and drawing upon decades of research and observations from one of the most prominent and prolific scholars of the contemporary Chinese city, *Creating Chinese Urbanism* locates the essence of China's urban revolution in the passing of longstanding modes of social relations and their replacement with new institutions of governance in which the state led-urbanization remakes the nature of state power itself.'

Mark W. Frazier, New School for Social Research

'In this pathbreaking study of the diversity and heterogeneity of neighbourhood life in urban China, Wu Fulong asks readers to reflect on the seemingly simple question what distinguishes the rural from the urban. But rather than foregrounding paired comparisons of the material conditions and built environments, Wu focuses on comparing social relationships within four types of urban residential areas: alleyway or courtyard neighbourhoods built before 1949, socialist era workplace apartment blocks, peri-urban villages now physically incorporated within cities, and suburban gated communities. And rather than foregrounding contemporary debates about agglomeration and capital accumulation, Wu asks readers to concentrate on the degree to which grassroots sociality and social relationships have departed from Fei Xiaotong's concept of differential modes of association (差序格局 *chaxugeju*) developed during fieldwork in rural China during the 1930s. Thus, for Wu the "fading of rurality is urbanization" (p.231) and the absence of a placed based moral order marks entry to city life. A remarkable, original and bold interpretation of China's recent warp speed urbanization.'

Deborah Davis, Professor Emerita of Sociology, Yale University, USA

Creating Chinese Urbanism

Urban revolution and governance change

Fulong Wu

First published in 2022 by
UCL Press
University College London
Gower Street
London WC1E 6BT

Available to download free: www.uclpress.co.uk

Text © Author, 2022
Images © Author and copyright holders named in captions, 2022

The author has asserted his rights under the Copyright, Designs and Patents Act 1988 to be identified as the author of this work.

A CIP catalogue record for this book is available from The British Library.

Any third-party material in this book is not covered by the book's Creative Commons licence. Details of the copyright ownership and permitted use of third-party material is given in the image (or extract) credit lines. If you would like to reuse any third-party material not covered by the book's Creative Commons licence, you will need to obtain permission directly from the copyright owner.

This book is published under a Creative Commons Attribution-Non-Commercial 4.0 International licence (CC BY-NC 4.0), https://creativecommons.org/licenses/by-nc/4.0/. This licence allows you to share and adapt the work for non-commercial use providing attribution is made to the author and publisher (but not in any way that suggests that they endorse you or your use of the work) and any changes are indicated. Attribution should include the following information:

Wu, F. 2022. *Creating Chinese Urbanism: Urban revolution and governance change*. London: UCL Press. https://doi.org/10.14324/111.9781800083332

Further details about Creative Commons licences are available at https://creativecommons.org/licenses/

ISBN: 978-1-80008-335-6 (Hbk)
ISBN: 978-1-80008-334-9 (Pbk)
ISBN: 978-1-80008-333-2 (PDF)
ISBN: 978-1-80008-336-3 (epub)
DOI: https://doi.org/10.14324/111.9781800083332

Contents

List of figures	viii
List of tables	xvi
Preface	xvii
Acknowledgements	xx
Introduction: leaving the soil	1
1 Changing residential landscape: a new urban social geography	23
2 The end of (neo-)traditionalism	58
3 Transient space with a new moral order	117
4 Residential enclosure without private governance	172
5 Rethinking urban China in an urban debate	219
Conclusion: a visible state emerging from urban revolution	247
References	263
Index	277

List of figures

1.1 Shanghai Pudong new area, showing the Lujiazui Financial and Trade Zone, which symbolises China's ascent in the global economy. Taken in 2008. 27
1.2 Fashion and foreign brands symbolise a new era of consumption and consumerism. Daning Plaza in former Zhabei District, the low-end of Shanghai, has totally transformed the area. Taken in 2017. 30
1.3 The lane houses in Zuopu Road, Shanghai, showing the high-density residential neighbourhoods. The original quality of the housing shown in the photo is comparatively higher than usual lane houses. The multiple occupancies of lane houses further increase the population density, making a crowded urban world. Taken in 2016. 31
1.4 The staff housing in No. 1 Village, Xi'an Jiaotong University. This part was constructed in the late 1970s but it deteriorated quite significantly as shown in the photo. Taken in 2016. 32
1.5 The work-unit compound of Baiwanzhuang, Beijing, before the area was demolished in 2014. The quality of housing was relatively higher as it was for the staff living quarters of the central government ministries. The layout was influenced by the Soviet super neighbourhood block. Taken in 2014. 32
1.6 An urban village, Zhucun (Pearl Village) in Guangzhou. The photo shows how new self-built rental housing maximises the use of space within individual housing plots. The communal area is under-maintained. Taken in 2012. 34
1.7 A dormitory for rural migrant workers, by private factory owners, in Shantou, Guangdong province. The photo shows crowded living conditions, standardised structure, and strict management as all windows are protected by safety nets. Taken in 2013. 35

1.8 An ordinary commodity housing estate in Tianjin Sino-Singapore Eco-city. The area was previously low land in an industrial area. The photo shows some modest security and the gate. Taken in 2014. 36

1.9 Informal gathering of villagers playing cards in Xiaozhou Village, Guangzhou. Such leisure activities are also widely seen in old and traditional urban neighbourhoods, and so is dancing in public squares. Taken in 2010. 41

1.10 A small city near the seaside, Ningde in Fujian province. The city used to be at a 'remote' frontier due to the lack of a railway. The photo shows that the city was just being connected by high-speed rail, crossing the bay. Taken in 2014. 47

1.11 An old rural village, Xiaba Village in Dongguan. The villagers left this village and relocated to the adjacent new village. The old village was renovated while some original features have been carefully kept for artists and creative industries, as well as tourists. Taken in 2012. 54

1.12 The new area of Xiaba Village in Dongguan. The living quality is much improved with spacious villas for the original rural villagers. In contrast to crowded urban villages, this new rural village, built by the farmers themselves, indicates economic benefits to farmers in the fast-urbanising area in the Pearl River Delta. Taken in 2012. 54

2.1 The deterioration of *longtang* (alleyway housing) in Shanghai. This lane, near Tiantong Road in Hongkou District, remained a densely populated area until the early 2000s and has entirely disappeared since urban redevelopment. Taken in the late 1990s. 59

2.2 Subdivision of single-family lane houses into multiple occupancies, making the courtyard extremely crowded. The photo shows many electric meters for this lane house near Tianjin Road, Shanghai. Taken in the late 1990s. 59

2.3 Alleyway housing near Tianjin Road, Shanghai. This area is just behind Nanjing Road (the high street). Although the density is very high, the area is relatively well maintained and has not been demolished. In 2021, this area was included in the new phase of redevelopment. Taken in the late 1990s. 63

2.4 A family dinner with multiple generations in alleyway housing in Tiantong Road, Shanghai. Taken in 2002. 65

2.5 The shared corridor for multiple tap-water basins near Tianjin Road, Shanghai. Kitchens were also shared, often in the courtyard corner. Taken in the late 1990s. 66

2.6 Alleyway housing near the Xintiandi area was demolished as Shanghai entered a property boom in the early 2000s. Developer-driven redevelopment intensified housing demolition and conflicts. Taken in 2003. 68

2.7 Caoyang Workers' New Village in Shanghai, constructed between 1951 and 1977. This terraced housing with relatively lower density compared with crowded alleyway housing areas was distributed to industrial workers nearby. Taken in 2014. 71

2.8 The entrance of the Fifth Village, Nanjing. The original was replaced by a new gate to control cars because of the lack of parking space inside the residential 'micro-district'. Taken in 2014. 73

2.9 The southern gate of the inner compound reserved for work-unit staff in the Fifth Village, Nanjing. Although the gate is not strictly controlled, it is served with a security guard room. This rather rudimentary 'gated community' reveals the attempt to maintain social order through management rather than neighbourhood self-governance in an urbanising mobile society in China. Taken in 1997. 74

2.10 Signs of deterioration in the Fifth Village, Nanjing. The original internal sewer pipes were blocked and an external duct had to be built. Housing privatisation does not enhance estate maintenance but rather has led to the withdrawal of workplaces' responsibility for maintenance. Taken in 2014. 76

2.11 The reconstruction of courtyard housing in Nanchizi, Beijing. The redevelopment was quite significant as the project also replicated the original courtyard housing and hence is less seen as *hutong* heritage preservation. Taken in 2004. 78

2.12 The redevelopment of alleyway housing into an entertainment and shopping district in Xintiandi, Shanghai. The photo shows the reconstruction of 'stone portal gate' housing into a cafeteria, bars, restaurants and boutique shops. Taken in 2003. 80

2.13 The traditional *shikumen* style housing in the Xintiandi area, Shanghai. The *shikumen* housing has been carefully refurbished since the late 1990s. The photo shows the 'stone portal gates' leading to an internal courtyard. The style is actually a hybrid

2.14 The clubhouse and core area of Xintiandi, Shanghai. The photo shows that as early as the early 2000s the area had become a popular and fashionable place in Shanghai. Taken in 2005. 82
2.15 Besides the low-rise *shikumen* bars and restaurants, Xintiandi also built high-rise shopping malls and office buildings. The photo shows the Xintiandi Plaza. Taken in 2019. 83
2.16 Chuangzhi Tiandi, Shanghai, is a mixed-use area with smart office buildings and technology firms. The place aims to build a 'knowledge and innovation community', with a brand of Tiandi. Taken in 2014. 84
2.17 Tianzhifang, Shanghai, is another alleyway housing neighbourhood turned into an arts, creative and entertainment district. The photo shows small restaurants in Tianzhifang. Compared with Xintiandi, Tianzhifang is more 'ordinary' and less elite. Taken in 2011. 85
2.18 The conversion of stone portal gate housing to artists' workshops and display rooms in Tianzhifang. The redevelopment of Tianzhifang has been driven more by smaller developers rather than as a single mega project. Taken in 2011. 86
2.19 Yongqingfang, Guangzhou, has been renovated from a traditional inner-city neighbourhood into a tourist and small business district through 'micro or incremental redevelopment'. Taken in 2018. 88
2.20 The central area of Huajin residential district in Wuhan has been renovated as a neighbourhood incremental redevelopment project. The project was designed by a team at Wuhan University and involves neighbourhood participation. Taken in 2019. 94
2.21 The community (*shequ*) centre of the Fifth Village, Nanjing. The photo shows the gradual development of social services into a professionalised structure at the neighbourhood level. Taken in 2014. 97
2.22 The courtyard housing has deteriorated into a crowded residential area with the influx of rural migrants and private

LIST OF FIGURES xi

	rentals. The photo shows self-construction inside a courtyard in central Beijing. Taken in 2004.	101
2.23	Staff housing tenants and municipal housing residents do not have much interaction. The photo shows a resident in the inner compound of staff housing in the Fifth Village, Nanjing. Taken in 2002.	102
2.24	The office building of Hongkou SoHo in the Hongkou district, Shanghai. The remaining alleyway housing is disappearing due to the new wave of urban redevelopment. Taken in 2016.	105
3.1	The urbanised village of Hancunhe in southern Beijing. The villagers built not only their villas but also a central square for tourism. They captured the opportunities of the construction materials business and informal housing markets in Beijing. Taken in 2004.	125
3.2.	'Small property rights housing' in Hancunhe village, Beijing. Without a property deed from the government, these properties only have village-certified ownership documents. The informal housing, however, cannot be detected from its appearance. Taken in 2004.	126
3.3	'Small property rights housing' in the northern outskirts of Beijing. The photo shows the scale and formal appearance of the informal housing built by villagers. The standard, judged from the style, is lower and more modest compared with 'commodity housing'. Informal housing construction has been widespread. Taken in 2010.	132
3.4	Garment workshops in 'Little Hubei', Guangzhou. The ground floor of village buildings is usually used by workshops and warehouses, while migrant workers may live on the upper floors. The photo shows a production function of urban villages. Taken in 2010.	132
3.5	The entrance of Tangjialing village, Beijing. The photo shows a booming village at the time of demolition. The area had many markets and restaurants, due to the agglomeration of IT migrants. Taken in 2010.	137
3.6	The alleyway of Tangjialing village, Beijing, before its demolition. The photo shows that the residential density is generally lower than in self-extended urban villages in southern China. Taken in 2010.	138
3.7	Purpose-built rental housing in Tangjialing, Beijing. The village lent the land to small developers to construct standard	

	rental housing which appeared quite popular owing to the low cost and better conditions. Taken in 2010.	139
3.8	The decent living conditions of purpose-built apartments constructed by small developers in Tangjialing, Beijing. The photo shows how natural light is introduced into the corridors. Taken in 2010.	140
3.9	The main road leading to Tangjialing village, Beijing, at the time of demolition. Banners show the campaign to 'vacate' the urban village, as villagers affected were mostly accommodated in nearby Tangjialing new town. Taken in 2010.	141
3.10	The demolition of Tangjialing village, Beijing. The demolition and redevelopment were rather swiftly completed owing to the programme of affordable housing provision in Beijing, which is largely for registered Beijing residents. Taken in 2010.	143
3.11	The small entrance leading to a large urbanised informal housing area in Gaojiabang, Shanghai. Taken in 2010.	145
3.12	The low-rise informal housing of Gaojiabang, Shanghai. The photo shows rather modest self-built housing and redevelopment. Most houses had only two floors in the place where the former village was partially absorbed into the urban fabric and institutions. Taken in 2010.	147
3.13	After many informal houses were demolished, some original self-extension became visible. The building was dangerously increased to four and a half floors. The original ground floor house was still visible and had a rather weak foundation and structure. Taken in 2013.	148
3.14	Two images from Google show the disappearance of Gaojiabang, Shanghai. The central area of the photo shows Gaojiabang. In the 2021 image the site still appears vacant, while a nearby informal housing area was transformed into commodity housing estates (left corner). (a) captured in 2011; (b) captured in 2021.	150
3.15	Reconstructed ancestor hall in Liede village, Guangzhou. The redevelopment of the village has been extensively studied, owing to its exceedingly high plot ratio after reconstruction and its central location along the Pearl River. Taken in 2010.	154
4.1	The magnificent decorative gate of Beijing Sun City, Beijing, mimicking neoclassical styles. This neighbourhood, however, is a rather 'ordinary' commodity housing estate. Taken in 2004.	180

4.2 An upper-market gated community, Garden of Kindred Spirits, Wenzhou. This gated estate mainly consists of villas and was once the most expensive area in Wenzhou. Taken in 2014 by Tingting Lu. 181
4.3 Housing estates near Hongkou Football Stadium, Shanghai. The photo shows the high-rise buildings of the City Garden estate built in the mid 2000s. Taken in 2017. 185
4.4 A small-gated estate, Liulin Court, among many large gated communities near Hongkou Football Stadium, Shanghai. The photo together with the overview of the City Garden estate shows a quite spatially subdivided residential structure in Chinese cities. Taken in 2009. 185
4.5 A rather exotic style as seen in China, but quite 'ordinary' detached houses in North America, in the 'Orange County' estate, Beijing. Taken in 2004. 187
4.6 The highly decorative gate of 'Orange County', Beijing. The gated community strives to use the gate to symbolise its high-quality housing and residential environment. Taken in 2004. 188
4.7 The gated housing estate in Thames Town, near Songjiang in Shanghai. The estate together with the 'new town' aims to follow the style of a British market town. Taken in 2010. 189
4.8 The gated community is often associated with new town development. Many are built into high-rise form rather than detached or semi-detached houses, owing to the land cost. The photo shows one in Jiading new town, northern Shanghai. Taken in 2013. 190
4.9 Neoclassical decoration in the compound of a gated community in Guangzhou. The compound is also carefully landscaped. This, however, is not at ground level but is a platform. Underneath are two floors of shopping and car parking spaces. Taken in 2000. 191
4.10 The highly decorated lobby of an apartment building in the gated community in Guangzhou shown in the previous photo. Taken in 2000. 192
4.11 A professionally managed upper-market housing estate in Beijing. The estate has spacious garden and villa-style housing. Taken in 2003. 204
4.12 A gated housing estate, Southern Lake Garden, in Shantou. The estate has a reasonable density compared with another high-density estate in the same city. Taken in 2013. 211

4.13 A high-density housing estate, Star Lake City, in Shantou. The plot ratio is much higher than Southern Lake Garden. These two photos show that gated commodity housing is now a mainstream product with varying densities and qualities. Taken in 2013. 211
5.1 The area near Xintiandi, Shanghai, showing an upgrading process in central Shanghai. Taken in 2019. 220
5.2 The dilapidated central area near the 'Little Park' in Shantou, showing a different trajectory from Xintiandi. Inner-city decline is rather rare in China. Taken in 2014. 221
5.3 A rural village left vacant near the convention centre in Wuxi new town. This area was originally planned for Wuxi eco-town. The place is not far from Kaixiangong village in Wujiang, also near the Taihu Lake, which is the setting for Fei Xiaotong's book *From the Soil*. The photo shows the disappearance of *Rural China*. Taken in 2017. 232
5.4 A private club near Xintiandi, Shanghai. The club, on the upper floor of a jewellery store with the same owner, has become a venue for fashion and business. Taken in 2019. 241
5.5 Taking a photo and strolling in Daning Park, Shanghai. Near the park are new commodity housing estates. The area is being upgraded with large shopping malls and green amenities. The scene shows everyday life in urban China. Taken in 2018. 242
5.6 Dancing in a public park, Shanghai. Dancing in public spaces is an ordinary event. Owing to the high-density living environment, residents tend to use spare space for exercise, less for socialising and club formation. The elderly prefer free public space rather than commercially run gyms and clubs. Taken in 2019. 243
5.7 A club, as the shop sign reads, for gymnastics, yoga and coffee. The commercially run club is becoming very popular with the Chinese middle class who are increasingly aware of health and a healthy lifestyle while facing high work pressure and busy urban life. This photo can be seen in comparison with the earlier photo of dancing in parks. Taken in 2019. 244

List of tables

1.1　The historical stages of urban redevelopment in China　49
3.1　Facilities in urban villages in Beijing, Shanghai
　　　and Guangzhou (in percentages)　123

Preface

Geography is a science subject in China. Students of Urban Planning in Geography in the 1980s had one thing in common: they did not take Geography or any humanities subject for their university entrance examination. Interested in physics, but for leisure reading, by chance I found a small book, *Rural China*, by Fei Xiaotong. Fei was an internationally renowned anthropologist and sociologist. At that time he was striving to re-establish Sociology in Chinese universities after its earlier abolition. But I did not know any of this. To me, the book, only about 100 pages in Chinese, is appealing because it provides a grand overview of the characteristics of Chinese society, offering synthetic narratives of complex social phenomena.

The 1980s, a liberal era in China, saw an intellectual renaissance. The discourse of Western market economics was introduced, though aggressive marketisation occurred a decade later. Disillusioned by the Cultural Revolution, the whole of society reflected on its root causes and on the nature of Chinese society. Based on my own experiences of life in the two urban worlds described in this book – alleyway neighbourhoods and work-unit campuses – I could not help but feel their resemblance to traditional societies. Instead of thinking of the order as externally imposed, I aimed to identify the foundation – an endogenously generated social order.

I began to think about *danwei* (workplace) as a basic social environment. But at that time I did not know of the publication of Andrew Walder's book, *Communist Neo-traditionalism* (1986). By 1989, I thought that I had discovered a physics-like dynamic for the longevity and super-stability of Chinese society, despite periodical peasant revolutions. But the idea seemed quite ridiculous to me. I put the draft paper aside. Some years later, the editor of a Chinese journal, *Chengshi Yanjiu* (Urban Research), visited the University of Hong Kong, where I was a PhD student. I passed the manuscript to him and published it in the journal. Of course, the idea was neither controversial nor received much attention. On the other hand, based on some life experience and imagination, another article on the 'types and characteristics of Chinese urban communities', published in 1992, was actually widely noted in China, because it was one of the earliest articles on the community (*shequ*), which only became a major topic in the 2000s.

While I later have observed two other types – 'commodity housing' estates and urban villages – I have no direct living experience and have only studied them as empirical research objects. It is more difficult for me to imagine urban life without close engagement. They are 'new' types. However, I do not suggest that they represent a contrast between the old and the new. All types of neighbourhoods are subject to a similar context of emergent urbanism, which was not observed in a traditional and 'totalised' (*zongti*) society. For the word 'totalised', there is also a translation problem because *zongti* is perhaps better translated as 'comprehensive'. Here my position is perhaps slightly different from neo-traditionalism. I intend to attribute stability to the nature of the under-bureaucratised and embedded state–society relationship.

As for governance change, in advanced capitalist economies neoliberalisation is seen as a process of welfare state retreat. China had a much smaller sphere of welfare provision only for industrialised workplaces (*danwei*). Thinking in terms of traditionalism, the state was embedded in the society, perhaps also owing to the deliberate practice of the 'mass line' (*qunzhong luxian*) – maintaining association with the mass. The state was temporarily pushed out by the process of marketisation it initiated as a practical solution to economic growth. To understand the changing social order through a new coordination approach (governance), I go beyond marketisation *per se*. Again, from a microscopic view of urban neighbourhoods, the way I was thinking about China in the 1980s, what we have observed since is an 'urban revolution'. Because of the slow development of society, for whatever reasons, intended or unintended, society's self-protection is not characterised as social movements, leading to a self-organised society but rather by a more visible and professionalised state. In the sphere of urban planning, I noted in my earlier book that *Planning for Growth* (2015) perhaps should not be seen as for the market interest but rather as dealing with the problems created by market development and pursuing an overall legitimate goal of national prosperity and modernisation. In this book, from the vantage of neighbourhoods, I observe urban revolution at the grassroots and explain governance changes in this context.

The book was written during lockdown. Unable to travel to do the fieldwork, what I could do was a virtual journey. I stopped watching the depressing news about infection rates and the death toll – they are not a football match score deserving constant attention. The virtual tour is of course full of images. I wished to revisit these places to take new pictures for the book. But this is still not possible. Now, looking back, what makes these photos interesting is time. The sense of history adds some appeal. My intention is just to show the reader what I have seen on the ground of very ordinary places.

Now completing this book in London, I am pondering what it is about. Perhaps as the saying, 'in the past three thousand years, a fundamental change has occurred' (此三千余年一大变局也 *ci sanqian yunian yi da bianju ye*), the book depicts a landscape that 'differential relation persists but its mode perished' (差序依在、格局无存 *chaxu yizai, geju wucun*).

Acknowledgements

It has been a long journey though the book was written up quite quickly during short lockdowns. My first expression of thanks goes to my mentors along this journey, Gonghao Cui, Anthony Gar-On Yeh and Chris Webster. Professor Cui at Nanjing University is a pioneer in the studies of China urbanisation. Professor Yeh at the University of Hong Kong is one of the first Western academics on social areas of Chinese cities. Professor Webster inspired me on gated community research, although our work at Cardiff University was mainly on urban simulation and morphologies. I had the privilege to co-edit *Restructuring the Chinese City* with Laurence Ma, who pioneered Western academic research on the geography of China. I participated in and greatly benefited from the Urban China Research Network, of which John Logan is the founding director. His insights on housing and residential segregation in China are a major source of inspiration. I thank Zhigang Li who did research on residential segregation with me and hosted and accompanied me on many journeys to interesting sites. Shenjing He studied urban regeneration, poverty and neighbourhood governance together in related research projects. Nick Phelps, Yuemin Ning, Chaolin Gu, Yuting Liu, Yuan Yuan, Jian Feng, Zhen Wang, Sainan Lin, Yuqi Liu, Ningying Huang collaborated on various research related to neighbourhoods or governance. Lan Zhou, Yanjing Zhao Guofang Zhai, Mingfeng Wang, Yang Xiao, Jie Shen, Guohui Long, Xigang Zhu, Tianke Zhu, and the late Qiyan Wu helped with various field visits. I thank Tingting Lu for her photo from her PhD research on the gated community in Wenzhou and wonderful assistance. Among many research trips, the journeys to urban villages in the hottest summer with Fangzhu Zhang were unforgettable. I also thank my classmate and friend, Qing Deng, who was a senior real estate consultant, for opening my eyes to the real estate market. My friends Jinying Lin and Zhong Tang gave me chances to see their homes and businesses. My extended family, uncles and aunts, and their friends helped find contacts in various neighbourhoods. On urban China research and on the topics related to this book, I learnt from stimulating conversations with Yixin Zhou, Cecilia Wong, Yaping Wang, Si-Ming Li, Youqin Huang, Alan Smart, George Lin, Cindy Fan, Youtien Hsing, Weiping Wu, Xuefei Ren, Ben Read, Deborah Davis, Min Zhou, Hyun Bang Shin and the late Choon-Piew Pow. I collaborated with Jennifer Robinson on her project of Governing the Future City, through which I discovered more about comparative urbanism and her insights on governance. I also thank Roger Keil for involving me in his Global Suburbanism project, which prompted me to pay more attention to suburban governance. Mark Frazier and Yawei Chen hosted my visits and provided me with great chances for research dissemination. On urban studies, I had beneficial conversations with Ananya Roy, Chris Hamnett, Simon Parker, Talja Blokland, Setha Low and the late Ray Forrest. I thank Bruce Hunt for reading my manuscript. I thank colleagues at my home institution, Bartlett School of Planning, the Bartlett Faculty of the Built Environment, especially Alan Penn, Nick Gallent and Claudio de Magalhães, for their collegial support, in particular to the China Planning Research Group. I incidentally discovered a chapter by our Dean of the Bartlett, Christoph Lindner, on postmetroplis urbanism in Hong Kong and the film of Wong Kai-Wai; I enjoyed both the film and my time in Hong Kong. Writing with anonymous reviewers in mind is often a disturbance. However, now I wish to thank these reviewers because their reviews were insightful and constructive, which helped me think further about the key message of this book. I thank the commissioning editor at UCL Press, Chris Penfold, who made efficient editorial and publication arrangements. I am grateful for being entitled to open access under UCL Press. Finally, among many research projects, I particularly acknowledge the funding support from the European Research Council (ERC) (Advanced Grant – ChinaUrban, grant agreement No. 832845).

Introduction: leaving the soil

Rural China: a society from the soil

Fei Xiaotong, a renowned Chinese sociologist, described the foundations of Chinese society as 'earth-bounded' (Fei 1947/1992). In such an earth-bounded society the social structure was characterised by the order of so-called *chaxugeju* (the differential mode of association), which is the basic organisational principle of rural China. Different from clearly defined social boundaries in Western society, traditional Chinese society was 'just like the circles that appear on the surface of a lake when a rock is thrown into it. Everyone stands at the centre of the circles produced by his or her own' (p. 62). Rural society is essentially a society of acquaintance, in which one is 'differentially associated' with the inner circle of family members, then the outer circle of extended family members, and further out, the ring of villagers. These differential associations integrate individuals into a society with dense social networks. Because of close but varying associations, rural villages were governed by social norms rather than laws or regulations. While the concept indicates the characteristic of Chinese culture in terms of differential relations, it concurs that the rural society is built upon tight-knit primary relations. The concept is applied in this book with an emphasis on collectivism derived from association instead of the nature of 'differentiation'.[1] Although villages did not represent a special spatial scale, they were meaningful places in which families, extended families and clans lived together. The rural village thus is presented as an ideal type, representing characteristics opposite to those of urbanism defined by Louis Wirth (1938).

However, Fei's earth-bounded village is not confined to rurality. It is a cultural interpretation of the entire Chinese society. In this sense, his concept of differential mode of association is not a Weberian ideal type to present a concept but rather depicting the empirical world.[2]

The differential mode is an abstraction of the social relation of China's rural families and kinships.[3] He presented a rather unique Chinese cultural feature beyond the generic contrast between urban and rural social characterisation (for example, the classic sociological notion of *Gemeinschaft* and *Gesellschaft* by Ferdinand Tönnies[4]). The social relations are not only close but also differentiated, stronger with close social proximity. Because of limited geographical mobility, such social proximity also turns into territorial bonding. As a cultural and social description, the differential mode of association transcends the distinction between the rural and the urban. In other words, although mainly referring to rural China, the mode can be extrapolated into the description of Chinese cities in the imperial era, which was a predominantly 'earth-bounded' society.[5]

Although the differential mode of association can be a base to suggest that social relation (*guanxi*) widely exists in modern China,[6] the original purpose of Fei's conceptualisation is to make a contrast between rural society and market society, as explained by Jack Barbalet (2021b):

> Perhaps the most pertinent element of Fei's treatment of chaxugeju, however, that deflects its viability as a model for guanxi is his prognosis mentioned earlier in this article, that with the development of market society in China the days of chaxugeju are numbered. This reflects the way Fei juxtaposes rural society and market society. (p. 376)

In the same way, Fei's concept is used in this book as a defined self-centred relation that lacks individualism. While rural markets were well developed in China, and commercial activities were flourishing and accommodated in market towns, forming the urban system and regional economies as early as in the Tang and Song dynasties as shown by William Skinner (1977), the commercial activities did not introduce market logic into the dominant principle of social relation. China had not been thoroughly 'urbanised' in Fei Xiaotong's time.[7] Fei's concept refers to social relations that are often called 'traditional' (particularistic, ascriptive) in contrast to the supposed 'modern' relations of impersonalism and legal-based norms.[8] Here, Fei was influenced by the Weberian idea of Occidental modernity. But he also tried to depict the world of rural China that was constructed upon families and lineages. They formed place-based attachment and moral order. Besides lineage, a native-place association commonly found in late imperial and republican China is another example of the differential mode of association affecting urban governance.[9] These territorially based or related social relations have been severely impacted in China's 'urban revolution' today, though the native-place identity and relation continue to exist in urban villages. This book examines these changes of territorial relations at a close distance in typical residential neighbourhoods.

The city in imperial China was mainly an administrative centre. But the differential mode of association as an indigenous, self-centred, bottom-up and decaying-with-distance governance mechanism necessarily deters the escalation of bureaucratisation in society. In imperial China, the power of the emperor did not intrude into vast numbers of rural villages. Nor was it visible in the everyday life of ordinary people living in the city. Fei observed that:

> Rural society is a small-scale peasant economy, and, if necessary, each peasant household can become self-sufficient, except for a few items of daily necessity. The household may simply close its doors on the larger economy. When this occurs, we can imagine that the scope of consensual power would also decrease. Judging from the reality of people's lives in agrarian societies, then, we can see that the power structure, although it may be labeled a 'dictatorship', is actually loose, weak, and nominal. It is a government that does not actively govern at all. (Fei 1947/1992, 113)

The county seats were the lowest base of administrative power. The vast rural area was governed by the gentry, representing the social order – and the consequential morality acceptable to its associated members.[10]

The gentry had the 'legitimacy' to govern, because they were a moral exemplar rather than being endorsed by a procedure, either externally (for example, appointment) or internally (for example, voting). 'Self-governance' was buttressed by *baojia* – an administrative organisational system (see later discussion). Although *baojia* represented a formal institution, its principle was more a decentralised system of local responsibility, making neighbourhood and village leaders accountable for anti-government political actions. Most of the time, this formal institution did not operate on routine neighbourhood governance or reciprocal social support. Therefore, the society from the soil is an organic one, maintaining order not chaos, but not a bureaucratised society. It is in this context that we should understand the (lacking) role of the city in social governance.

As the seat of administrative power, the city had a salient element: *yamen* (the government compound).[11] But beyond this confined space of formal bureaucracy, other activities were 'suppressed' or found it difficult to flourish, because the Confucian elites all preferred to pursue their careers in the government rather than becoming merchants.[12] While in the Song Dynasty (960–1279) China saw an embryonic urban culture brought about by booming commerce, the city as a space outside traditional governance by gentry and with limited yet effective administration was absent; professional associations were not developed into a 'civil society' and community in the modern sense. The Chinese city can still be regarded as an earth-bounded society.

As mentioned earlier, the conceptualisation of earth-bounded society based on the differential mode of association is not exclusively applied to the system of agricultural production but rather originates from a social and moral order. The vast area of the Chinese city was occupied by traditional cellular neighbourhoods, which were alleyway housing neighbourhoods. The residents had occupations different from agricultural production as merchants and craftsmen, but differential mode of association applied well to this kind of society.

The Chinese title of Fei's book is transliterated directly as *Rural China,* and the published English title is *From the Soil*. The book is not about the countryside, but rather about a social construct of villages originating from the specific field site of his anthropological investigation (Kaixiangong village in southern Jiangsu province). It represents Chinese society at that time. As argued earlier, this characterisation can be extrapolated to include the city although the city was rather peripheral and China was not really urbanised. In *Rural China*, the city is not a generic term. This book will further argue that differential mode of association can also be extrapolated temporally into industrialised cities under socialism. Despite revolutionary change after 1949, Chinese society was not fully urbanised until after the economic reform. From the perspective of urban studies, particularly urbanism, I will revisit how differential mode of association – represented as 'communist neo-traditionalism'[13] – continued to maintain a society from the soil.

There has been a long tradition of thinking of cities in the Orient as different from the European city, or the 'Occidental City', as in sixteenth-century Europe in the account of Max Weber. Hartmut Haussermann and Anne Haila (2005) explain that, according to Weber:

> The role of city dwellers also differentiated European cities from cities in Asia. Whereas in Europe citizens participated in the local administration, in China urban dwellers belonged to their families and native villages, while in India urban dwellers were members of different castes.

> For Max Weber, cities were special kinds of societies. In Europe, the contrast between the city and the countryside was clearly defined. Up to the beginning of modernity, the border between the urban and the rural was demarcated by walls. The walls also separated different types of societies. Cities distinguished themselves sharply from the surrounding feudal countryside. Inside the city walls, economic and political life flourished and cities became the breeding ground for the new mode of production – capitalism – and Occidental modernity. (p. 51)

In other words, the development of the city in the West represents the advancement of modernism. The implication of modernisation for everyday life is the bureaucratisation of social relationships. Social and cultural innovations fostered capitalism.

In contrast, the Chinese imperial city was the site of administration with limited commercial activities. Laurence Ma (2009) explained:

> As seats of administration and local political power, cities were walled for defence and local population control. Aside from city walls, the most salient spatial element of the cities was the government district consisting of a set of local government buildings (*yamen*) that served as the nerve centre of a city. Other key spaces in the cities included official residences, military compounds, drum and bell towers, granaries, schools, temples, and commercial areas. (pp. 66–7)

Urban markets were marginal in location and restricted in their time of operation until the nineteenth century. Although commercial activities were no longer restricted and became dispersed across the city, 'significant commercial capitalism failed to appear in Chinese cities because the most profitable commodities such as salt and tea were monopolised by the state and the Confucian elites all preferred to pursue government service as their career goal'.[14]

This landscape changed dramatically after the establishment of the treaty-port cities following the Opium War. International settlements and foreign concession areas were set up. Foreign merchants and entrepreneurs formed their own spaces outside the walled Chinese cities, showing a contrast between the under-serviced Chinese part and the European quarters with modern building codes.[15] The influx of rural migrants and war refugees and a growing working class in Shanghai led to an increasing urban population in the 1920s and 1930s. The rich

Chinese began to seek the protection of Western extraterritorial power in international settlements and concession areas, creating a mix of Chinese and foreigners in these places. The real estate boom in Shanghai created a landscape of *shikumen* – a 'stone portal gate' style of terraced housing with an internal courtyard.

The quality of the housing and public services in international settlements and French concession areas was superior to the Chinese walled city.[16] The development of foreign residences led to citywide residential differentiation – as in Shanghai, the residential areas were differentiated into upper and lower quarters. In upper-market areas, cultural entertainment and amenities flourished, symbolising a new middle-class culture.[17] In the peripheries of cities, slums became widespread, accommodating the influx of migrants from the countryside which suffered from constant wars and became impoverished in industrialisation driven by Western imperialism.

China's efforts to modernise its cities were short lived. In the 1920s and 1930s, as a semi-colonial treaty-port city, a thriving financial capital, and an early industrialising city, Shanghai arguably developed a 'cosmopolitan' culture.[18] This 'middle-class' culture was built upon material comfort, as re-emerging consumerism has been since the 1980s.[19] Learning from Western city planning, Chinese planners trained in the West even envisioned in the Greater Shanghai Plan of 1927 the building of a new civic centre in Jiangwan, Shanghai's exurb at that time, to serve the public. The public facilities were to include a library, a stadium, a museum and a hospital to enhance the quality of life. At the centre was the city hall. From the perspective of city planning,

> The new civic centre was planned to combine Chinese architectural style with a Western planning concept. This would be a new monumental civic centre, not like a traditional Chinese government compound – *yamen*, which symbolises imperial or magisterial power. The central square was to be surrounded by 'public buildings' such as the library and stadium and open to the public, which aimed to enhance the quality of everyday life. (Wu 2015, 10)

Except for a few buildings, the civic centre did not materialise, due to the Japanese invasion. The city hall was completed and survived but became the administration building within the 'work-unit compound' of Shanghai Physical Education College after 1949. The building was therefore not open to the public. In fact, outsiders could not even access the place as it was a work-unit territory. The extent of the influence of Western modernist planning and middle-class cosmopolitanism on neighbourhood structure and governance in Shanghai before 1949 is unknown. We can only speculate about this past life from observing the lane housing neighbourhoods in old Shanghai.

As a fusion of traditional courtyard and modern terraced housing, *shikumen* alleyway houses were real estate projects to maximise profits from rent and were uniformly constructed.[20] The residents were an emerging 'middle class' of small workshop owners and foremen or forewomen in factories, as Jie Li (2015) observed:

> The Republican-era residents of Alliance Lane also led hybrid lifestyles – as compradors (intermediaries) whose livelihoods depended on foreign industries, as dandies who danced in jazzy ball-rooms with Western clothes, and as Confucian patriarchs and matriarchs who maintained strict domestic hierarchies and imprisoned daughters-in-law in their inner chambers. (p. 36)

Although designed for multiple occupancies, these lane houses initially had a lower density than the later crowded houses created through subdivision and densification after 1949. We can only speculate that these lane houses in the republican era maintained a certain privacy while, as a popular and mixed residential environment, neighbourhood interaction increased through the length of residency. These neighbourhoods, in their architectural style, had a strong social imprint of rural communities. Still, perhaps time was too short for the Chinese city to evolve into self-organised communities. After 1949, alleyway housing neighbourhoods became marginalised as their petit-bourgeois urbanities were not at the centre of state-led industrialisation.

This brief historical review of Chinese society and its urban history shows that despite commercial activities, limited administrative functions and the short-lived cosmopolitan middle-class culture in treaty-port cities, Chinese society, including rural and urban places, remained as an earth-bounded society from the soil. I will show in the next section that the Chinese city in the socialist era still maintained such a character, even though the economy experienced state-led industrialisation.

The neo-traditionalism of the Chinese socialist city

If the Chinese city in the imperial era is not a theoretically meaningful object, then what is the meaning of the 'socialist city' for China after

1949? This question has a theoretical implication. For the European city, or the capitalist city more generally, Manuel Castells (1977) asked 'the urban question', arguing that the city had lost its meaning as an ecological contrast to the rural area, empirically researched by the Chicago School. The city was integrated into the national economy by the Keynesian welfare state. Under the welfare state, the (capitalist) city has lost its meaning as a distinctive form of social life. The main 'urban' function was the venue for the welfare state to organise 'collective consumption' through its redistribution.

After the communist revolution, the Chinese city was transformed from a consumption base to a production site for state-led industrialisation.[21] In contrast to the countryside, the city represented the domain of the state. The level of formalisation or bureaucratisation, however, varied between the old urban core with private housing and the new industrial areas. The latter more thoroughly reflect socialist planning principles. However, compared with Eastern European and Soviet cities, China witnessed a much lower level of industrialisation and the lack of a thorough transformation of its cities. I argue that, because consumption was constrained, the Chinese city did not see an emergent urbanism along its industrialisation during the socialist period. Like the earth-bounded society from the soil, the socialist city maintained an organic order from differential mode of association. In addition, this order of traditionalism was deliberately maintained through its work-unit system.

The city remained peripheral in industrial organisation. Instead, state work-units (*danwei*) became the basic unit for organising economic activities, consumption and housing provision. The city, as a spatial form, is more or less a collection of work-units plus traditional neighbourhoods built before the revolution. City-wide bureaucratisation was much underdeveloped. Strong evidence comes from city planning. In China, development control under the city/municipality was not established until 1990 when the first city planning ordinance was enacted.[22] It is therefore difficult to conceive of Chinese city planning as planning in the 'public domain',[23] not because of state authoritarianism and the lack of civil society, but because such a vocabulary implies a city-based politics.

In contrast, although the city is a territory of local government, sectoral administration has always been strong. The absence of civil society and the influence of the state over everyday lives through its work-units meant that the state had strong influence over urban development. But such language of the state controlling society is inappropriate, as will be seen from an 'urban' perspective, because the Chinese state was deeply embedded into its society. For example, in terms of land use control, state work-units played an important role in self-regulation through their discretionary decision-making power over land uses. The role of the city government was to supplement work-units through citywide infrastructure provision, to fill the gaps between work-units. Comprehensive urban development was rare.[24]

Despite revolutionary change after 1949, traditionalism continued, formalised and in some aspects strengthened by work-unit socialism. There are two related conceptualisations by Andrew Walder (1986) and Liping Sun (2004, 2008). Both disregarded state socialism as an 'authoritarian state' and tried to find a description of how the state organises social life, respectively from industrialisation and its organisational form, and social organisation. Their studies do not particularly focus on urbanism; but both are related to the socialist city and point out the absent space outside the collective/public/state realm. Walder examines labour processes and welfare within work-units; Sun stresses pervasive, penetrating, wide-ranging state functions and resource controls which displace and overlap with society. They paid attention to the local sphere and provided a picture of urban life in the socialist city. In the planned economy, the state organised collective consumption through state work-units. These work-units were more than production units; they were 'totalised social entities' carrying out service provision, housing development and distribution, and social management.

Walder criticised both the totalitarian interpretation and 'interest groups' (e.g., fraction or civil society) explanation of the Chinese state. Because the membership of the work-unit was permanent and the interaction between the state and individuals occurred closely within a short distance of the work-unit, the work-unit was a societal organisation, in which the relation was particularistic rather than impersonal. Because the state controlled the resources of work-units, within which workers were obliged to live, this created 'organisational dependence', which led to the concentration of state power. Walder describes the dominance of state work-units in social lives as 'communist neo-traditionalism'. On this point, this particularism resonates with Fei's differential mode of association because in the society from the soil, relationships are differentiated. Although Walder did not regard neo-traditionalism as in continuity with traditional society, the territorial aspect of the work-unit compound as a combination of living and work implied a replication of similar relations of dependence and of the comprehensiveness of social relations (and hence difficult to maintain as 'impersonal' and universal).

The concept of the 'totalised society' proposed by Chinese sociologist Liping Sun (2008) describes the omnipotent state that totalises its relation with the society. The concept is less about the power of the state in total control (authoritarianism) and more about its ability to control resource management – 'near monopoly of resources', which 'engenders a total social system where the state controls everything'. Sun describes how:

> Such a total society is constructed on a series of institutions. For instance, in addition to the monopoly system, the urban work-unit system and the rural commune system were important organisational institutions in China during the socialist period. Since these two institutions were actually extensions of the formal bureaucracy, the fact that their members heavily relied on them meant that they actually heavily depended on the state. Consequently, to strengthen the state's total control over society, it was necessary for the Chinese government to eliminate any social forces that tended towards independence from the state. Thus it was that all the previously independent social forces in China were deprived of their independence after 1949. The state-society relationship in such a country undergoing transition involves a ceaseless weakening and disassembly of the total social system, the formation of a civil society, and the rebuilding of society. (Sun 2008, 96)

While Sun emphasised bureaucratisation and control through resource management, thinking of work-units as part of formal state organisation, it is equally possible to read this totalised society as a society with 'under-differentiated social structure', in which 'the state controls the economy and monopolises all social resources. Further, politics, society and ideology are highly overlapped with each other'.[25] Further, related to Fei's differential mode of association and Walder's particularism, the totalised society can be read as the modern adaptation of traditionalism, and perhaps an essential outcome of underdeveloped urbanism. 'Total' does not refer to the degree of entirety of state capacity but rather to the comprehensiveness of relations, in terms of the absence of partial and impersonal relations. These relations are dense and confined in a local space. Similarly, in traditional urban neighbourhoods, Martin Whyte and William Parish (1984) reveal a comprehensive function of residents' committees, which combined the state and society. Compared with the state workplaces, the official state organisation was not fully developed in these traditional urban neighbourhoods. Despite the penetration of the state into the grassroots and multiple functions of the residents' committees such as political mobilisation, the state–society relationship maintained a high degree of informality as the committees were not formally staffed but served by volunteers. Thus these neighbourhoods bore more features of traditional rural China than of modern industrial societies.

This book will pursue this perspective, arguing that the totalised society is characterised by the embedding of the state in society. The concept of 'communist neo-traditionalism' indicates its socialist tradition. Indeed, the close relationship between living and work was deliberately designed as a planning concept for the socialist city, seen in Eastern Europe. Alison Stenning (2005) described everyday life in the town of Nowa Huta in southern Poland and depicted social life built upon the state steelworks:

> Soviet town planning and social policy ideals were imported to establish microdistricts which would serve many of the residents' daily needs – schools, medical facilities, playgrounds and food shops – within a small area… . The social and cultural facilities offered by the steelworks, the Party and its youth organisations provided workers and their families with opportunities to socialise and be entertained within the community. (p. 117)

> The restrictions placed on mobility by the state were reinforced by the integration of so many spheres of life around the workplace which meant that moving was a complicated process. Long waiting lists for accommodation also slowed the mobility process. The structuring of social lives in this way shaped a tendency to stability and meant that mobility was often unnecessary and difficult… . The immobility was coupled with the migrants' more recent peasant past to create a 'small-town climate', the intimacy of social relations within families, blocks and neighbourhoods more reminiscent of rural Poland than cosmopolitan Krakow. Low levels of housing mobility and the association of housing tenure with the workplace have meant that networks of acquaintance and friendship tend to be long-standing and stable. (p. 122)

The public housing system centred upon the state workplace reinforced the nature of traditional neighbourhoods.

Compared with cities in Eastern European countries and the Soviet Union, Chinese cities share similarities of low mobility, neighbourhood stability, intense neighbouring and strong attachment, suggesting that traditionalism is not limited to Chinese society as one from the soil. Walder's conceptualisation is certainly not linked to the Chinese imperial past, as Fei's differential mode of association is. Both China and socialist economies in Eastern Europe tried to contain urbanism while fostering industrialisation. They presented similar features of neighbourhood traditionalism. But different levels of industrialisation have meant that China has perhaps preserved more traditional features like those old urban areas and witnessed less pervasive state service provision, partially because compared with the European socialist economies, the Chinese urbanisation level was even lower, and partially owing to the Chinese culture of differential mode of association. In China, the advantage of public service provision was actually concentrated on state key development projects. Similarly, the socialist city was built within a shortage economy and underdeveloped consumption and missing consumerism. China's traditionalism was maintained in its cities, perhaps also due to a much lower level of urbanisation than in their socialist counterparts in Eastern Europe. Urban life only began to flourish after the economic reform when migration and urbanisation accelerated.

Urban revolution: the society leaving the soil

Neither in its imperial time nor in the socialist era was the Chinese city the spatial scale for organising production and social life. The pivot of urban life under socialism was the residential micro-district as the world for socialist workers. The economic reform in 1978, however, started an urban revolution. The Chinese city became the engine of economic growth. Under the catalyst of globalisation, China joined the global production network and became the 'workshop of the world'. While socialism has not officially ended, the transformation of production and reproduction has led to society 'leaving the soil' – away from its neo-traditionalism. The state has reinvented its role in economic promotion and acts through various state-owned enterprises and agencies in the market.[26] The state persists in neighbourhood governance through 'community building' but its relation with society is different – the state is no longer embedded in society through (neo-)traditionalism.

The 1949 revolution was the first socialist revolution, which radically transformed the means of production, nationalising and controlling the economy through administrative commands; a comprehensive approach to urban development through city planning was missing until the 1990s. The second urban revolution which started in 1978 reorganised the city as the spatial scale of production, consumption and the pivot of urban life. China turned from state-led industrialisation to urban-based accumulation.²⁷ The level of urbanisation has risen from about 18 per cent in 1978 to over 50 per cent in 2015.

Development zones were initially set up near the large cities in the coastal region but soon spread over the country. In southern China, as a result of globally driven industrialisation, densely mixed rural and urban land uses appeared.²⁸ Initially, workshops, warehouses and the living space of factory owner and workers were combined into the same building, known as 'three in one' (*sanheyi*), which created a convenient place for rural workers to live on site. Later, larger factories built their own workers' dormitories. To maintain an effective management factory regime, these dormitories deliberately disrupted the social networks of migrants and allocated different accommodation to fellow migrants from the same place of origin. Both the rudimentary accommodation combined within workshops in villages and more advanced workers' dormitories in factories were very different from traditional village neighbourhoods or socialist workers' villages in that they are not a socialised space or a community for life. The relation with the living place is 'contractual', even if there is no formal contract.²⁹

The early stage of economic reform had already begun to transform Chinese urban life, creating an embryonic yet more liberal and vibrant culture in the 1980s. Deborah Davis and her co-editors (1995) were perhaps among the first to speculate on the potential implications of new urban spaces for 'personal autonomy' and found the tendencies in many spheres such as urban form, leisure, film-making, arts and workers' associations to develop 'associational ties that signalled emergent urban communities or non-state institutions' (p.10). Despite greater autonomies brought about by urbanisation and emergent urbanism, concepts such as 'civil society' or the 'public sphere' do not fit properly in the Chinese city. Chinese cities in the 1980s were characterised by a persistently dominant state-owned economy, emerging private sectors led by township and village enterprises (TVEs), and limited and low-value-added foreign and overseas investment, in contrast to experimental policies to introduce markets and urban consumption. Yet full-fledged market development was not initiated until 1992. Housing and land development were not commercialised in the 1980s.

After a more radical reform was launched by Deng Xiaoping's southern China tour in 1992, the tendencies of the 1980s were strengthened by a booming urban consumer market; the market development was less ideologically oriented but more pragmatically focused on profit-making, which was deemed beneficial for national revitalisation, as the slogan suggests – 'it is glorious to become rich'. The full-fledged marketisation after 1992 seemed to develop a 'market society',[30] while Deborah Davis (2000) referred to the change in society as 'the consumer revolution' with profound implications as 'an increasing reliance of urban residents on horizontal ties of friendship, kinship, or informal sociability that challenge the vertical relationship between subject-citizens and state agents' (p. 3). And if this were true, then the consumer revolution would be 'a story of how changing consumer behaviour can enlarge the social space for urban residents to invest in nonofficial initiatives'.[31]

The change, namely the emergence of autonomous urban space, would be profound, as this would break up the 'hegemony' imposed by the state in the past, described here as:

> Politicised ties between subordinates and superiors in the workplace could define the quality of one's personal life, and it was virtually impossible for employees or their family members to prosper without the active support of enterprise leaders. If an employer denied or failed to provide a benefit, there was rarely an alternative source. (Davis 2000, 5)

As can be seen from this perspective, traditionalism and informal social networks were thought of as forces countering authoritarianism.

However, this was very different from the understanding of neo-traditionalism because for the latter, it was this 'traditionalism' that tended to strengthen the state's role. Although the strong influence of the state over urban life has been found in neo-traditionalism by Andrew Walder (1986) or urban life under work-unit socialism studied by Martin Whyte and William Parish (1984), their perceptions were quite different. They did not regard state control as 'vertical' and operating outside the urban space; rather that the state was closely linked and embedded within the workplace community. For neo-traditionalism, it is the tightly intertwined relations in workplaces that made it possible to govern rather than simply operate through coercive forces.

Unlike the state apparatus, the nature of traditionalism was not in force, although the setting of undifferentiated urban space through a neighbourhood system such as *baojia* made control more effective. In other words, the close proximity between the state and society in a neighbourhood setting makes it more convenient and effective for monitoring, because the social order is not established by monitoring – the latter is very much a modern view of the state. In the Chinese urban setting, according to Fei's differential mode of association, which describes a society from the soil, order and coherence were indigenously generated, hence it was a moral order.

In this sense, the study here does not seek marketisation or its related manifestation such as residential differentiation or consumer-driven diversity as the explanation for changing governance. In other words, the 'consumer revolution' does not directly transform the order. We need to explore how consumerism together with other social and institutional changes have played out in a spatial setting – neighbourhood changes – in order to understand how urban China is 'leaving the soil', which finally separates state and society. This is not to deny that interpersonal networks, kinship and lineage continue to play a role, for example in the formation of migrant settlements by migrants from the same place of origin.[32] Nevertheless, these relations have been changed by emergent urbanism. The Chinese urban society in the post-reform era is very different from a 'totalised' society.[33]

A note on methodology

Compared with research monographs based on in-depth single-case studies,[34] this book adopts a holistic approach built upon my three decades of observations and research on Chinese cities. Some of my studies are quantitative through neighbourhood surveys and population censuses at a fine spatial scale. Others include long-term observation and detailed case studies (such as the Fifth Village in Nanjing or the Gaojiabang neighbourhood in Shanghai). The overall argument made in the book is not associated with a specific research project. But I take a broader historical and interpretive stance to develop new concepts and claims, based on hundreds of research site visits over many years.[35] While nowadays abundant journal articles aim to fill a gap in specific literature, there is a lack of an overall picture of the Chinese urban landscape. Existing studies often focus on a specific type of neighbourhood. For example, 'urban villages' have been extensively studied, mostly examining informal development. Few studies cover the aspects of governance and social life across different neighbourhoods. Most studies on housing tenure are cross-sectional and do not provide a longer history of neighbourhood changes.

On the other hand, historical books depict more general political, economic and social changes,[36] lacking attention to specific neighbourhoods[37] and, with few exceptions, to ordinary life and public space. This book tries to view general social change from multiple sites – various types of urban neighbourhoods – while not being a rigorous historical study. As an urban scholar, I have paid more attention to urbanisation. Although the changing urban landscape is depicted in the context of political changes, the book does not cover Chinese politics and social movements.[38] Rather, my intention is the other way round, to speculate on the implications of urbanisation for politics, especially changing governance, from place-based neighbourhood observations.[39]

On urbanisation, this book is not a population study concerned with the increasing percentage of urban population, regardless of how the urban is categorised or 'defined' statistically or administratively. I refer to the transformation of social relations as 'urban revolution' after Henri Lefebvre (1970/2003). This change in social relations has been triggered by the introduction and more pervasive use of market logic in Chinese society. This revolutionary change, that is, China becoming urban, has generated profound political implications. In a way, it represents how social change at the level of the urban neighbourhood (in a sense of particularity) creates a more macro and regime-wide pattern (in the sense of universality). Some aspects of this trend are surprisingly similar to what we have observed in the contemporary world beyond China. Therefore, the book has a comparative intention in mind,[40] although I do not situate the study outside China. In fact, these several sites are concentrated in coastal China, in super large cities, which manifest the trend in a more visible way. The neighbourhoods observed in this book are understandably concentrated in large cities such as Shanghai, Beijing and Guangzhou in the coastal region. Some have a history of being treaty-port cities and thus are quite special in China. But the general trend observed here should be applicable to other smaller or remoter cities in China. While there are some studies on cities in remote regions,[41] very few provide neighbourhood-level studies.[42]

Finally, I have encountered great difficulty in presenting certain terms to the world outside China. My original intention was to preserve the precise and 'authentic' meaning of Chinese terms. The most frequently used term in this book is Fei Xiaotong's *chaxugeju*. The question is whether I should keep translating it throughout the book. English translation was used to help to reveal meaning, for example, *fengbi xiaoqu* (sealed estates) for gated communities. This helps to point out some essential differences, indicating that the term 'gated communities' in its English version is often loaded with 'private governance', which may not exist for the Chinese 'sealed estates'. But I admit that this could create some readability problems. Then, I tried using the English term first and supplementing it with the Chinese *pinyin* specification, for example, gated communities (*fengbi xiaoqu*) to limit the meaning of gated communities here in this book. The constant reminder of the limitation of the English term (actually as the 'concept') seems to apply a Western concept to China and test its validity. But this is not necessary as my intention is not to bring in Western theory to explain China. In the end, for the sake of readability, I gave up double translation and sometimes only use the English terms with the occasional *pinyin* specification. In this way, I do not treat them as concepts but rather as commonly used expressions.

The outline of this book

This introductory chapter discussed the concept of *chaxugeju* developed by Fei Xiaotong, a renowned Chinese sociologist, which describes the social order of rural China as a society 'from the soil'. In contrast to the 'Occidental City', the Chinese residential settlement largely maintained the features of rural society throughout China's imperial history. Despite a short-lived thriving urban culture in the republican era, the Chinese city has not evolved into a structure of separated state and society. The socialist city after 1949 experienced state-led 'industrialisation without urbanisation'. This neo-traditionalism built upon state work-units (*danwei*) created a 'totalised society', resembling an 'earth-bounded' society. The economic reform started China's urban revolution. The Chinese city has become the engine of economic growth. As China urbanises, the social typology of the residential world has changed.

Following the introduction of the perspective of differentiated mode of association, Chapter 1 examines China's changing residential landscapes, which reveals a new urban social geography of four types of neighbourhood. That is, a dualistic one of traditional and work-unit neighbourhoods is expanded into a fourfold one with two new types: migrant and middle-class neighbourhoods. For a long time, the Chinese social areas had revealed a mixed nature of social classes but separation by occupation. The market reform and housing commodification introduced a pattern of housing characterised by tenure-based differentiation. Chinese cities experience greater heterogeneity and diversity. But at the same time, the four types of neighbourhoods show the path-dependent logic of development. Each presents different residential dynamics and governance changes. A new Chinese urbanism arises from not just residential segregation but also neighbourhood changes. Chinese cities thus see social relations with greater heterogeneity, superficiality and diversity. These relations are less place-bounded and impose great challenge to form a social order, particularly when the society has been underdeveloped and remains passive. Echoing the classic research on urban life and social mentality, the chapter also introduces some survey results to reveal that the new urban China is organised with greater informality, networks and urbanity of social mentality. In the three chapters that follow this overview chapter of neighbourhoods, these neighbourhood types are examined in detail with cases.

Chapter 2 investigates two types of traditional neighbourhoods – inner-city alleyways neighbourhoods developed before 1949 and work-unit neighbourhoods built in the socialist era. Inner-city neighbourhoods were largely left untouched after 1949 and remained organic. Consisting of an inferior type of public housing, these neighbourhoods were not thoroughly 'bureaucratised' in the socialist era. Many traditional neighbourhoods have vanished since urban redevelopment began in the 1990s. Work-unit compounds and a larger version of the workplace neighbourhood – the workers' new village – have seen collective consumption organised by the state and their workplaces. Both traditional and workplace neighbourhoods have seen large-scale urban redevelopment since the 1990s. The chapter examines some redeveloped neighbourhoods such as Ju'er *hutong*, Nanchizi and Nanluoguxiang in Beijing, Xintiandi in Shanghai, Yongqingfang in Guangzhou, the Fifth Village in Nanjing and Huajin in Wuhan to understand neighbourhood changes. Many old neighbourhoods had deteriorated into an overcrowded and dilapidated condition. Yet very few courtyard and alleyway houses were upgraded through residential gentrification. Instead, low-income migrants moved into inner-city neighbourhoods and to a lesser extent workplace neighbourhoods. Social interaction and participation declined. The traditionalism has come to an end. Along with the task of dealing with the problems created by marketisation, the state apparatus has been formed, improved and upgraded at the neighbourhood level. Through the 'community construction' movement in the 2000s and more recently 'grid management', neighbourhood governance has seen professionalisation. The new state–society relation is now more administratively oriented. The change is a reaction of these traditional neighbourhoods to market development – a social protection mechanism. But this mechanism of social self-protection has eventually transformed society itself – beginning with the restoration of some state redistributive functions. In order to redistribute social welfare, the nature of the society 'from the soil' has been transformed. We see a more procedural and bureaucratic state apparatus in a Weberian sense in traditional parts of urban China.

Chapter 3 investigates a new type of migrant neighbourhood – 'urban villages' – which has evolved out of former rural villages near the city. Migrant enclaves are created as informal settlements on the socialist urban topography of inner-city and workplace neighbourhoods. The informal housing is built by villagers or their shareholding cooperatives. The corporatisation of village land has led to disappearing traditional collectivism. Building urban villages means 'business'. The chapter looks into how Little Hubei in Guangzhou is transforming into a space of production, and how the relation of native places (*laoxiang*) is different from the close social relation of traditional villages. Urban villages are places of transience, as seen from Tangjialing in Beijing, changing from an 'ant tribe' enclave to a new town; Gaojiabang in Shanghai, vanishing into a business park; and Liede in Guangzhou, experiencing corporatisation and massive redevelopment. A new moral order is based on property rights rather than organic social engagements. Although rural migrants maintain neighbourly social interactions, they are not incorporated into village governance. Different from a rural village, the urban village is a 'limited' society, a mixture of production activities and partial social relations. The rural village has been physically transformed and disappeared. There is a temptation to interpret the change as a result of Chinese authoritarianism – strong state authority and a weak society under socialism. However, the main problem with this view is the inappropriate assumption about state and society relations in the past. There is a need for a more spatialised view to understand the Chinese residential landscape. We need to understand both broad urban changes and how the state and society co-evolve under the impact of marketisation, generating significant impacts on the traditionalism of rural society. Urban villages represent not only residential differentiation but also the process of differentiation between the state and society, through which the state is separated from the society in the process of urbanisation. The state has been 'forced' out of its embedded position in a totalised society and then takes over new functionality – partly as a social protection mechanism to respond to the threat of a marketised society. The urban village is an exemplar of disappearing traditionalism, which had been remaining strong due to urban–rural dualism under state socialism until the Chinese urban revolution.

Chapter 4 investigates the middle-class gated communities. Residential enclosure is a ubiquitous landscape of Chinese cities. Gated communities are the mainstream residential form for the middle class. Residents seek greater personal privacy rather than collectivism in these neighbourhoods. These neighbourhoods are spaces moving away from a 'totalised society'. However, private governance is not a defining parameter of Chinese gated communities. A closer look into the development process reveals that the residential form of enclosed super-blocks is a cost-effective approach to property development, as a built environment product for residential privacy. This chapter examines cases such as Sun City Beijing and 'Orange County' to understand service packaging and decorative design. The emergent homeowners' association and the property management company complicate neighbourhood governance. The solidarity of Chinese gated communities is built upon shared property interests rather than a world of acquaintances. Reflecting Fei Xiaotong's distinction between the public and private in China, the book concurs with the idea that the development of gated communities is a process of 'individualisation' accompanying the Chinese urban revolution. As residents left traditional and workplace neighbourhoods and moved into gated communities, the differential mode of association and neo-traditionalism has come to an end. Property owners do not replicate their social relation of previous traditionalism in new places. Choosing a gated community is basically a choice of consumer products, with different degrees of security, services and prices; the gated community is a micro consumer society. It is not a *public* choice for different governments or governance modes. The extent of self-governance is quite limited. The gated community is a new type of 'community' of property owners. Different from the rural village based on the differential mode of association, it is an imagined community that has little actual social interaction but common interests in property rights. It is not evolving into a 'civil society' that can exert political demands for governance. The construction of these gated neighbourhoods started with the market provision of housing and consequent property management services. But the state still plays an important role in neighbourhood governance. The configuration of governance mode becomes even more complicated when there are different combinations of actors such as the property management company, the homeowners' association, the residents' committee and street offices in diverse neighbourhood types.

Chapter 5 summarises the findings from residential neighbourhoods in China to shed light on the 'nature of cities'. Placing urban China in three recent debates in the field of urban studies – the 'nature of cities', the city as concentrated form versus the urban as assemblages, and particularism versus generalisation – the book adopts a historical and contextualised view of neighbourhood changes to show that Chinese society has embarked on a journey towards greater complexity, diversity and heterogeneity. Fei Xiaotong developed an ideal type of rural China – a 'society from the soil' – from Kaixiangong village in Jiangsu province. In contrast, observations from these Chinese urban neighbourhoods show a common trend of 'leaving the soil' in the new urban China. The consumer revolution has not led to a self-governed society, nor has the building of residential communities by the state managed to recreate an entirely totalised society. Rather, urban revolution leads to a necessarily modernised and more visible state in China. Residential transformations in China over recent years have not only changed cities but changed state governance itself.

The Conclusion suggests that new urban China is no longer confined to the differential mode of association or the principle of (neo-)traditionalism. It is no longer earth-bounded. Introducing the market mechanism, along with urbanisation, has generated significant impacts on Chinese society. Echoing earlier research on the 'consumer revolution' in China, this book understands Chinese social changes as an urban question and explores the implications for governance. The purpose of this book is to understand the origin of the strong state in its urban context. The urban revolution does not lead to the dominance of the market, nor a self-governed society, but rather triggered a Polanyian turn – social self-protection achieved through consequential rising state action. In the Chinese case, we see the rise of 'state entrepreneurialism' with professionalised and technical governance, which have established a wide range of formal neighbourhood governance institutions. Thus, a visible state emerges from China's urban revolution.

Notes

1. The original use of Fei Xiaotong stresses the differential pattern. But from its application to an earth-bounded rural village, an overall mode can be inferred, as all residents are associated by the territorial network of social relation based on kinship and lineage. This book interprets the pattern as an overall order derived from differential associations. In this way, I tend to interpret *chaxugeju* as 'the mode of differential associations'. That is, the emphasis is placed on an order of differentiation. See Barbalet (2021a; 2021b) for further elaboration on the usage of the concept.
2. See Barbalet, 2021a: 360.
3. Barbalet, 2021a: 360.
4. The notion was related to the contrast between rural and urban life, back to Ferdinand Tönnies about *Gemeinschaft* (community) and *Gesellschaft* (society) whereby *Gemeinschaft* refers to more closely knit and localised social ties, while *Gesellschaft* refers to indirect interactions, social norms and formal values. For Fei Xiaotong, the contrast is also between Chinese and Western societies. For relational networks (*guanxi*) derived from Fei Xiaotong's concept in Chinese society, see Bian (2019).
5. See Esherick, 2000.
6. For example, Bian (2019) developed sophisticated social network analysis based on the belief that Fei's differential mode of association lays down the validity of *guanxi* in China.
7. Although this does not mean that the Chinese urban ecology is totally static. For example, from the sixteenth to the mid-eighteenth centuries, Beijing saw the development of two distinct centres, 'one serving merchant and tradesmen and the other host to China's scholar-official elite' (Belsky, 2000: 54).

8. Thanks to the reviewer for suggesting this sentence.
9. Thanks to the reviewer for reminding me on this point. For native-place associations, see Belsky, 2005.
10. Esherick, 2000.
11. Ma, 2009.
12. Ma, 2009.
13. This concept was coined by Walder (1986), which will be discussed in detail in Chapter 2.
14. Ma, 2009: 67.
15. See Wu, 2015 for city planning in different areas.
16. Strand, 2000.
17. Yeh, 2008.
18. Lee, 1999.
19. Davis, 2000.
20. Li, 2015.
21. Wu, 1997.
22. Wu, 2015.
23. Friedmann, 1987.
24. Wu, 2015.
25. Sun, 2004: 31.
26. Wu, 2018b.
27. Wu, 2003.
28. Lin, 2006; Wu, 2016b.
29. Wu, 2016c.
30. Wu, 2008.
31. Davis, 2000.
32. Ma and Xiang, 1998.
33. Sun, 2004.
34. See for example Smith (2021) on Chongqing; Kipnis (2016) on Zouping city in Shandong province.
35. Thanks to the reviewer for the suggestion to stress this point.
36. See Lincoln (2021) for an overall introduction.
37. With exceptions, for example, Lu (2006) and Liang (2014).
38. There are extensive studies on labour movements and social contexts. Frazier (2019) linked social movements such as riots, strikes and protests with place-based politics.
39. In this sense, it is similar to *The Power of Place* (2019) by Mark Frazier, who compared urban social movements in Shanghai and Mumbai and their impacts on their respective political regimes.
40. As Fei Xiaotong, his rural China is also in contrast with 'Western' society.
41. For smaller cities, see He et al. (2018); Qian and Tang (2019); Qian and Wei (2020); and Su (2015) on border cities in Yunan. Woodworth and Wallace (2017) and Su and Qian (2020) for the city of Ordos in Inner Mongolia.
42. On the urban morphology, Gaubatz (1996) examined the cities in China's north-western region. Not all cities in China have alleyway housing as in Beijing and Shanghai.

1
Changing residential landscape: a new urban social geography

In order to understand the spatial setting of China's urban transformation, we should explore its social geography at a finer neighbourhood scale. Before census data were made available to provide an 'ecological' portrait of Chinese social areas, the complexity of urban space under socialism and in the earlier stage of economic reform in the 1980s was noted. There were some observations about four generic residential types, which include:

> (a) traditional neighbourhoods in the old city area, mainly developed in the pre-1949 periods; (b) single work unit living quarters, largely associated with industrial development, with clear boundaries (walls) defining land uses, and mainly developed in the period from 1949 to 1978; (c) mixed comprehensive communities, in the suburban areas, jointly developed by work units or through comprehensive development by municipality, and developed since the late 1970s; (d) rural–urban fringe villages, related to urban encroachment on rural villages, developed spontaneously and sometimes 'illegally' since the late 1970s. (Wu 2002b, 162)

In other words, the *urban* residential landscape under socialism is in essence characterised by two types: the pre-socialist legacy of more 'informal' and organic neighbourhoods (type a) and socialist formally built residential areas (type b). The latter enjoyed the welfare benefits redistributed from the state but at the same time were subject to a more modern hierarchical management. This pattern was complicated by the introduction of market development and the change in development organisation (types c and d).[1]

A new urban social geography

In the earlier stage of reform when the market approach to housing production was introduced, the role of the municipality was strengthened. Housing was not fully commoditised until 1998 when the allocation of welfare housing was abolished. The housing was market produced but administratively allocated.[2] Nevertheless, this new development approach allowed joint development, which transformed the landscape of work-unit compounds. New housing estates developed into more mixed communities. Later, with the progress of housing reform, 'commodity housing', which is purchased as properties under the real estate boom, led to the development of 'gated communities' in Chinese suburbs. In the peripheral urban areas, informal development by rural villagers interrupted the pattern of discrete urban and rural areas and introduced a space 'in-between'. These urbanised villages in former rural areas not only extended the built-up area, informally and irregularly, but also became a ubiquitous and distinct Chinese residential landscape.

One of the earliest studies on Chinese urban social areas by Anthony Yeh and his colleagues, using transport, population and land use data from small areas in Guangzhou, revealed that the 'differentiation' of urban space exhibited as the difference between land uses rather than social stratification (Yeh et al. 1995). In this sense, the patterns identified by the factorial ecology are not really 'residential differentiation' created as spatial manifestation of socioeconomic stratification. The study of Guangzhou revealed the variation in terms of population density, education, employment, house quality and household composition. Along with these differences, five types of areas were identified: high-density and mixed function areas; cadre areas; workers' areas; intellectual areas; and scattered agricultural areas. The first and the last categories refer respectively to pre-1949 traditional neighbourhoods and rural settlements. The three categories in between are different work-unit residential areas.

These areas reveal the characters of the employers (work-units) as government offices and institutions, manufacturing industries and universities. For example, the difference between factory and university living quarters is in the nature of land use rather than residential 'segregation' between workers and teachers as different social classes. In fact, within the university staff quarter, workers employed by the university (for example, workers for canteens and estates) lived in the same compound. Through work-unit housing provision, the workplace and residence maintained a strong link. The Chinese residential landscape thus presented a cellular structure; the variation between these units should be seen more as statistical difference in terms of their characteristics. The spatial pattern identified reflects under-differentiated and integrated residential landscapes in the 1980s. The most striking feature is that these identified 'ecological units' are not class-based social areas.

Through the development boom that started with Deng Xiaoping's southern China tour in 1992, such integrated spaces began to be broken down. Using 2000 population census data at the fine resolution (*juweihui*, the residents' committee), Zhigang Li and Fulong Wu (2008) provide a portrait of the residential landscape of Shanghai after its great urban expansion in the 1990s. The spatial variation of housing tenure is becoming prominent; the starkest contrast being between 'commodity housing purchased' and 'public housing rental', with the index of dissimilarity[3] reaching 0.7. By comparison, this index when measuring black and white segregation in the United States in the 2000s is around 0.6. This indicates a quite significant level of differentiation between different housing tenures. As mentioned earlier, 'residential differentiation' in the early reform period represented the statistical variation of neighbourhoods in terms of residents' occupation. Except for this difference, other socioeconomic attributes did not show significant spatial differentiation. Residential differentiation between rural migrants and local residents is rather modest, even with an increasing rural migrant population. In other words, in the 1990s Shanghai had not yet seen the obvious spatial concentration of rural migrants, who were more scattered and mixed with local residents either in traditional inner urban neighbourhoods or peri-urban villages.

Residential segregation had not occurred in a significant way before the 2000s when more rural migrants began to concentrate. It was observed that:

> Most communities are characterised by homogenous tenure and heterogeneous population. In all, post-reform urban China is characterised by tenure-based residential segregation. Through market-oriented housing consumption, a new stratified sociospatial structure is in the making. (Li and Wu 2008, 404)

Residential differentiation in Shanghai in the 1990s was led by housing changes – the relocation of residents into commodity housing estates in contrast to public housing tenants. While the overall pattern of rural migrant population in peri-urban areas was obvious, residential differentiation was finer grained and caused by different housing tenures. Residential relocation driven by new housing consumption broke the tightly integrated work-unit compounds and established new neighbourhoods.

Studies suggest that neighbourhoods are the appropriate spatial scale for understanding residential segregation and the neighbourhood changes that have laid down the mechanism of a new urban social geography.[4] To understand 'tenure-based residential segregation', it is important to examine neighbourhoods composed of different types of housing. Such a finding echoes earlier observations of four generic neighbourhood types and reflects the division between the first two 'traditional' and socialist types and the newly developed neighbourhoods of middle-class, owner-occupied housing and private rental housing.[5] But in order to understand the new residential landscapes and their mechanism, we need to examine these neighbourhoods more closely.

The mechanism of migrant residential segregation was strengthened with the large-scale influx of rural migrants into major Chinese cities in the 2000s after China joined the WTO and became the 'workshop of the world' (Figure 1.1). Also in the 2000s, large-scale and substantial housing commodification reshaped the residential landscape. China entered a real estate boom following its drastic policy to end the provision of welfare housing in 1998. The policy was to use domestic property development to rescue the economy after the Asian financial crisis. The development of the real estate market strengthened the role of residential choice in sociospatial differentiation.

Using 2010 census data, again at the fine spatial resolution of residents' committees, Jie Shen and Yang Xiao (2020) find that residential segregation based on educational attainment (an indicator of human capital and highly related to income- and market-based social stratification) has become more obvious. The massive construction of commodity housing estates in the suburbs has attracted the middle class to move there, starting a process of suburbanisation and perhaps 'professionalisation' in the suburbs. Meanwhile, under economic restructuring and globalisation, the central area of Shanghai has been redeveloped for the tertiary sector, while suburban districts have experienced the relocation and development of manufacturing industries.[6] The provision of jobs for migrants in the suburbs and the difficulty of finding accommodation in the central area have led to further concentration of migrant workers in the suburban area. Rural villages have turned into migrant enclaves. Consequently, the suburb became highly heterogeneous and differentiated in socioeconomic status.[7]

Figure 1.1 Shanghai Pudong new area, showing the Lujiazui Financial and Trade Zone, which symbolises China's ascent in the global economy. Taken in 2008.

Three consequent studies reveal that the segregation of migrants from the local population continued to grow throughout the 2000s.[8] Moreover, educational attainment and migrant status were two major dimensions of residential segregation found in 2010.[9] Compared with 2000, in terms of educational profiles, the central area has seen the rise of high-status neighbourhoods, while university towns in the suburbs have led to the concentration of high-education population in selective places. In terms of migrant status, the replacement of former mixed neighbourhoods in the suburbs with migrant neighbourhoods is the most apparent change in the residential landscape. Suburban neighbourhoods became the most segregated places.

The two dimensions are actually related to and reinforce each other. Highly educated migrants can turn their migrant status into new citizens through the route of merit-based scoring which has been implemented by the more relaxed system of household registration to absorb the 'elite and talents'. The policy is known as 'migrant integration' (*shiminghua*) but the actual outcome is very selective. Shen and Xiao (2020) observed the impact of these two dimensions on the residential landscape in Shanghai:

> The central areas have witnessed the emergence of many mixed neighbourhoods where migrants and *hukou* holders live. But the development of high-status neighbourhoods along the inner ring road has led to a great increase in educational segregation. In the suburbs, along with the emergence of both high-status neighbourhoods and migrant neighbourhoods, the suburbs have become more heterogeneous. Accordingly, the level of segregation is greater in the suburbs than in central areas. (p. 1351)

In short, the residential landscape in 2010 shows that two emerging trends identified in the 1990s have been enhanced in the 2000s: segregation due to first housing relocation and second the influx of migrant population. These two mechanisms have eventually consolidated the development of two entirely new types of neighbourhood: migrant enclaves and gated communities.

Together with researchers from Shanghai, John Logan investigated residential segregation in Shanghai across different spatial rings (inner Shanghai, inner suburbs and outer suburbs) at the whole metropolitan scale. Their study confirms that local Shanghainese, urban and rural migrants literally live in different urban worlds – their neighbourhoods having distinctive composition of housing tenures. They found that '… some tenure types rarely overlap at all in the same neighbourhoods' (Gu et al. 2021, 90), as these housing tenures are spatially fixed by their pre-socialist and socialist development histories. For example, 'rural fixed locals (those with a rural Shanghai *hukou* who live in their registered place) are far less likely to live in a commodity housing neighbourhood', 'extremely unlikely to live in a public housing or mixed public and commodity housing neighbourhood'. But 'in contrast, they are very likely to live in neighbourhoods that consist of predominantly self-built housing' (p. 91). They stress the continuation of segregation, explaining that

> the patterns attributable to the market reform period mostly did not supplant the socialist urban structure, but rather used it as its foundation. Segregation today can be attributed less to current class inequality than to state policies in the distant and recent past that have determined when, where and for whom housing is built. (Gu et al. 2021, 80)

They argue that, although increasing income inequality and housing prices tend to 'create a potential for the emerging settlement patterns to resemble the Western model of class-based segregation, … institutional forces continue to be more important than market forces in creating the particular (and complex) pattern of segregation and spatial distribution of social groups in Shanghai' (p. 96).

All residential segregation studies suggest that it is meaningful to use neighbourhoods as a basic unit to observe urban changes. The social typology of the residential world has turned from the dualistic one of traditional and work-unit neighbourhoods into a fourfold one with two new types: migrant and middle-class neighbourhoods. If the difference between the first two types of neighbourhoods under socialism reflects the pre-socialist historical legacy, the variation of state welfare provision and degrees of formalisation and bureaucratisation, the contrast between the two new types of neighbourhoods in the post-reform era is sharp, producing a profound impact on urban China. They reflect two different residential worlds with entirely different physical appearances, composition of residents, housing tenure and governance.

Some residents of traditional neighbourhoods managed to move into work-unit compounds through formal job recruitment by state work-units. However, it is rare for a migrant worker in an urban village to move into a gated community; this route is only for successful migrant entrepreneurs. For highly educated migrants, the pathway is again their employment. In other words, although they may temporarily stay in urban villages, their remuneration from human capital enables them to purchase property and move into gated communities just like their fellow staff living in the work-unit compound. In other words, residential mobility between urban villages and gated communities is low; when such mobility does happen, it is the same as residential mobility from the central area to the suburb within the city, while urban villages are treated only as temporary accommodation.

After depicting a picture of residential differentiation, it is possible to examine individual types of neighbourhoods to understand how 'traditionalism' has been broken down. China has seen a rising consumerism (Figure 1.2).[10] However, the collapse of an organic society is not simply caused by consumerism that challenges state authority. As will be seen later, the homeowners' association does not play this role, as might be expected, by injecting the private realm. The urban village is not a world without rules, as its informal appearance might suggest. We need to understand how governance is simultaneously transformed and enhanced and how order is maintained. In the following discussion, the features of these four generic neighbourhoods are explained first before the internal dynamics and governance are subjected to closer examination in the respective chapters.

Figure 1.2 Fashion and foreign brands symbolise a new era of consumption and consumerism. Daning Plaza in former Zhabei District, the low-end of Shanghai, has totally transformed the area. Taken in 2017.

Four types of neighbourhoods

Traditional neighbourhoods were less bureaucratised because street offices – a quasi-government agency under the district government – and their subsidiary 'mass organisations' called residents' committees (*juming weiyuanhui*) provided the basis of governance. This was less formal than state work-units under formal government departments. Traditional neighbourhoods were less incorporated into the state system than work-unit compounds, factory living quarters or large industrial-residential complexes.

In terms of housing tenure, a large proportion of traditional neighbourhoods comprised public housing converted from pre-1949 private housing but under the management of municipal housing bureaux. This is a relatively inferior type of public housing compared with 'work-unit housing'.[11] Because the residents in traditional neighbourhoods stayed there for a long time, they were familiar with one another and developed close relationships. Courtyard housing (*siheyuan*) in alleyways (*hutong*) in Beijing and *shikumen* housing in lanes or alleyways (*lilong* or *longtang*)

Figure 1.3 The lane houses in Zuopu Road, Shanghai, showing the high-density residential neighbourhoods. The original quality of the housing shown in the photo is comparatively higher than usual lane houses. The multiple occupancies of lane houses further increase the population density, making a crowded urban world. Taken in 2016.

in Shanghai all present the features of traditional neighbourhoods and intense social interaction (Figure 1.3).

Work-unit neighbourhoods were usually built by state work-units as staff living quarters (Figure 1.4). Larger employers were able to build their own exclusive work-unit compounds (Figure 1.5). Smaller work-units needed to jointly develop accommodation for their workers or relied on workers' new villages developed by the municipal government. Workers' new villages were an upscale version of work-unit compounds for multiple work-units. Residents lived in work-unit neighbourhoods owing to their employment and affiliation to a work-unit. They all belonged to the community of the work-unit but at the same time stayed in the same living environment. This configuration combined the secondary and economic relationship with the territorial social relationship. Along with socialist life-long employment came residential stability and tenancy security.

Work-unit neighbourhoods were therefore a world of acquaintances, although neighbouring relations also overlapped with professional

Figure 1.4 The staff housing in No. 1 Village, Xi'an Jiaotong University. This part was constructed in the late 1970s but it deteriorated quite significantly as shown in the photo. Taken in 2016.

Figure 1.5 The work-unit compound of Baiwanzhuang, Beijing, before the area was demolished in 2014. The quality of housing was relatively higher as it was for the staff living quarters of the central government ministries. The layout was influenced by the Soviet super neighbourhood block. Taken in 2014.

interactions. Compared with traditional neighbourhoods, work-unit neighbourhoods may not have stronger neighbourhood social interactions. There could be several reasons for this. First, neighbourhood interaction might be substituted by workplace interaction. Because of concern over the complication of work relationships, especially during constant political movements, neighbouring might be deliberately kept minimal and informal by residents, in order to stand away from workplace relations.

Second, because the estate department of a work-unit was responsible for estate maintenance, residents needed less mutual help. The work-unit compound is a reinvention of the society 'from the soil' in an environment in which residents perform industrial and modern economic activities which are impersonal and secondary in terms of social relationships. Although the 'totalised society' rather successfully maintained a low cost of information collection and monitoring, there was hidden tension between the need for partial relations and private space, and all presence and comprehensive relations extended from working relations into the neighbourhood. Work-unit compounds had some security features such as gates and walls, but compared with the new gated communities of commodity housing, the security was rather lax.

Due to tight social integration, the work-unit compound was truly a place of 'neighbourhood watch'. It did not need 'surveillance' as a technical and professional service. Such an exclusive environment integrated with living and work had significant implications for social life,[12] for example 'organised dependence',[13] because workers were dependent upon collective consumption organised by the work-unit. Work-units organised social life and provided a wide range of amenities such as cinemas and canteens to their residents. Because of this form of material provision and social organisation, traditional features were preserved, replicated and strengthened in work-unit neighbourhoods.

The post-reform era witnessed the emergence of two types of neighbourhoods. First, rural villages near the city evolved into a new category of social area in urban China. These urbanised rural villages are called 'urban villages' (*chengzhongcun* in Chinese) (Figure 1.6). Their residents – farmers – lost their agricultural land during land acquisition but managed to keep their housing plots because it was cheaper to acquire farmland than to obtain the land of village housing through relocating farmers. Hence, rural villages remained and were encircled by the city. With the influx of migrants from other rural areas, these villages literally became migrant settlements providing low-cost housing to migrant workers.[14] The concentration of migrant population in peripheral urban areas is due to the lack of affordable rental housing in the urban areas themselves. In residential

Figure 1.6 An urban village, Zhucun (Pearl Village) in Guangzhou. The photo shows how new self-built rental housing maximises the use of space within individual housing plots. The communal area is under-maintained. Taken in 2012.

areas formerly built by state work-units, homeowners who were sitting tenants of former public housing did not have spare property. In central areas, although much low-quality housing could be used for private rental housing, residents usually lost their property when they were relocated by urban redevelopment projects to suburban settlements. Thus, the supply of rental housing in former urbanised areas became limited.

When migrants came to the city, they could not find sufficient private rental housing in work-unit compounds or traditional urban neighbourhoods. Rather, they had to find accommodation at the periphery of the city, usually in urban villages. When villagers saw the opportunity to make an income from renting out spare rooms, they began to extend their housing or even rebuilt their property into multi-floor buildings. Because of relatively lax land regulation and development control in rural areas, the scale of redevelopment was massive, creating a distinctive feature of extremely narrow alleyways between buildings as every house owner tried to build right up to the boundary of their land plots. The influx of migrant renters transformed the rural community into a migrant enclave. The proportion of the migrant population is much higher than that of local villagers. Some villager landlords have moved into new nearby resettlement

Figure 1.7 A dormitory for rural migrant workers, by private factory owners, in Shantou, Guangdong province. The photo shows crowded living conditions, standardised structure, and strict management as all windows are protected by safety nets. Taken in 2013.

villages and use their properties especially for rental. The ratio of migrant population to locals could be as high as 20 times in some cases.

The media have tended to describe the physical environment of urban villages as dirty and chaotic, and the government is seriously concerned about the crime rate in urban villages because migrant tenants have high residential mobility and are not under the usual neighbourhood management. Nevertheless, urban villages are not a lawless world; landlords usually have no problem collecting rents, and most migrant tenants are employed, coming into the city for work. Many live with their families, compared with those who lived in factory dormitories. Because of the informal living environment, migrant tenants encounter each other and maintain intense social interaction. But they are not able to participate in neighbourhood activities, even if these social activities exist. Migrants are excluded from neighbourhood affairs and decision-making, because the local villagers are the property owners and the shareholding company of the village is the 'executive board' of village business. In short, the urban village is an economic space of rental housing for rural villagers and a cost-effective shelter for migrant workers (Figure 1.7). But the traditional rural community has been broken down.

Besides the urban village, the second new type is 'gated community', which is a term originating from North America, referring to 'privately governed and secured neighbourhoods'.[15] The concept consists of two aspects in its definition: first, security features surrounding the neighbourhood, for example, gates and walls; and second, private governance which is associated with privatisation and governance, for example, 'contractual constitution'. It would be difficult to apply the full definition to the Chinese context in which gating is ubiquitous while 'private' governance by the community is questionable. We use the security component of the definition to refer to the enclosed estates in China as gated communities without endorsing a view that they follow private governance.

Most commodity housing estates for Chinese middle class are secured; many are built in the suburbs, but inner areas also see the development of gated apartments or condominium compounds (Figure 1.8). In Chinese, these secured estates are called 'enclosed micro-districts' (*fengbi xiaoqu*). The concept of *xiaoqu* is a planning concept, which means that these estates are developed by planning, similar to workers' new villages – the 'micro-district' planned for socialist workers. Later

Figure 1.8 An ordinary commodity housing estate in Tianjin Sino-Singapore Eco-city. The area was previously low land in an industrial area. The photo shows some modest security and the gate. Taken in 2014.

all planned residential neighbourhoods beyond the compound of single work-unit are called residential *xiaoqu*. The term *fengbi* means 'enclosed'. The combination of these two words indicates that these estates were designed before they were developed and earmarked with a boundary. These are new neighbourhoods, often developed from scratch by real-estate developers. As such they are not memorable places, even lacking a place name before they were built.[16] Therefore, exotic names such as Orange County, Yosemite, Beverly Hills, Fontainebleau and Thames Town were invented to hint that these were upper-market housing estates.[17] Some are decorated in ostentatious or neo-classical building styles. Considering the namelessness of these places, it is understandable that their developers have had to brand the place and 'package' the services to attract homebuyers.

Residents in gated communities are all homeowners; except in premium central locations, rental is rare. The property owners may consider them as second or third homes for occasional use, but they are mostly for investment purposes if the owners do not live there. Many properties in gated communities have been sold but are left empty, because rental income does not justify the huge investment and the cost of redecoration after renting out. Gated communities are built into micro-districts based on large parcels divided by main roads. It is the cheapest and fastest way to divide land into large parcels because they require fewer infrastructure networks and are also suitable for land sale. The developer enclosed the land after buying it from the municipal government, which is the only legitimate seller. Because gated communities were developed quickly during suburbanisation and the real estate boom, social services have not been fully developed. Property management companies were introduced to maintain the estates.

Initially, the developer of gated communities was responsible for appointing and supervising property management companies. But soon after the completion of development projects, many developers wished to offload this burden, although some developers may continue to manage the neighbourhood for the sake of the company brand. Homeowners' associations were set up to manage property-related issues and supervise property management companies. Residents are homeowners and associated with the gated communities through property rights, which formed a community of consumers. They have an attachment to the neighbourhood based on this interest in property and are sometimes mobilised to defend their rights during property disputes with the developer or property management companies. On the other hand, the governance of gated communities is very different from that of traditional neighbourhoods or work-unit compounds. However, in terms of neighbouring and social interaction, residents keep a comfortable distance from each other, although they may participate in leisure activities in communal space.

Urban life and social mentality

Associated with urbanisation and the making of the 'metropolis', according to George Simmel (1903/2002), is a new social mentality. This mentality, in response to the nature of the metropolis as a place of higher density and intensive encountering, is a 'blasé attitude' or indifference to other dwellers. Individuals tend to explore their own freedom and personality rather than caring for the lives of other people.[18] This 'sensory over-stimulation' or 'overexposure of the senses to external stimuli' eventually leads to more rationalisation, objectivity and indifference, as well as to autonomy and the self-identity of individuals.[19] This thesis of the 'blasé metropolitan attitude' tends to build upon the generic nature of the metropolis.[20] However, rather than thinking of this as the 'natural' trait of life in the metropolis, here these characteristics are described as socially constructed along with residential changes and marketisation in China. This book describes the social and historical process behind this development in diverse contexts. While largely confirming this overall trend – the decline of parochialism along with the loosening of the bonds of collectivism – its manifestation is variegated and contextually dependent.

The Chicago School largely extended Simmel's tradition, as shown in Robert Park's research on the changing moral order in cities and Louis Wirth's famous notion of 'urbanism as a way of life'. Borrowing an older German proverb of 'city air makes men free (*stadtluft macht frei*)', Park (1915) described the 'advantage and alluring characteristics of the city such as better chances of social mobility and individual freedom'.[21] But at the same time the increasing mobility of the population and the extension of industrial organisation led to 'impersonal relations defined by money'.[22] Population is defined into vocational groups, breaking down social groups and the traditional social structure based on family ties and local associations and substituting them for the organisation of vocational interests.[23] Louis Wirth (1938) further elaborated that the division of labour and the proliferation of different professions are driven by the 'segmental character and utilitarian accent of interpersonal relations in the city' (p. 13).

In short, while the traditional moral order is defined by shared sentiments and memories and based on primary and neighbourhood relations, that order is modified by the peculiar characteristics of the city with secondary relations characterised by anonymity and personal interest. The moral order differs between the city and the rural society (village).[24] The Chicago School attributes the difference to the nature of the city – as the site for industrial production and high population mobility, rather than the capitalist mode of production in history. But later studies found that even in large cities such as Boston, the Italian-American ethnic working-class neighbourhood demonstrated the characteristics of the village. The village-like life of 'urban villagers'[25] is represented as a subculture of the metropolis. In the post-war United States, the existence of close residential communities was threatened by large-scale inner-city renewal.[26]

The Chicago School of sociology invented a human ecology perspective to understand the city and the characteristics of urban life. The city is distinctive and is defined by these ecological characteristics. This approach was criticised for its lack of attention to other political economic factors. For example, Manuel Castells (1977) suggests that the city should be understood as the basic unit for social reproduction through collective consumption organised by the state. David Harvey (1978) developed the concept of the spatial fix to see the production of the built environment (the city) as an extension of capitalist production and its function in sustaining capital accumulation. In other words, these social areas are not 'naturally' formed by human ecological processes of invasion and succession. The distinction between the city and the rural is not just in terms of agricultural and industrial or commercial activities but is also defined by the territory of state governance. In the thesis of 'planetary urbanisation', developed by Neil Brenner and Christian Schmid (2011), the urban is not a bounded spatial unit, but exists in relational terms through the process of urbanisation created by the everyday life of urban dwellers.[27]

This book aims to understand urban China in this context of changing urban life and social mentality. It does not characterise the Chinese city as having 'concentric zones' or natural 'social areas' to be discovered by factorial ecology, which has been extensively studied in China.[28] But rather, generic neighbourhoods are discovered within the context of specific urban history, the changing relation between the state and capital, and reorientation of social relations and organisation.

Looking back at the history of urban development in Central and Eastern Europe, the socialist city hoped to create a new built environment to create a new mentality or personality – 'socialist man'[29] – committed to collectivism and further to the state. The concept of neighbourhood was applied to develop the micro-district, the residential district consisting of neighbourhoods provided with community facilities such as nurseries and primary schools. It was hoped that by using public facilities in a small territory, the effect of alienation from large-scale industrialisation could be avoided.[30] The development of the socialist city reduced private consumption in neighbourhood life and in turn fostered collectivism. However, the result was that while street life became politicised, residents turned to a more family-oriented life within their houses.[31] The residential neighbourhood was a social space organised by the state. The actual development was implemented by smaller administrative units, hence creating fragmentation between industrial sectors and territorial administrations.[32]

China adopted a similar strategy of 'industrialisation without urbanisation'. Therefore, the level of urbanisation was low because only the urban population enjoyed state collective consumption. The extent of urbanisation was limited and urbanism as a way of life was absent because of the collectivist characteristics of urban neighbourhoods. 'Informal' social relations were maintained in alleyway neighbourhoods or invented and grafted onto industrialised and formal workplaces. Bureaucratisation was incomplete, not only because full entitlement was available only to the 'insider of the system' but also because residential neighbourhoods retained reciprocal relations. In this sense, before China started its market reform the country was quite 'rural' (Figure 1.9).

The socialist transformation triggered and further facilitated the process of 'individualisation', freeing people from clan and extended family relations.[33] However, collectivism was maintained through particular urban settings. Now after the economic reform, urbanisation has led to greater residential mobility and wider social encountering. Residents have been emancipated from the constraints of traditionalism which still existed before marketisation. Social relations based on traditional ties have become weaker and extend into networks beyond the bounded territory, becoming increasingly translocal. Traditional alleyway neighbourhoods and new urban villages have seen fragmented social composition. The division is not just between rural and urban *hukou*, as in urban villages; although both landlords and renters have the official status of rural *hukou*, they present a different social class. The social relation between migrant tenants and local landlords is more based on the rental market and calculated profits or expenses. Even when living at close quarters, residents no longer retain their relations through parochialism or

Figure 1.9 Informal gathering of villagers playing cards in Xiaozhou Village, Guangzhou. Such leisure activities are also widely seen in old and traditional urban neighbourhoods, and so is dancing in public squares. Taken in 2010.

particularism (the differential mode of association – a social order from a recognition of the self to caring for the community through differentiated social relations).

Social relations become more universal, although the personal relation (*guanxi*) between individuals still exists. But what is the meaning of *guanxi* in a transformed urban world? In the urban world, informal and reciprocal relations still exist.[34] In Chinese gated communities, residents still socialise in leisure and entertainment activities and even jointly take action to defend their property rights. The retired elderly dance and socialise in public squares and parks. But *guanxi* as used in the urban world has a special meaning as a connection for the parties involved to perform a transaction – a utilitarian function – while in a setting of rurality, association is simply a relation existing through family and within a local territory. Because *guanxi* now is centred more upon the benefit than on the relation itself, a moral order cannot be built simply from such social relations or connections. It must resort to a third party, a guarantee, or an arbitrator. It is now the state that plays this role in market transactions. For example, residential disputes in gated communities or residents' quarrels with the developer cannot be resolved within their relations (between fellow residents or between the customer and business owner).

From observations in different neighbourhoods, we hope to understand how residential communities are dismantled[35] and territory-based social capital is underdeveloped. Below, several studies are pieced together for a general picture of urban life, interaction and integration, and social mentality. First, low-income neighbourhoods experienced a departure from an organic society of greater social participation and place attachment.[36] In order to understand their particular conditions, different social groups are examined, with their statements on place attachment, social participation, and willingness to stay. While retired people still maintain a strong neighbourhood attachment, working household heads show lower attachment to the neighbourhood because they have more connection outside their residential communities. Rural migrants show the lowest attachment because they are excluded from social participation. The workplace neighbourhood demonstrates the strongest place attachment among its residents. Next is the traditional neighbourhood, which still maintains place attachment. In contrast, urban villages have the lowest level of place attachment.

In short, migrants and their places of living show the lowest place attachment. In terms of social participation, retired people are involved in neighbourhood social activities to the highest extent, while migrants show the lowest level of involvement. The workplace neighbourhood shows the highest percentage of participation among their residents, while urban villages show the lowest percentage because migrants are excluded from neighbourhood activities. Because urban villages are mainly places for rental housing, there are fewer neighbourhood social activities. But in terms of willingness to stay in these neighbourhoods, migrants are not the lowest social group. For economic reasons (e.g., closer to work and cheaper rent), they are more willing to stay in the existing neighbourhood. Similarly, retired households demonstrate the strongest willingness to stay in their current neighbourhoods. The workplace neighbourhood is the most stable residential community with the highest percentage of residents wishing to stay in the same place. In contrast, the traditional neighbourhood shows the lowest percentage of households willing to stay, reflecting poorer living conditions and the longing for a more modern estate. Interestingly, urban villages still have a large percentage of households preferring to stay – as migrant renters they moved into the current place based on their preference and calculation of economic cost.

Rural migrants in these neighbourhoods are less territorially bonded, and their social networks are more translocal and less embedded into an existing neighbourhood.[37] In contrast, state-sector employees in their workplace neighbourhood, either retired or still working, are more integrated into their neighbourhoods. Despite a large proportion (in the survey over 60 per cent) of migrants already living with their family members in the city, they have low participation. Their low participation is not due to their status of being single and hence not able to participate in family-oriented neighbourhood activities. They wish to stay in their current neighbourhoods but remain detached from these places due to social exclusion. In contrast, residents who have been in a traditional neighbourhood for a long time prefer to leave their current place. For them, despite the location in a faraway and less convenient place, suburban gated communities are often perceived as more desirable places.

Second, a citywide random survey in Shanghai reveals that rural migrants retain a great deal of localised social interaction.[38] Migrants visit their neighbours more often than their local counterparts. A large proportion of migrants greet or help their neighbours. Similar to the study on Beijing,[39] a large share of migrants continue to have strong neighbourly interactions with fellow migrants. Further distinguishing households' *hukou* status indicates that rural migrants tend to interact more with local residents compared with locals who later interact less frequently with migrants in the neighbourhood. The reasons are twofold: rural migrants are more likely to live in migrant-dominant neighbourhoods, and migrants are more willing to interact with locals in order to get better access to the labour market and gain social integration.[40]

The survey suggests that more than half of migrant respondents report that they exchange support with native neighbours on a frequent or occasional basis while only a quarter of native residents exchange help with migrant residents. Nearly 80 per cent of migrant respondents state that they frequently or sometimes exchange greetings with their native neighbours.[41] Frequent neighbourhood interactions enhance the way rural migrants construct their sense of social solidarity, which contradicts Park's assertion that social solidarity in an urbanised world would disappear or be based on common interest rather than sentiment and habit.[42] The result shows that rural migrants have stronger feelings of mutual care, trust and amity toward native residents in Shanghai, with whom they also frequently exchange support and visits.[43] Migrants tend to be generally more trustful toward the native population,[44] indicating that good neighbourly relations with their native neighbours may also affect their general sense of trust and sentiment toward the urban population.⁴⁵ In Park's original thesis, industrialisation and labour market formalisation underpin the moral order of the city, which is based on the 'organisation of vocational interests'.⁴⁶

Since migrant workers joined the urban labour market in China, according to this thesis, rural migrants might be causing the decline of territorially based social capital. On the contrary, as Fulong Wu and John Logan (2016) observed:

> They are a factor countering the process of 'modernisation'. They bring a traditional element of society into the city, especially into their enclaves. Being constrained by access to public resources, they interact with neighbours, who are probably in the same category of 'floating population'. Rural migrants are developing a social space of their own. Greater neighbouring is accompanied by a higher propensity of helping neighbours, and based on neighbouring they do not have a significant lower evaluation of the social relation in the neighbourhood. In a sense, the neighbourhood is still relevant to rural migrants, even against a background of declining neighbouring and increasing privacy as in middle-class commodity housing. (p. 2988)

Third, a national survey of migrants provides valuable information about the extent of social integration of rural migrants.⁴⁷ The survey allows mapping of migrants' social interaction and neighbourhood evaluation with their housing tenures and types, from which the generic neighbourhood can be inferred. It is found that migrants living in commodity housing neighbourhoods (largely gated communities) manage to achieve the highest level of social integration in terms of socioeconomic achievement, neighbourly interaction and social relationships.⁴⁸ Migrants living in urban villages show a lower level of social integration, although they earned on average a higher income than those staying in factory dormitories and old neighbourhoods. In other words, moving into private rental housing in urban villages indicates an economic achievement.

Considering the higher degree of neighbouring in urban villages,⁴⁹ the survey results further suggest that migrants living there do not manage to go beyond neighbourly interaction to achieve better social integration. Urban villages 'serve as a stepping-stone' for migrants to earn an income but cannot eventually provide a pathway to greater social integration.⁵⁰ This concurs with the earlier findings that migrants in urban villages lack stronger place attachment and social participation. Using the indicator of migrants' place attachment to their 'host city' rather than to the neighbourhood itself, the limitation of urban villages in social integration becomes even more apparent. Migrants living in commodity housing (largely as gated communities) are more likely to feel attached to their cities in contrast with those who live in urban and rural villages.[51]

From the close investigation of different neighbourhood types in this book, the effect of homeownership on urban life, social mentality and further integration of migrants can be better understood. Being a renter in an urban village does not hinder the migrant from neighbouring and socialising with other migrant tenants because urban villages are predominantly inhabited by rural migrants and the informal setting of the built environment even replicates some 'organic' features of the traditional alleyway neighbourhood.

However, the neighbourhood is not governed by a social order of collectivism emerging from migrants' everyday life. Although neighbouring may contribute to sentiment towards the urban village,[52] rural migrants living in informal housing do not manage to claim their right to the city: they are physically living in the city and are actors in the process of urbanisation yet they do not identify themselves with the city, achieve stronger 'place attachment', or influence the course of urban development.[53] Instead of suggesting that the neighbourhood itself has a causal effect or can determine urban life, social mentality and integration, here generic urban neighbourhoods are regarded as different 'urban worlds' which present similar trends of urbanisation but in a variegated way because of their historical and political economic differences.

From these observations, we can begin to understand the changing urban life and social mentality in urban China. Despite strong place attachment and existing higher levels of participation, the traditional neighbourhood (often a low-income neighbourhood) has witnessed neighbourhood decline along with the residential preference to leave for less engaged social relations and a better quality of housing and built environment; the residential community is weakened by changing housing consumption and commodification, or is 'dismantled' not only by physical demolition but also through the mass everyday life of long-term residents.

To a lesser extent, the workplace neighbourhood, especially in low-income industrial areas, suffered similar impacts, with better-off residents moving into suburban commodity housing estates. In general, we see the transformation of working-class communities – declining solidarity and the consequential marginalisation of residents.[54] These long-term residents are replaced with incoming migrant renters, new graduates and other low-income families, a process that does not fit into 'gentrification'. Although low-income families show a strong preference for living in these places, because of their housing 'preference' and residential 'choice' they are not actively involved in neighbourhood life and have low place attachment. Low participation and attachment indicate the transformation of residential communities, even though these residential areas demonstrate a bustling atmosphere of everyday life. The residents, especially low-income migrants, maintain social interaction – neighbouring and networking across neighbourhood boundaries. But social interaction in these places differs both from rurality, or what Fei Xiaotong described in imperial China, and from 'socialist solidarity' as observed in working-class neighbourhoods. To be precise, these neighbourhoods today are not 'sterile places' but accommodate a variety of social activities. However, they are no longer confined to the mentality of collectivism and are evolving as the new urban China.

The development of urban villages and gated communities as two entirely new types of neighbourhoods, respectively for rural migrants and the urban middle class, is creating a profound residential segregation by housing tenure. As discussed earlier in this chapter, urban villages are created out of the rental economy. Social interaction between migrant tenants and rural landlords is superficial, and governance remains within the original village structure and operates through new shareholding cooperatives. The governance thus is exclusionary. The only way to be incorporated into the city and urban governance is through demolition and resettlement, as shown in Chapter 3. Hence, despite local interaction, territorial social capital has not been developed.

For gated communities, as discussed in Chapter 4, place attachment to these neighbourhoods does not disappear, as might be implied by the Chicago School or concern for the disappearance of small places or residential communities.[55] However, strong place attachment is largely built upon the identity and image of the enclosed neighbourhood,[56] common interests in property rights[57] and the quality of services now provided through the market.[58] Social interaction in commodity housing estates becomes superficial and the overall intensity is comparably lower than for the traditional alleyway neighbourhood or the informal neighbourhoods of urban villages. Despite the formation of homeowners' associations in gated communities, the homeowners' association encounters significant challenges because of weak territorial social capital.[59] Neighbourhood participation is not driven by social capital or frequent interactions[60] because residential privacy is highly respected. In other words, although gated communities are strikingly different from urban villages in the sense that the latter encounter much everyday bustling and are rental places, the former are also created by the housing market – a regime of

Figure 1.10 A small city near the seaside, Ningde in Fujian province. The city used to be at a 'remote' frontier due to the lack of a railway. The photo shows that the city was just being connected by high-speed rail, crossing the bay. Taken in 2014.

property ownership. Instead of seeing the neighbourhood itself having a causal effect, as seen in both urban villages and gated communities, the impact is generated from marketisation and social changes in a traditional society which had a great deal of remaining rurality.

Accompanying marketisation is a process of urbanisation – disappearing rurality and emerging urbanism (Figure 1.10). There is a significant extent of diversity, superficial encountering, interest calculation and social exclusion. In one way, from neighbourhood observations in China, this book shares a long tradition of concerns over the rise of modern industrial capitalism and its impacts on society and social mentality – Durkheim's 'anomie' as the result of losing a spontaneous and organic social order or the loosening of community ties as claimed by the Chicago School of Sociology[61] – the detrimental impact of large-scale urban renewal for urban communities,[62] the dystopia created by the postmodern condition,[63] the decline of community in social and political life, rising control through private governance[64] and the loss of the public realm,[65] and the threat posed to the neighbourhood as a small and cherished place.[66] But this book explores changing urban life and social mentality in a specific Chinese history of development and geographies of urban spaces and neighbourhoods. In short, urban life and social mentality are not reduced to isolation within fragments but rather each segment and the social relations of residents across these neighbourhoods are being transformed. It is precisely this transition, or 'leaving the soil' from being territorially based to a network form, that is described in this book. In other words, the book does not discuss the generic urban and rural 'ecological' difference but rather the urbanisation process in particular historical and cultural Chinese geographies and specific governance institutions encountering now worldwide commodification.[67]

Destroying old China by property-led redevelopment

Chinese urban neighbourhoods have experienced significant impacts of real estate development. They have been literally destroyed by property-led redevelopment.[68] After the introduction of housing market and real estate development, urban redevelopment has shifted from dilapidated housing rehabilitation to property-led redevelopment since the late 1990s.[69] In the 2000s, property developers became major actors in urban redevelopment. The renewal was funded through land value capture as part of property development. In Shanghai, urban renewal shifted its priority from the rehabilitation of dilapidated housing to demolition and off-site relocation. In short, urban redevelopment was combined with and facilitated by housing commodification and property rights redistribution.[70] Fulong Wu (2016d) provides a simplified periodisation of urban redevelopment in China (see Table 1.1), which is punctuated by major global historical events such as China's joining the World Trade Organisation (WTO) and the 2008 global financial crisis.[71]

The redevelopment of the central city has shifted from housing refurbishment, to property development, to the development of the service sector. This change echoes what Neil Smith called the transition from middle-class–driven sporadic residential gentrification to the redevelopment of old areas as a 'global production strategy' seeking economic competitiveness by state-led initiatives or growth coalitions between the state and developers.[72] Although the state has always been prominent in urban redevelopment in China, the actual organisation of development has shifted from state work-units themselves, or comprehensive municipal renewal (such as the development of the Fifth Village) in the 1980s, to developer-initiated real estate development (such as the Xintiandi redevelopment) in the 1990s, to state-owned development corporations

Table 1.1 The historical stages of urban redevelopment in China

Periodisation	Historical conditions	Policy aims	Approaches and main actors	Features of redevelopment projects
1979 – 1997	Economic reform in 1979	Housing renovation	State work-units Municipal housing bureau	Housing refurbishment
1998 – 2008	Asian financial crisis in 1997 WTO membership in 2001	Housing commodification Attracting foreign investment Land revenue	Property developers Entrepreneurial local states	Demolition, displacement and property-led redevelopment
2009 – 2014	Global financial crisis in 2008	Urbanisation and economic upgrading	Entrepreneurial local states State-owned development corporations Property developers	Mix-use development Mega urban projects
2015 – present	Fiscal stimulus package Enlarged financial risk	New urbanisation plan Social stabilisation Urban heritage	Policy mandates Multi-scalar states Social mobilisation and neighbourhood participation	Incremental or micro-urban redevelopment Regeneration and innovation

Source: developed from Wu (2016d) and Wu et al. (2022)

(such as the Lujiazui financial centre and Hongqiao Transport Hub) in the late 1990s and 2000s.

The outcomes of urban development have expanded from renewed housing estates to newly developed gated communities and the 'mix-use urban complex' characterised by super-blocks, combining shopping malls, offices and businesses, and condominiums. Consequently, the central city has changed from residential neighbourhoods to financial centres, government offices, research and development and logistics uses. This later stage of large-scale land use change is also referred to as commercial or 'retail gentrification'[73] but the redevelopment is very different from the classic form of residential gentrification. The sheer scale of these redevelopment projects means that they are organised more by development corporations and developers through urban regeneration programmes. The later stage has also seen selective preservation of original architectural styles but conversion of original residential uses into creative cultural industries, tourist shopping districts, and entertainment venues under so-called 'culture-led regeneration'.

Since 2015, urban redevelopment has resorted to financial means or those of so-called financialisation.[74] To reduce the stock of unsold housing and to stimulate the housing market in smaller cities,[75] the government initiated the large-scale demolition of dilapidated housing, providing monetary compensation to residents for them to buy new commodity housing. In the central areas of large cities, earlier demolitions had created social tension, and redevelopment became increasingly costly due to rising land prices and compensation. A new redevelopment approach, called 'incremental redevelopment', has been introduced to replace wholesale demolition: this converts original residential uses into mixed uses with boutiques, shopping, restaurants, museums and tourist attractions. Overall, market-oriented real estate development has completely transformed the landscape of Chinese cities.

The coming of heterogeneity, superficiality and diversity in new urban China

As can be seen from the earlier description of generic neighbourhood types in China, the trend that Chinese urban society is 'leaving the soil' is not due only to greater residential differentiation. Leaving the soil – or urbanisation in a social sense – has been materialised through the dynamics of neighbourhood changes. To repeat, creating a new Chinese urbanism and transformation of urban life arise not only from emerging class-based residential differentiation and residential segregation, breaking up previous socially integrated traditional neighbourhoods, but also from the changes in neighbourhoods themselves, together with changing neighbouring interactions, relations and governance, and finally the development of a new social geography. In other words, in order to understand the creation of urbanism, we need to understand not only space and spatial processes but also place and place-based changes.

In post-reform China, the profound transformation is that heterogeneity, greater superficiality and diversity, as the essential traits of urbanism, have finally arrived. Built upon the differential mode of association, Chinese society maintained an organic and intimate nature of 'village' from the soil. The socialist city did not break down the village; instead, by developing workplace compounds and workers' new 'villages', the socialist city was a collection of 'villages' and was socially engaged. The private realm was reduced by state-organised collective consumption. In the work-unit compound, residents were familiar with each other because they were affiliated with the same workplace. In traditional neighbourhoods, former single-family houses were converted into multiple tenements. The privacy of courtyard living was eroded because of increasing living density and multiple occupancies, as we see in the story of '72 tenant families under a single tenement building' and the spread of gossip about residents in Shanghai's alleyway neighbourhoods.[76] Residents often had to share facilities and communal spaces. In a sense, the socialist city was a totalised society, because everyday life was totalised into a residential sphere.

The development of commodity housing provided a chance for the new middle class to escape from the totalised society. The aspiration of the new middle class for social engagement in the neighbourhood is low. Rather than seeking a community life, they desire a good environment with higher privacy. For them these gated communities maintain a certain anonymity.[77] Thus, relocating into these places gives them a sense of freedom, escaping from the intense social engagement, gossip, control and monitoring of traditional neighbourhoods. Although the property management company sometimes promotes neighbourhood activities, residents are generally willing to keep a comfortable distance from one another. Professional services can be provided by property management companies rather than neighbours' assistance. Their places thus are a more 'purified' living space, without too much uncertain interaction between neighbours or nuisances.

To suggest that the Chinese city in the post-reform era has seen greater heterogeneity, a greater level of superficiality in social life (anonymity), and diversity does not mean that it lacks order; nor was rural society entirely without administration. In the imperial era, the system of feudal governance primarily relied on self-containment and self-monitoring through the mechanism of *baojia* invented by Wang Anshi in the Song Dynasty (960–1279). *Baojia*, a household and neighbourhood-based control, consisted of two basic units: one *jia* consisted of 100 households, and 10 *jia* formed one *bao*. So *bao* was a rather large unit, reaching a population of five to six thousand. But through *jia*, the large unit of *bao* managed to achieve a governance order. The leaders of *bao* and *jia* took responsibility for social order, while the household within the same *baojia* shared community duties. As can be seen later, in the socialist period, *baojia* was replaced by another two scales: in traditional inner urban areas *baojia* was ended with the establishment of street offices and residents' committees; in newly industrialised areas, the new system of work-units was set up.

In the post-reform period, through consolidating smaller residents' committees into larger *shequ* (residential communities, or enlarged administrative neighbourhoods), this self-governed mechanism continued. However, compared with the underdeveloped society, the capacity of state at the grassroots level has been quickly developed. The system of residential communities has evolved into a more bureaucratic government. The budget is allocated by the street office. In the early days of residential communities, neighbourhood services were provided on a commercial basis to subsidise the operational costs. But later the state required these businesses to be separate from the governance organisation, making the residential community entirely a governance device.[78] Residential communities are served by professional social workers, and the process of 'community building' is literally the professionalisation of social services and neighbourhood governance. This conversion from neighbourhood self-governance to professional regulation during the process of urbanisation and urban development has eventually changed the nature of the society from the soil.

Conclusion: the Chinese city and emergent urbanism

In China, there is a long tradition of the differential mode of association (*chaxugeju*) derived 'from the soil'.[79] 'Rural China' is a sociocultural construct in Fei Xiaotong's conceptualisation. It is related to rural–urban ecological dualism but is not entirely confined to this dualism. It is not an economic description of agricultural production and political consequential mode of governance. In the differential mode of association, self-centred but differentiated association does not lead to individualism as individuals are so tightly knitted into the web of relations. At the village level, the web is sufficiently strong to maintain a world of acquaintance as a socialised structure. In this world, lawsuits and business transactions were difficult – as Fei observed, villagers had to deliberately meet outside the village in order to talk about business. In theory, *chaxugeju*, if it is a sociocultural construct, could survive even when Chinese society is 'urbanised', as the Chinese city might still bear a Chinese culture in their social relation. The question is, then, to what extent the differential mode of association could be maintained when more and more people began to live in the city. This book demonstrates that it is not the ecology of the city *per se* (with higher density and anonymous encountering) that destroyed this mode of association. It is the marketisation widely occurring throughout Chinese society and deeply penetrating into everyday urban life that finally brings the mode of association to an end – the sociocultural aspect of Chinese society has thus been profoundly transformed.

The features of the society from the soil were even maintained under state-led industrialisation. Partially this is due to the lack of urbanism, as described by Ivan Szelenyi (1996), in the generic socialist city. Partial persistent traditionalism was recreated through the residential form of the work-unit. The notion of 'communist neo-traditionalism' captures some features of labour organisation, reproduction and state control.[80] The governance of the work-unit compound is a combination of hierarchical state control and residential management.[81] Attention has been duly paid to the modern state apparatus. But we need to understand that this was not solely achieved by the authoritarian state; rather it is a process of space construction, in its specific residential form resembling the soil from which the differential mode of association is derived, and upon which the 'totalised society' was built.[82] Both traditional and work-unit neighbourhoods have features 'from the soil'. Chinese society up to the economic reform had seen limited bureaucratisation and a more organic residential space – due to the work-unit construct and left-over traditional neighbourhoods. The governed live together with those who govern in a world of acquaintances, in which the state is embedded.

China's market-oriented reform has transformed the residential landscape through residential differentiation and diversity (Figure 1.11 and Figure 1.12). Two new types of neighbourhood – urban villages of migrants and gated communities of the middle class – have been created. However, it is not sufficient to focus only on residential differentiation

Figure 1.11 An old rural village, Xiaba Village in Dongguan. The villagers left this village and relocated to the adjacent new village. The old village was renovated while some original features have been carefully kept for artists and creative industries, as well as tourists. Taken in 2012.

Figure 1.12 The new area of Xiaba Village in Dongguan. The living quality is much improved with spacious villas for the original rural villagers. In contrast to crowded urban villages, this new rural village, built by the farmers themselves, indicates economic benefits to farmers in the fast-urbanising area in the Pearl River Delta. Taken in 2012.

led by marketisation; we need to investigate the concrete dynamics within these neighbourhoods in order to understand how their governance has been experiencing a departure from 'neo-traditionalism'. The market reform transformed urban governance into 'entrepreneurialism', treating the city as a machine of capital. Urban demolition and redevelopment physically destroyed the traditional neighbourhood. Overall, neighbourhood social interaction declined. On the other hand, the state has enhanced its governance through a new set of structures. So far, this has been understood more as state control and the extension of its 'nerve tips' as a continuation of authoritarianism,[83] which has not paid sufficient attention to the *new* governance feature. The strengthened neighbourhood governance can also be understood as a social protection movement, mobilising the agencies of society to deliver practical services, as can be seen from this book. The new way of delivery, different from the traditional approach – under 'traditionalism' – finally breaks down the foundation or the 'soil' on which traditionalism relied. In Chapter 2, we examine the institution of the neighbourhood – an urban social geography, or its spatiality, to understand how the foundation of earth-bounded China has been destroyed.

Notes

1. See also Rowe et al. (2016) and Jacoby and Cheng (2021) for residential communities and neighbourhood studies.
2. Wu, 1996.
3. The index of dissimilarity measures the spatial relation between two groups in small residential areas. The index ranges from 0.0 (complete integration) to 1.0 (completely segregated by these small residential areas). The index over 0.6 is regarded as a high level of differentiation. See additional information for its application to Chinese cities: Li and Wu, 2008, 417; Shen and Xiao, 2020, 1346; Gu et al., 2021, 86.
4. For residential segregation, see also Monkkonen et al. (2017) and He et al. (2021) for the studies of multiple cities. Also Li and Gou (2020) for rural migrant segregation, and Ren (2021) for a general reflection on comparative studies on residential segregation in China.
5. Wu, 2002b.
6. For residential suburbanisation, see Feng et al., 2008; Shen and Wu, 2013; Wu and Shen, 2015.
7. Wu and Shen, 2015.
8. Li and Wu, 2008; Liao and Wong, 2015; Shen and Xiao, 2020.
9. Shen and Xiao, 2020.
10. Davis, 2000.
11. Wu, 1996.
12. Whyte and Parish, 1984; Bray, 2005.
13. Walder, 1986.
14. Zhang et al., 2003.
15. Glasze et al., 2006: 1.
16. Tomba, 2005: 939.
17. Wu, 2010a.
18. See Parker, 2015: 14–15.
19. Parker, 2015: 14–15.

20. For an interesting application of this notion, see Lindner (2011), which illustrates this blasé metropolitan attitude through Wong Kar-Wai's cinematic presentation in the post-metropolis Hong Kong.
21. Originally, Park, 1915: 584; also see Wu and Wang, 2019: 44, in China.
22. Park, 1915: 586.
23. Park, 1915: 586.
24. See Wu and Wang, 2019: 45, for elaboration and figure to contrast the difference.
25. Gans, 1962.
26. Jacobs, 1961.
27. Also see Brenner and Schmid, 2014; 2015.
28. There is an extensive literature on Chinese urban social areas: see Chapter 1 and Yeh et al., 1995; Li and Wu, 2008; Feng et al., 2007. This list is understandably selective.
29. French and Hamilton, 1979.
30. Hirt, 2012; Stenning, 2005.
31. The notion of the Soviet kitchen as a place for social life, Argenbright, 1999.
32. Hence the notion of 'fragmented authoritarianism', Mertha, 2009.
33. See Yan, 2003 for an in-depth study of a rural village in Northern China; also for the theoretical discussion, see Yan, 2010.
34. Simone and Pieterse, 2018.
35. Although there are different views about the communities, Wellman and Leighton (1979) suggest three different scenarios: the lost community, the liberated community and the saved community. Putnam (2000) described the decline of American communities.
36. The feature is revealed in a survey of low-income neighbourhoods in six Chinese cities in the mid 2000s (Wu 2012). Gated commodity housing neighbourhoods are not included in this sample.
37. Liu et al., 2015; Wissink et al., 2014; Sheng et al., 2019.
38. For the details of the survey, see Wang et al., 2017a, b; Wu and Wang, 2019: 52–3.
39. Wu and Logan, 2016.
40. Wang et al., 2016.
41. Wu and Wang, 2019: 53.
42. Park, 1915.
43. Wang et al., 2017b.
44. Wang et al., 2017b.
45. Wu and Wang, 2019: 54.
46. Park, 1915.
47. Lin et al., 2020, 2021.
48. Lin et al., 2021.
49. Wu and Logan, 2016; Wang et al., 2016.
50. Lin et al., 2021.
51. Lin et al., 2020: 1. Also see Liu et al., 2022.
52. Wu and Logan, 2016.
53. Liu et al, 2022; Xu et al., 2022.
54. Wu, 2007a; Wu, 2012.
55. Friedmann, 2005; 2007.
56. Zhu et al., 2012.
57. Zhu et al., 2012; Zhu, 2020; Lu et al., 2020.
58. Lu et al., 2018.
59. Fu and Lin, 2014. See also, Lu et al., 2022.
60. Zhu, 2020.
61. Parker, 2015: 44.
62. Jacobs, 1961.
63. Davis, 1990.
64. Low, 2003.
65. Sennett, 1977.
66. Friedmann, 2010.
67. This is therefore a conjunctural analysis. See Peck, 2015.
68. There is an extensive literature of urban demolition in China, see He and Wu, 2005; 2007; 2009; He et al., 2009; Meyer, 2009; Shao, 2013; Shin, 2016; Wu, 2016d; Wu et al., 2013; Zhang, 2018.

69. He and Wu, 2005; 2009.
70. See He and Wu, 2005; 2007; 2009; He et al., 2009; Wu et al., 2007.
71. It should be noted that the policy shift has been more gradual and the rising interest in property remained rather than entirely disappeared.
72. Smith, 2002.
73. See Hubbard, 2018.
74. See He et al., 2020; Wu et al., 2020.
75. In China, these medium and small cities are called third- and fourth-tier cities according to their location and the level of economic development.
76. Li, 2015.
77. Wu, 2010a.
78. Wu, 2018a.
79. Fei, 1947/1992.
80. Walder, 1986.
81. Bray, 2005; Read, 2012.
82. Sun, 2004.
83. Read, 2012.

2
The end of (neo-)traditionalism

Introduction

When the Chinese city inherited the capitalist city core in 1949, the socialist government did not radically transform the inner areas of private housing except for turning private housing into public rentals. Rather, the government shifted its development priority to industrial areas and added a new layer of work-unit residential compounds to the urban social geography. More precisely, industrial development was extended to the periphery where 'decentralised clusters' and satellite towns were built. In the 1950s, both Beijing and Shanghai prepared their urban master plans for peripheral industrial areas.[1] The standard of services and facilities was, according to the socialist planning guidance, kept to a minimum owing to the lack of investment. In existing urban areas, new workers' villages were built. Except for a few slums renewed into 'model neighbourhoods', the old urban areas were untouched (Figure 2.1). Housing demand was mainly accommodated through residential densification by subdivision of single-family houses into multiple occupation (Figure 2.2). Near the production site, factories self-built their workers' living quarters. Similarly, the staff of government institutes live in close proximity to their workplaces.

The inner urban areas were characterised by courtyard housing in *hutong* areas in Beijing, alleyway housing in lane (*lilong*) neighbourhoods in Shanghai and traditional housing of the style of the Ming or Qing Dynasty in Nanjing.[2] Walled workplaces and their staff compounds mixed with traditional neighbourhoods comprised the major residential landscape in the urban area, which was roughly equivalent to the residential area developed before China embarked on market reform. As mentioned in Chapter 1, the residential forms of the urban area include the first two neighbourhood types in our generic classification of Chinese

Figure 2.1 The deterioration of *longtang* (alleyway housing) in Shanghai. This lane, near Tiantong Road in Hongkou District, remained a densely populated area until the early 2000s and has entirely disappeared since urban redevelopment. Taken in the late 1990s.

Figure 2.2 Subdivision of single-family lane houses into multiple occupancies, making the courtyard extremely crowded. The photo shows many electric meters for this lane house near Tianjin Road, Shanghai. Taken in the late 1990s.

urban social areas. This chapter describes the disappearance of alleyway housing neighbourhoods and the transformation of work-unit neighbourhoods in the post-reform era. Their disappearance and transformation are presented not only as physical changes in bricks and mortar but also as the social transformation of an 'organic' and 'totalised' society.

This chapter focuses on these two neighbourhoods rather than the whole inner urban areas where they are located, because in the existing urban areas we can also see other types of development – urban villages and gated communities of condominiums, which will be addressed in, respectively, Chapters 3 and 4. Changes in the residential areas where traditional and workplace neighbourhoods are located are mainly narrated in the literature by the theme of demolition and displacement[3] – these terms are described as the variegated and concrete forms of gentrification.[4] But even if gentrification is an appropriate characterisation of the broad urban changes in China, whether these neighbourhoods have experienced exactly the same process is subject to interrogation. Rather, attention is paid here to these neighbourhoods before their redevelopment, as most inner neighbourhoods have seen an influx of migrant renters.

The traditional neighbourhoods experienced physical changes. Some were demolished. Some saw neighbourhood changes as original residents left and existing structures became private rental housing for new migrants in the city. Physical disappearance and conversion into commercial and new residential estates are read as newly built gentrification.[5] But recent 'incremental redevelopment' (*weigaizao*) aims to promote the preservation of culture and heritage. Such redevelopment projects require a reliance on land-use changes into commercial and condominium development to recover their huge redevelopment costs.

As for privatised work-unit compounds, their conditions quickly deteriorated into 'old and dilapidated estates' (*laojiu xiaoqu*).[6] Especially, those near industrial areas became 'poverty-stricken neighbourhoods'.[7] Some basic refurbishment was needed, such as installation of elevators for the ageing population in five- to six-storey buildings. Many work-unit compounds remain. Better resourced workplaces such as universities still help their staff to buy properties in the area, where they manage to obtain land through negotiation. The properties are sold to staff at a discount price. But neighbourhood governance, especially estate management, has been transferred to local administration. Linkage to the workplace has been important for housing purchase. But new buyers now may not have a workplace affiliation.

Increasingly, large-scale urban demolition is becoming more difficult, and an alternative small-scale regeneration approach, known as incremental regeneration, has been introduced.[8] It is likely that some traditional neighbourhoods will persevere and remain for the foreseeable future. Similarly, it has been almost impossible to redevelop the modern workers' villages and multi-storey walk-ups built between the 1950s and the 1990s before housing reform. The questions concerned here are what do these traditional and workplace neighbourhoods look like now and what changes have they experienced?

Looking at these existing neighbourhoods helps us understand both residential changes and social transformation. In *Neighborhood Tokyo* (1989), Theodore Bestor described continuing 'traditionalism' in a downtown neighbourhood – in fact, the reinvention of neighbourhood life by the old middle class (the petty bourgeoisie, merchants) who, threatened by a rising modern economy and salarymen, act as community leaders to define their meaning and identities. These old-fashioned social relations, often read as Japanese culture from the Western perspective, attracted wide attention. As the most modernised/Westernised society in East Asia, Japan seems to present a scenario of stable and well-functioning neighbourhoods. As mentioned in Chapter 1, Chinese workplaces continued to present what Andrew Walder (1986) called 'neo-traditionalism'.[9] In *Social Space and Governance in Urban China* (2005), David Bray fully explored these features in the neighbourhoods of work-units, and in *Shanghai Homes: Palimpsest of Private Life* (2015), Jie Li provided a vivid personal account of neighbourhood life in traditional alleyway neighbourhoods. These studies seem to suggest a similar landscape of densely knitted social relations and neighbourhood activities up to the socialist period. Echoing 'traditionalism' and 'neo-traditionalism', this chapter concurs that low residential mobility and stable neighbourhood life in the socialist era tended to distinguish the Chinese neighbourhood from vibrant urbanism in a market society. Even in modern larger workers' villages, some traditional features were maintained in China. The term 'village' reflects the nature and intention of these working-class neighbourhoods. In other words, the Chinese city seemed to confirm the absence of urbanism in the socialist city model. To what extent has this feature changed since China's market reform? This chapter explores the exact changes in traditional alleyway and workplace neighbourhoods.

Alleyway neighbourhoods

Inner urban areas built before 1949 generally have no access restriction. Despite modest gates occasionally installed at the end of alleyways, many residential areas remain open neighbourhoods. Residential differentiation, however, happened at the city scale and is still obvious. In the upper residential quarters, villas and large houses were enclosed with walls. These compounds were gated. However, the neighbourhood, as a purely residential area, has no gates or walls and is openly accessible. The bankruptcy of the rural economy in the late 19th century and early 20th century led to an influx of migrants and refugees into the cities. Poor migrants were expelled into shack settlements in the periphery of the metropolitan area, while craftsmen, small landlords and corner shop owners, together with many lower 'middle-class' office workers, lived close to the downtown. Industrial workers were accommodated in dormitories near the factory area, which was perceived as 'lower quarters'. In treaty-port cities like Shanghai, Tianjin and Guangzhou, international settlements or foreign concession areas were built.[10] Foreign company employees, petits bourgeois and rich local businessmen moved into the 'upper corner' in the foreign concession areas.

In Shanghai, such residential differentiation between the 'upper and lower quarters' is deeply embedded in historical memories, indeed is long lasting and has been recently revived by 'Shanghai nostalgia'.[11] The former colonial area retained a relatively good quality of housing after the socialist transformation, while the lower quarter of industrial areas or shantytowns remained marginalised except for a few model regeneration neighbourhoods. In Shanghai, industrial workers from northern Jiangsu province (*subei*) were consciously and unconsciously discriminated against.[12] However, the inner urban areas generally remained outside the state system of work-units, except for a few villa houses and 'garden houses' which were reassigned from their former owners to government cadres in the 1950s.

After 1949, through socialist transformation, private housing in inner urban areas became public housing. However, neighbourhoods were largely left untouched except for a few slum regeneration projects.[13] Compared with work-unit housing, alleyway housing came mainly from previous private housing and was an inferior type of public housing, which was managed by the municipal housing bureau and was seriously under-maintained. It had poorer quality and deteriorated conditions, because of the lack of continuing investment and maintenance.[14]

In Beijing, the courtyard housing (*siheyuan*) formed alleyways (*hutong*). As a Chinese vernacular form of dwelling, a small compound is surrounded by four sides of houses to provide a multi-generation single-family occupation with maximum privacy and comfortable access to a natural environment in the courtyard.[15] From the imperial period in the

Qing dynasty (1644–1911), courtyard housing declined in the late Qing and during the war of Japanese invasion, because of housing shortages and courtyard houses being rented out to multiple families.[16] From the 1950s onwards, multiple occupancy became the norm. But since the 1990s, with urban renewal, courtyard housing has been demolished on a large scale.[17] The influx of rural migrants into central Beijing also led to the additional expansion of informal rental housing inside the courtyard. Despite efforts in the 1990s to replicate the spirit of the courtyard in new, multi-storey courtyard housing, preservation has been rather limited and too late. The main challenge seems to be the deterioration of the built environment of *hutong* where courtyard housing is situated and the pressure for land use conversion from residential to commercial, leisure and tourist uses. The preservation plan introduced in the 2000s began to encourage the retention of the courtyard form but did not manage to restore the social style of traditional courtyard and *hutong* neighbourhoods.

In Shanghai, the dominant style of traditional housing is 'stone portal gate' (*shikumen*) built into lanes (*lilong*) neighbourhoods (Figure 2.3).

Figure 2.3 Alleyway housing near Tianjin Road, Shanghai. This area is just behind Nanjing Road (the high street). Although the density is very high, the area is relatively well maintained and has not been demolished. In 2021, this area was included in the new phase of redevelopment. Taken in the late 1990s.

The *shikumen* residence is thus a hybrid form of Chinese vernacular and Western row housing, as Chunlan Zhao (2004) observed:

> [It is] a 'perfect' match to satisfy nostalgia for traditional Chinese living and the demand for modern urban dwelling with great concern for economy. Chinese families who had just given up the bygone way of life and tried to start a new life in a modern city welcomed such a type. For them, it was then possible to live in a bustling city, enjoying the convenience of new urban infrastructure and facilities, and meanwhile finding some comfort and tranquillity at home behind the heavy gate and high walls. (p. 59)

Gregory Bracken (2013) described the Shanghai alleyway house:

> A nineteenth-century commercial development, the alleyway house was a hybrid of the traditional Chinese courtyard house and the Western terraced one. Most were speculative real estate ventures and consisted of large blocks, typical of inner-city Shanghai, which were divided into three or four smaller blocks of approximately one hundred dwelling units each and developed separately. (p. 1)

Jie Li (2015) provides a vivid account of neighbourhood life and describes the built form of traditional *shikumen* housing:

> Built throughout Shanghai from the 1870s to the 1930s, *shikumen* alleyway homes were hybrid in their architectural planning. The individual houses had a traditional courtyard layout, south-facing orientation, and local decorative motifs. (p. 29)

The later increasing density in new style alleyway housing was a result of maximising real estate profits by rationally planning and uniformly constructing them into lanes rather than freestanding Chinese courtyards through natural accumulation.[18] A more nuanced understanding of alleyway housing reveals that these neighbourhoods actually consisted of traditional courtyards (multiple or single bay) of a more native dwelling mixed with corner shops and the so-called 'new-style neighbourhood' originated from Western terraced housing as a purer residential environment for foreign sojourners, though later welcomed by locals.[19]

Because of limited housing construction in inner urban areas, housing demand due to population growth was mainly accommodated by densification. Often several generations lived in the same house (Figure 2.4). In traditional neighbourhoods, former single-family

Figure 2.4 A family dinner with multiple generations in alleyway housing in Tiantong Road, Shanghai. Taken in 2002.

houses were converted into multiple tenements. The privacy of courtyard living was eroded because of increased living density and multiple occupancy. Residents often had to share facilities and communal spaces. In inner urban areas, several households had to live in a house that was previously built for a single family, with shared facilities. Most residents lived there for a long time. The neighbourhood was therefore a 'society of acquaintance'. They shared an open kitchen and communal areas (Figure 2.5).

These traditional neighbourhoods maintained intimate relations among neighbours. The moral order was partially maintained through informal knowledge of 'private life', or 'gossip'. The acclaimed novel, *The Song of Everlasting Sorrow,* by Wang Anyi, describes how gossip brewed in the alleyways:

> Gossip not just as speech, but also as 'landscape' and as 'atmosphere' that 'sneaks out through the rear windows and the back doors'…. Gossip is heteroglossic, has collective authorship, and generates its own communities: 'It does not stand in opposition to society – it forms its own society', and it 'deviates from traditional moral codes but never claims to be anti feudal.' Gossip erodes privacy at the same time that it is the essence of the alleyway's intimacy. (Translated by Li, 2015: 148)

Figure 2.5 The shared corridor for multiple tap-water basins near Tianjin Road, Shanghai. Kitchens were also shared, often in the courtyard corner. Taken in the late 1990s.

These untold stories of the city, flowing from the neighbourhood, form 'the "trivial" experience of ordinary people in the cramped spaces of *longtang* neighbourhoods'[20] and maintained an organic social control. The alleyway neighbourhoods were thus social spaces for the then middle-class or little urbanites in Shanghai, as Xudong Zhang (2008) observes:

> As an architectural, social, and psychological space, the longtang is the embodiment of middle-class Shanghai, its privacy (or lack of it) and its material culture (or its 'transcendence'); it records the ways and gestures by which this middle class shelters itself from the brutal forces of history. (p. 202)

While it might be possible to see the novel as unfulfilled bourgeois modernity, as Shanghai nostalgia has seemed to rediscover the cosmopolitan characteristics of colonial Shanghai in now globalising Shanghai,[21] the socialist period remarkably preserved and even strengthened this nature of the society from the soil. Densification and conversion to multiple occupancies strengthened the atmosphere of intimacy and informal moral control. Because of the sharing of communal areas and the dense living environment, the alleyway space continued to be 'a milieu for gossip'.[22] Informal small talk serves a purpose, as Jie Li (2015) shows in an in-depth account of gossip in Shanghai alleyway homes:

> With the establishment of neighbourhood committees, however, gossip about alleyway residents also became an instrument of surveillance as professional or recreational busybodies informed the police about their neighbor's private affairs, from how their ancestors made a living to what they had for supper last night. As the revolution's mass campaigns divided and subdivided the housing of once privileged households, as household registration made mobility and anonymity increasingly difficult, each family's privacy depended increasingly upon their neighbors' discretion and compassion. (p. 147)

Here there is a temptation to follow environmental determinism to suggest that the built environment determines the characteristics of traditional neighbourhoods. However, the feature is related to their residents as more marginal social groups. Residents in inner urban areas worked for collectively owned enterprises or small state-owned enterprises which lacked the capacity to provide housing to their staff. Many residents worked in social services and retail trades. Their marginal position in the political economy of socialist urban development ironically retained –intentionally or unintentionally – the characteristics of traditional society.[23] The state lacked the capacity to fully transform them into a modern industrial system, and consequently there was a lack of a comprehensive system of welfare provision. Otherwise, the need to deliver such provision would necessarily require a more 'efficient' bureaucratic system as in the 'community construction' movement in the 2000s. The world of acquaintance was effective for governing relatively stable, stagnant traditional neighbourhoods, and is a low-cost approach to information gathering through semi-official residents' neighbourhoods. Despite the mess and intimacy of social life in traditional neighbourhoods, as shown in the spread of gossip, the structure and agencies of traditional neighbourhoods are quite 'simple', limited to the everyday routines of a politically under-mobilised society. Reading the story of 'gossip' of neighbourhoods, I wish to emphasise the 'informal' social order rather than an authoritarian state machine. Or, at most, the formal social control was built upon and extended by traditionalism.[24]

These neighbourhoods may have had an important function of social reproduction and even performed rudimentary production in the quasi-formal economy as in the 'street collective economy',[25] but they

Figure 2.6 Alleyway housing near the Xintiandi area was demolished as Shanghai entered a property boom in the early 2000s. Developer-driven redevelopment intensified housing demolition and conflicts. Taken in 2003.

were not pivotal in socialist urban development and remained peripheral in decision making in the socialist city, in contrast to the powerful workplaces of state-owned enterprises, which were also governed in a hierarchical and sectoral way. Similarly in old Nanjing, houses in the styles of the Ming and Qing Dynasty were widely constructed in the southern part of the city including places like Pingshijie, Mengdong (the east side of the gate) and Mengxi (the west side of the gate) near the Gate of China. Very similar to Beijing and Shanghai, these traditional neighbourhoods are under the pressure of redevelopment. Today in Chinese cities, the unfulfilled socialist transformation of traditional neighbourhoods is now being achieved through urban redevelopment. Many traditional neighbourhoods have vanished (Figure 2.6).

Workplace neighbourhoods

The concept of work-units takes its origin from revolutionary military bases to allow them to act as an operational unit. The work-unit was deemed the most effective organisational form of state-led industrialisation. The form fits well in the planned economy which presents a command route through the administrative hierarchy. Its social form, as a unit to organise collective consumption, also remarkably resembles a traditional village society. The implementation of work-unit construction was thorough in large-scale industrial projects which constructed new staff living quarters. They were often built into self-contained compounds with facilities accessible only to the staff. To reduce the cost of construction, work-unit housing was subject to a more modest and industrialised standard. Samuel Liang (2014) noted:

> Modern-style apartments in socialist China did not create private retreats similar to the bourgeois home or the nuclear family home in the capitalist city. Their architecture features included porous and airy interiors compared with the sealed interior space in Western urban apartments.... Both party cadres and new workers just migrated into the cities from rural areas. Their former concept of home as the peasants' simple hut was reproduced in the city as the simple and often temporary shelter: a small room (usually no larger than 20 square meters) that included all necessary functions and other improvisational uses. This type of simple shelter was now mass-produced in the new urban environment; it negated the old ideas of urban home that represented the gentry, merchant, and bourgeois classes. (p. 76)

The typical workplace neighbourhood was the residential quarter of a single work-unit, usually a large enterprise or government institute, such as the residential estate of Baiwanzhuang, built in the 1950s for staff working in the central government.[26]

In the socialist period before the economic reform, housing construction adopted very low standards. The conditions of work-unit housing were incredibly cramped because priority was given to production rather than consumption. According to Andrew Walder, workplace activists and loyalists to the party were given access to scarce rationed resources like housing, which even created social cleavages as party members enjoyed access to housing and other resources and were resented by those outside such networks.[27] While the design of socialist housing tended to foster closer social relations, frequent interaction with neighbours and greater participation in workplace neighbourhoods, the level of bureaucratic intervention by the state in resource allocation was much stronger than in rural villages. After all, these workplaces were state-owned enterprises or organisations. The social order of these workplace neighbourhoods was not entirely built upon spontaneity and the differential mode of association. The combination of employment and residential resource allocation represented the advance of the state into social life and social relations, different from traditional rural China. Notwithstanding the development of the state in the socialist period, neo-traditional workplace neighbourhoods did represent an embedded state–society relation. Residents in tight-knit communities did not always present mostly frequent and friendly contacts but were involved, willingly or unwillingly, in constant political campaigns and movements. All-inclusive and inescapable social interaction and relations reinforced intense political struggles. It was this intrusive social control at the neighbourhood level that created a broad demand in the reform era for housing that provided privacy and intimate spaces together with ownership rights.[28]

Besides single work-unit neighbourhoods, an enlarged workplace neighbourhood is the workers' new village or later the micro-district (*xiaoqu*) for multiple work-units. While there are extensive studies on work-unit housing as a distinctive housing form in socialist China, workers' new villages have received less attention. The notion of 'village' indicates its traditionalism – to replicate the village in a new type of public housing estate for the working class, which bears the virtuous features of organic villages without the social alienation of capitalism. Workers' new villages are exemplars of socialist urban redevelopment, which selected former slum areas or places near industrial areas to provide convenient commuting and integrated residential-industrial complexes. But because of the lack of investment, workers' new villages are only exemplars – 'model communities' – and could not be replicated widely as mainstream housing under socialism. They were mostly developed in major cities such as Shanghai and Beijing where there was a severe housing shortage for industrial workers. Workers' new villages can be seen as enlarged work-unit compounds for multiple work-units. Housing allocation for these public housing areas, in some initial projects such as Caoyang New Village in Shanghai, considered meritocratic criteria such as 'socialist model workers' as well as housing needs.

The workers' new village perhaps represents the only planned feature of the socialist city, in addition to the industrial area, because the city as a whole was not subject to comprehensive development control.[29] Rather, planning had limited capacity to intervene in subdivisions and land uses within work-unit compounds. The implementation of urban planning relied on work-units to self-regulate their developments. In other words, regulation was more sectoral than territorial. Because these new villages were built for multiple work-units, their plan and design were more territorial, under the municipal government. Workers' new villages are a mixture of the features of alleyway housing and work-unit housing, as the housing was managed by the municipal housing bureau but a large proportion of residents were affiliated with work-units.

A well-known workers' new village is Caoyang New Village, which was the first workers' village built in Shanghai (Figure 2.7). The first phase started in 1951 and the final phase was finished in 1977, just before China launched the economic reform. The initial phase consisted of 48 two-storey buildings providing 1,002 apartments, with an area of 13.3 hectares. The total area of Caoyang occupied 94.6 hectares after its completion. The building style also includes two- to six-storey buildings. The residential area was later extended to 180 hectares with 718 buildings up to the end of the 1990s. Its population reached 107,000, which is a large residential district, consisting of multiple residential clusters. With such a scale, workers' new villages evolved into micro-districts (*xiaoqu*). The concept of micro-district has been extensively used in planned residential areas, in modern industrial areas, and later in suburban gated communities with distinctly marked boundaries.

Figure 2.7 Caoyang Workers' New Village in Shanghai, constructed between 1951 and 1977. This terraced housing with relatively lower density compared with crowded alleyway housing areas was distributed to industrial workers nearby. Taken in 2014.

In terms of neighbourhood social types, workers' new villages still belong to 'neo-traditionalism' communities, because they were public housing areas, despite a more modern layout, influenced by the concept of the 'neighbourhood unit' from the US. This origin of workers' new villages echoes the effort towards social protection through urban planning of the Garden City advocated by Ebenezer Howard's Garden City as well as the neighbourhood unit by Clarence Perry to reconstruct a sociable city in the aftermath of capitalist industrialisation.[30] The workers' new village was built largely with open access areas, and neighbourhood interaction and governance were strong, relying more on residents' committees and municipal service provision. As Caoyang introduced generous public green space, occupying 29 per cent of the total area, it was more urban than the industrial work-unit compound; the latter is more influenced by Soviet planning as micro-districts built into 'large neighbourhoods' subdivided by grand boulevards.

This generous urban planning standard was criticised in the 1950s.[31] In other words, the workers' new village remains a more traditional Chinese area than an industrialised residential area. Compared with commodity housing areas built as gated communities, workers' new villages are more similar to a mixed feature of alleyway housing areas in that they were under municipal control, and work-unit compounds because they were newly built into a more designed and planned space. Despite the look of terraced housing in the core area of Caoyang New Village, the workers' new village is served by public services. The evolution of neighbourhood lives shows a trajectory similar to that of alleyway housing and work-unit areas, as Mark Frazier (2022) observed:

> Aerial photo shows Caoyang New Village wedged amidst towering luxury apartment buildings, as a low-lying array of tiled roof dwellings across dense foliage. But few of today's Shanghai residents choose to live in what looks to be a quaint leafy neighbourhood when viewed from above. The dwellings that were once celebrated as spaces of emancipation are now deemed to be so small by Shanghai standards that the only residents who take advantage of the location and the low rents are migrant workers, whose landlords are the remaining original residents, the model workers of the past. (p. 77)

Because of high population density and the structure of multi-storey buildings, it would be costly to rebuild workers' new villages. Although the buildings are of low quality, the places are not sufficiently dilapidated and the tenancies are strong, which means that compensation would be enormous. Hence, gentrification in this type of area is rare. Workers' new villages remain largely as they were, unlike inner alleyway housing areas, which have been selectively built to be like the 'stone portal gate' housing in Xintiandi or Tianzifang and many other inner-city areas have seen the construction of gated communities of condominiums.

There are also hybrid forms of residential estates combining municipal and work-unit housing. The following is an example which was created under the 'comprehensive development' organised by the municipal government. The Fifth Village (a pseudonym) is an estate built in 1987 at the then periphery of Nanjing.[32] It is a good example to illustrate neighbourhood changes in public housing estates, because the so-called 'village' is in fact a mixture of public housing under the municipality and work-unit compounds (Figure 2.8).

Within the modern estate of municipal public housing, an enclosed residential compound was built for work-units. It has now become quite a mature neighbourhood in Nanjing, and in fact, according to the local government, 'an old and dilapidated neighbourhood' (*laojiu xiaoqu*). The estate is actually located not too far from the central city, within a bike ride of 20 to 30 minutes; but the connection, when it was built and

Figure 2.8 The entrance of the Fifth Village, Nanjing. The original was replaced by a new gate to control cars because of the lack of parking space inside the residential 'micro-district'. Taken in 2014.

THE END OF (NEO-)TRADITIONALISM   73

continued for the next two decades, was not very easy. The place was circled and confined by a river that was also used for sewer discharge, cutting off the roads to the city.

In the 1990s, residents had to use the rugged riverbanks to commute to the city. The area was close to the docklands along the Yangtze River, where manual workers lived. This was the edge of the city. The residents had lower socioeconomic status. Before 1949 rural refugees concentrated in this district of Xiaguan and built simple shacks. The place gradually evolved into shantytowns. In the 1980s the city of Nanjing decided to renew this area because the site was visible from trains across the Yangtze River Bridge to the city, and was near to the city but underdeveloped. The site had vacant land for vegetable cultivation and hence there was less pressure for resident relocation. In 1986 the city of Nanjing launched a large development project at this site to rehouse relocated households from old nearby areas. Two work-units contributed investment for six residential buildings for their staff, which were enclosed in a compound (Figure 2.9). The total area of the estate was 8.2 hectares and

Figure 2.9 The southern gate of the inner compound reserved for work-unit staff in the Fifth Village, Nanjing. Although the gate is not strictly controlled, it is served with a security guard room. This rather rudimentary 'gated community' reveals the attempt to maintain social order through management rather than neighbourhood self-governance in an urbanising mobile society in China. Taken in 1997.

the total building floor space was 104,000 square metres. The estate consisted of 35 residential buildings, one nursery, one primary school and some shops along the main road of the estate. In 2001, more buildings were added, totalling 52 buildings in the Fifth Village, accommodating 2,565 households with a population of 7,472 persons.[33]

As the name suggests, the estate is similar to a workers' village but includes residents with different occupations. As a micro-district, it has been entirely designed from the beginning of construction. The neighbourhood includes a public square, a statue and a gate, but with open access. It is therefore different from piecemeal development by workplaces themselves. It is a mode of 'comprehensive development' in which the municipality organises the development and individual workplaces contribute funds to obtain properties for their employees. The remaining flats were managed by the municipal housing bureau and later sold to sitting tenants during housing privatisation in the late 1990s.

When it was built, the Fifth Village was a modern estate with the best housing quality in the area, in contrast to the shacks and dilapidated houses outside its entrance. Next to the estate was the Nanjing Tungsten and Molybdenum Filament factory. In 1998, the factory, owing to the bankruptcy and restructuring of state-owned enterprises, gave up some land to the district government to build an indoor grocery market in which stalls were leased to hawkers. The neighbourhood was quite stable. But for work-units, there has been housing relocation of staff from this neighbourhood to other compounds, and new staff moved into this relatively inferior housing. The work-units are no longer involved in estate management. Although the workplace still provides some welfare entitlement to their retired residents, the neighbourhood is gradually deteriorating and lacks maintenance (Figure 2.10). The neighbourhood is thus a rather matured and to some extent crowded living environment.

Redevelopment of alleyway neighbourhoods

Through many years of densification, traditional neighbourhoods became overcrowded and deteriorated into dilapidated areas. In the 1980s, Chinese cities were confronted with severe housing shortages as well as dilapidated housing conditions in inner urban areas. Urban renewal programmes were initiated by the government to refurbish dilapidated housing. In Shanghai, the objective was to renovate 3.65 million square metres of old alleyway housing through the so-called '365 urban renewal'.[34] In Beijing, the programme was 'Old and Dilapidated Housing

Figure 2.10 Signs of deterioration in the Fifth Village, Nanjing. The original internal sewer pipes were blocked and an external duct had to be built. Housing privatisation does not enhance estate maintenance but rather has led to the withdrawal of workplaces' responsibility for maintenance. Taken in 2014.

Redevelopment' (ODHR).[35] In Guangzhou, urban renewal was combined with the construction of road and metro lines.[36] But these programmes lacked sustained investment and thus made slow progress until the abolition of welfare housing in 1998. As introduced in Chapter 1, China has seen large-scale urban demolition and renewal through real estate development. The social impacts and neighbourhood changes have been extensively documented. I will now introduce some neighbourhoods to illustrate the transformation of social life in these places.

In Beijing, *hutong* rehabilitation started in the 1990s, with experiments in preserving architectural style. These efforts largely failed because of the lack of funding, subsequently giving way to demolition and real estate development. But with the rising awareness of the cultural value of *hutong* and heritage, in 2002 the Beijing municipal government announced a strict preservation policy and designated 25 conservation zones in central Beijing. The conservation policy focused on the aesthetic value of courtyard housing and did not pay sufficient attention to the preservation of the texture of the built environment and neighbourhood life.

While the restriction policy did not entirely stop demolition and high-rise real estate projects, it did lead to the gradual conversion of some neighbourhoods into commercial and tourist uses like the place near Shishahai (known as Houhai) which became a night-time entertainment quarter of bars and restaurants. In the remainder of this section, some redeveloped neighbourhoods in Beijing, Shanghai and Wuhan are introduced.

In 1990, the first phase of the Ju'er *hutong* (Chrysanthemum Lane) rehabilitation project was completed. This aimed to create a prototype of the 'new courtyard' for the redevelopment of traditional *hutong* neighbourhoods.[37] The experimental project required a funding subsidy from the government but also involved the developer. Under the notion of 'organic renewal' avoiding total demolition, the new courtyard retained the original style but expanded the courtyard buildings into two- to three-storey walk-ups for multiple occupation. However, only 10 per cent of the original residents were able to afford the discount price and returned after the redevelopment. While still mimicking courtyard housing, this kind of new courtyard is in fact a new build.

After the completion of the second phase in 1994, the project proceeded no further. It was a failure because the design of the new courtyard housing paid too much attention to the living environment and neglected the changing neighbourhood in Beijing after the introduction of the real estate market. The government lacked funding to rehabilitate *hutong* – redevelopment projects had to consider market demand. The rehabilitation project was not sufficiently profitable to attract redevelopment when the overall plot ratio was still restricted. However, for those who could afford the renovated courtyards, the quality of housing and residential privacy are more desirable. Fundamentally, in the 1990s before full-fledged housing privatisation and consumer revolution, *hutong* in inner Beijing were not seen as a desired location for the 'middle class', or simply the middle class had not yet formed. At that time and later in the 2000s, the suburban villa style was a desirable style of the good life (see Chapter 4). The new courtyard housing, while of good quality, was not a luxury product that managed to retain a low-density development in such a central and premium location.

Nanchizi in Beijing, built in the early 2000s, is another project that tries to replicate the courtyard style of living (Figure 2.11). The project is to the east of the Forbidden City and hence at a very central location. The project restored the local temple, renovated 31 courtyards that were in good condition, and reconstructed 17 courtyards based on their original layouts.[38] But what is more controversial is that the project also built 301 completely new two-storey residential compounds, as the site is

Figure 2.11   The reconstruction of courtyard housing in Nanchizi, Beijing. The redevelopment was quite significant as the project also replicated the original courtyard housing and hence is less seen as *hutong* heritage preservation. Taken in 2004.

in a 'historic and cultural conservation area'.[39] The redevelopment not only refurbished housing but also improved infrastructure and facilities including gas pipes, embedded electricity lines, drainage, underground parking and a nearby park. The landscape of *hutong* has been maintained. Compared with Ju'er *hutong*, the rate of returning residents increased to 27 per cent, and the impact on the landscape was less dramatic than with larger courtyards in Ju'er *hutong*. But according to some critics the residential area is a *hutong* replica.

While Nanchizi still continues as a residential neighbourhood, Nanluoguxiang (Southern Drum Lane), not far from Ju'er *hutong*, has been experiencing commercialisation. Since the 2000s the place has seen the growth of trendy shops, tailor-made boutiques, bars and cafeterias developed by private entrepreneurs.[40] As a former residential area, Nanluoguxiang presents more of a *hutong* atmosphere compared with bustling bar areas near Houhai or the commercial street of Qianmen. Hyun Bang Shin (2010) observed:

> Landlordism is also prevalent in Nanluoguxiang. One after another, courtyard houses undergo refurbishment and facelift in order to

appear on the private rental market, eventually consumed by those who seek trendy living in historic quarters. (p. s49)

The redevelopment of Nanluoguxiang reflects an overall change from the real estate-oriented approach to the promotion of cultural, heritage and leisure districts in central and traditional areas of Chinese cities, similar to Tianzhifang in Shanghai (see later). Traditional neighbourhoods have seen depopulation for heritage conversion. The traditional neighbourhood has been transformed along with the departure of original residents and the consequent change in neighbourhood life associated with their living environment, as the residents were a more marginal population even in the socialist era and could not sustain the cost of redevelopment. The marginality of traditional neighbourhood residents is extensively studied in poverty research, but recently the study of oral history in old neighbourhoods like Dashalar near Qianmen reveals that these neighbourhoods have remained marginal.[41]

In Beijing, alongside demolition, the conservation of *hutong* areas did not retain the original residents and their neighbourhood life. Instead, we see the conversion of traditional neighbourhoods. Through imposing more stringent control over the redevelopment of *hutong* and promoting preservation, the local state actually facilitates the transformation from a residential neighbourhood to a culture and leisure street like Nanluoguxiang. It becomes more difficult to regenerate for residential purposes. Since the adoption of heritage conservation, we have begun to see gentrification in the specific form of displacement – courtyards have been bought by the super-rich. They have also bought vacant land or previously public spaces, such as primary schools or kindergartens, in *hutong* neighbourhoods, and converted them into private houses or clubs. This extreme version is more about the power of the elite rather than the middle class replacing the working class through housing consumption and residential changes. This is not an ordinary everyday life change. It would be too costly for middle-class homeowners to remove and assemble multiple households in courtyards when the intensity of development was controlled by *hutong* preservation. Indeed the 'new courtyard' has been created rather than preserved. But they are no longer part of residential neighbourhoods. Each of them is more like a hidden castle with very little interaction with neighbours who might also be a business owner or shop tenant.

In Shanghai, preservation has been selectively carried out by property-led redevelopment projects. Although demolition and displacement, driven by entrepreneurial governance, have been

Figure 2.12 The redevelopment of alleyway housing into an entertainment and shopping district in Xintiandi, Shanghai. The photo shows the reconstruction of 'stone portal gate' housing into a cafeteria, bars, restaurants and boutique shops. Taken in 2003.

widespread, since the 2000s Shanghai has begun to pay more attention to heritage conservation and has tolerated and even encouraged the self-refurbishment of alleyway housing in the original style. Residents discovered that, besides heritage value, their houses had become attractive to some expatriates and well-educated residents.[42] So some original residents even chose to rent a cheaper place for themselves, renovated their *shikumen* houses, and rented them out to newcomers or private businesses. Ironically, the awareness of heritage value does not enhance conservation. Rather, the increase in rent has led to landlordism and transformed traditional neighbourhoods. However, this process is also driven by the original residents themselves rather than intervention by the local government or real estate developers.[43] However, such *shikumen* housing upgrading is rather piecemeal. Major redevelopment projects have still been organised by real estate developers since the late 1990s.

Xintiandi (literally new heaven and earth) is a milestone in the history of urban redevelopment in Shanghai, treating stone portal gate housing as a heritage and preserving the *lilong* texture of traditional residential neighbourhoods (Figure 2.12).[44] Two factors contributed to the turning of redevelopment policy to selective preservation and

Figure 2.13 The traditional *shikumen* style housing in the Xintiandi area, Shanghai. The *shikumen* housing has been carefully refurbished since the late 1990s. The photo shows the 'stone portal gates' leading to an internal courtyard. The style is actually a hybrid of the traditional Chinese courtyard and Western terraced housing in order to be land efficient with increased density. Taken in 2019.

demolition. First, the Asian financial crisis disrupted the pace of the '365 Urban Renewal Programme'. The district of Luwan where Xintiandi is located lacked the capital to continue its redevelopment project. There was extensive dilapidated old alleyway housing in the district. It was difficult to carry out large-scale demolition. Luwan district government asked the Hong Kong-based developer, Shui On Group, to carry out property development.

Second, more specific to Xintiandi, one terraced house in the area of the former French Concession area was the CCP First Congress Memorial. Hence the area is subject to the restriction of height (Figure 2.13). To follow this planning restriction, the core area had to be preserved. The developer, Shui On, invited a Boston-based architect, Benjamin Wood, to design the area, following Quincy Market in Boston, preserving *shikumen* and adaptively turning these buildings into bars, restaurants and boutique shops (Figure 2.14).

Figure 2.14   The clubhouse and core area of Xintiandi, Shanghai. The photo shows that as early as the early 2000s the area had become a popular and fashionable place in Shanghai. Taken in 2005.

Before the Xintiandi redevelopment project, the government strove to preserve and recreate the memorial from an ordinary *shikumen* building. As Samuel Liang (2014) observed:

> The earlier preservation of the revolutionary heritage site anticipated Shui On's new 'conservation' project. There was a strange and puzzling parallel between the two projects: whereas Xintiandi reinvented the colonial past as a theme of consumption for the new transnational elite, the First CCP Congress Memorial retrospectively invests the revolution history as an ideological structure of the ruling class. (p. 200)

This echoes well with the slogan of Xintiandi, 'Let yesterday meet tomorrow in Shanghai today'. This is indeed a juxtaposition of the old and new. As can be seen from the layout, even the core area of Xintiandi has limited *shikumen* housing area. Xintiandi Plaza in the corner of the northern block and the entire southern block have been redeveloped into modern high-rises (Figure 2.15).

Figure 2.15 Besides the low-rise *shikumen* bars and restaurants, Xintiandi also built high-rise shopping malls and office buildings. The photo shows the Xintiandi Plaza. Taken in 2019.

But the core of Xintiandi consists of only two street blocks. The redevelopment, however, is a large project covering the whole Taipingqiao area, 52 hectares of 23 street blocks. The vast *lilong* area in the region simply disappeared. In terms of historical location, the place was at the edge of the French Concession area near the indigenous Chinese walled city. However, the success in branding Xintiandi as a trendy shopping, leisure and entertainment quarter to represent Shanghai's glorious colonial past – Shanghai nostalgia – has turned the place into up-market housing. The premium estate, Lakeville Regency, became the most expensive housing in Shanghai in the 2000s. In a real estate development sense, Xintiandi can be regarded as a success as a flagship project for property-led redevelopment, although the core blocks did not bring immediate financial income to the Shui On Group.

Since then, the developer has developed a good relation with the government of Shanghai and built a reputation in China. Xintiandi has become a brand of *tiandi*, replicated in over a dozen places such as Chuangzhi Tiandi (smart neighbourhoods) in Shanghai's Yangpu District (Figure 2.16), Xihu Tiandi in Hangzhou, Linnan Tiandi

Figure 2.16 Chuangzhi Tiandi, Shanghai, is a mixed-use area with smart office buildings and technology firms. The place aims to build a 'knowledge and innovation community', with a brand of Tiandi. Taken in 2014.

(southern China) in Foshan and Chongqing Tiandi. Such redevelopment is not interested in everyday urbanism that is described by Hanchao Lu (1999). Rather, attention has been exclusively paid to the architectural form. In Beijing's Houhai and Shanghai's Xintiandi, courtyards and *shikumen* housing are turned into more exclusive consumption and entertainment spaces.

While traditional *lilong* neighbourhoods allegedly accommodated almost 80 per cent of Shanghai's population by 1980,[45] they were demolished through large-scale urban redevelopment programmes in the 1980s and 1990s. Near Taikang Road, Tianzhifang is a rare case in Shanghai. Its preservation was due to the Asian financial crisis in 1997 which put the pace of redevelopment on hold. The bankruptcy of state-owned industries in the 1990s created pressure for reemployment. Shanghai began to seek the development of tertiary industries and to promote 'street commerce'. Small artists' workshops were also encouraged, and began to use the vacant street factories. The success of small studios and workshops was later recognised by the government, which now endorses the

Figure 2.17 Tianzhifang, Shanghai, is another alleyway housing neighbourhood turned into an arts, creative and entertainment district. The photo shows small restaurants in Tianzhifang. Compared with Xintiandi, Tianzhifang is more 'ordinary' and less elite. Taken in 2011.

cluster as a creative industrial area. The development is compatible with Shanghai's ambition to become a global city. The place could serve to preserve culture (the heritage of *shikumen*) and become a cultural quarter like SoHo in New York.

In terms of timing, the redevelopment of Tianzhifang came later than that of Xintiandi. As for the development approach, Tianzhifang is more bottom-up than Xintiandi, which was a large-scale, property-led redevelopment project initiated by Shui On. Xintiandi only preserved *shikumen* houses in its core shopping area while nearby residential neighbourhoods in the Taipingqiao area were demolished. The area preserved in Tianzhifang is larger than the limited core area of Xintiandi. Tianzhifang provides space for smaller restaurants and cafeterias rather than pubs and dining places in Xintiandi, the latter targeting the upper middle class, diaspora and business elites (Figure 2.17). When Tianzhifang started, artists' studios and workshops were located in the former factories of the collective economy of the street (Figure 2.18).

However, the cultural industries were outpaced by the growth of retail and businesses. Hai Yu and his colleagues noted that the

Figure 2.18 The conversion of stone portal gate housing to artists' workshops and display rooms in Tianzhifang. The redevelopment of Tianzhifang has been driven more by smaller developers rather than as a single mega project. Taken in 2011.

conversion from residential to commercial had almost been completed by 2014:

> Beginning from no leased space in 2004, one-third of the two- or three-storey *shikumen* houses were renting space to commercial tenants in 2008. Two years later, more than half the houses were renting commercial space, and by 2013, nearly 90 percent were doing this. Even more important, individual floors of these houses, owned by different landlords, were leased to separate businesses. (Yu et al. 2015, 69)

Eventually, the new retail businesses invaded the *shikumen* houses, turning the residential neighbourhood into a tourist and shopping area.

Guangzhou has experienced several waves of urban renewal. Shenjing He (2012) periodises them into dilapidated housing renewal, property-led regeneration, and redevelopment of old urban areas and villages. Starting in the 1990s, dilapidated housing has been demolished along with the construction of metro lines and roads in old urban areas. This first wave of urban renewal displaced original residents in traditional neighbourhoods and gave the land to real estate development. These redevelopment projects aimed to maximise profits without proper residential resettlement. Demolition aggravated social contests.

The Asian financial crisis in 1997 disrupted property-led urban redevelopment. While the original policy intention was to renovate the dilapidated built environment through the real estate market, in reality developers gained the most benefit from redevelopment, leaving the government with the burden of rehousing residents. In 1999, Guangzhou announced a new policy to prohibit the participation of private developers in urban renewal. However, the government lacked the capital to finance urban renewal. Until 2005 the process of urban renewal was halted.

From 2004 the tightening of land policy by the central government had begun to constrain the speed of urban expansion. Guangzhou also faced pressure to upgrade its economy from manufacturing industries to the tertiary sector, which increased the demand for space in central urban areas. To release more space to stimulate economic growth and restructuring, the provincial government of Guangdong managed to negotiate a special policy with the central government, to allow real estate development in the redevelopment of old villages, old urban areas and old factories, known as 'three-olds regeneration' (*sanjiu gaizao*) which started the second wave of urban redevelopment. Compared with the redevelopment of urban villages (see Chapter 3), it was more difficult to redevelop traditional urban areas because of the cost of compensation in areas of high population density.

However, redevelopment has been extended from dilapidated housing to traditional neighbourhoods with good locations. In other words, the motivation of redevelopment has shifted from the refurbishment of poor housing to property development. To host the Asian Games in 2010, the Guangzhou government speeded up the pace of urban redevelopment. The large-scale urban redevelopment caused huge tension between developers and residents, who demanded more appropriate compensation, as the booming real estate market made it difficult to be rehoused. Strong resistance to demolition and greater concerns over the loss of valuable heritage eventually exposed the controversies of redevelopment projects in the media, beginning to shift the policy agenda. The Global Financial Crisis in 2008 suddenly slowed down the pace of investment and economic development. The organisation of the Asian Games in 2010 created a heavy financial debt for Guangzhou. Large-scale demolition and displacement were halted. The government then wanted higher-quality development, and the agenda of cultural and historical preservation began to surface.

There was little progress in the redevelopment of traditional neighbourhoods until 2015. Uncompleted redevelopment projects turned

Figure 2.19 Yongqingfang, Guangzhou, has been renovated from a traditional inner-city neighbourhood into a tourist and small business district through 'micro or incremental redevelopment'. Taken in 2018.

inner areas into the sites of ruins. The pressure for the government to improve the built environment intensified. One inner urban resident commented, 'Facilities disappeared. In the night, mice run everywhere. It's scary. We are looking forward to demolition just as the poor people waited for the Liberation Army!'[46] In this context, in 2015 the Guangzhou government launched so-called 'incremental redevelopment' (*weigaizao*), which aimed to initiate small-scale redevelopment while preserving original residential buildings. This new approach allowed land use changes, including the conversion of existing residential uses into co-working spaces for creative industries which promote heritage values. Incremental redevelopment maintains the original architectural style and enhances both appearance and quality.

Yongqingfang is a pilot project from which the incremental redevelopment policy was derived (Figure 2.19). The residential block is located in the Enning Road area, which was a major redevelopment area in Guangzhou during the second wave of redevelopment from 2005 to 2010.[47] The residential block covers 11 hectares. The inner urban area of Guangzhou is known for the style of 'arcade housing' (*qilou*). The original plan before incremental redevelopment was wholesale urban renewal, which was strongly resisted by residents. Some residents had already been relocated which created an opportunity for this pilot redevelopment project. The redevelopment did not create more residential properties and hence no new residents came to the neighbourhood. In other words, this was not a housing renewal programme but rather a re-use of existing residential buildings for mixed uses. This was possible partly because previously uncompleted redevelopment had relocated some residents; public rental housing at the time of this new pilot project was largely vacant. The new redevelopment approach was still under the guidance of the district government, which meant, in this case, that the land was still under the control of public ownership. A comprehensive redevelopment plan was approved by the district government, but the actual development was carried out by one of China's largest developers, Vanke.

Different from other redevelopment projects, Yongqingfang adopted a model of build –operate – transfer (BOT). The developer, Vanke, does not own the land and properties, and thus cannot sell any real estate property from the redevelopment project. Instead, it refurbished the street block for the government and rented out these properties to business tenants. The district government selected Yongqingfang because a large proportion of the original residents were public housing tenants. It was easier to relocate them. The municipal housing bureau controlled public housing properties. In fact, these public housing tenants had already been relocated during the earlier phase of redevelopment. The core area of Yongqingfang remained empty. The pressure of residential relocation was lower. The project did not seek further residential relocation. At the time of redevelopment, the residential block had only a small number of households who were private housing owners. As the intention of redevelopment had changed from demolition to preservation, these households were not relocated and remained in Yongqingfang. In other words, Yongqingfang was not a real estate development project.

However, some residents were unhappy because after redevelopment the place was converted from a residential neighbourhood to commercial and business uses. Some complained that newly refurbished houses blocked the sunlight and that they were disturbed by noisy reconstruction and later on increasing numbers of tourists. Although they own the properties, they do not have the development rights to turn them into business premises or commercial outlets. The development rights have been franchised to Vanke.

The redevelopment of Yongqingfang was the first time the involvement of the private sector in urban renewal had been permitted since 1999, when restrictions on private developers were imposed in

Guangzhou. The district urban renewal office was responsible for selecting the developer through public procurement. After public tendering, Vanke managed to gain the right to operate this site for 15 years, with an obligation to complete refurbishment in less than one year.

Adjacent to Yongqingfang, the Cantonese Opera Museum has been reconstructed. Within the neighbourhood, small museums, including Bruce Lee's ancestral home, have been refurbished and preserved to show the traditional residential style. Public squares have been created to host activities and gatherings. The project has since been widely acclaimed for its commercial success and the preservation of traditional arcade housing and a traditional neighbourhood. The highlight was the visit of President Xi Jinping in October 2018, stressing that urban redevelopment should not be carried out through large-scale demolition but should, like Yongqingfang, carefully improve the built environment and preserve culture, heritage and memories, as if using an 'embroidery needle' on an artwork. Since then, there have been constant visitors from other cities to learn from its success.[48]

The business model of Yongqingfang is actually the public–private partnership. Vanke was willing to take on the project because it wished to use this pilot project to develop business relations with the government and gain development rights in the future for the larger area of Enning Road. It also wished to expand its experience from that of a mainly residential developer to that of a commercial developer. It could then further operate in the fields of property management and services contracts with the government. This was deemed particularly important by the developer as a change of business because the government is constantly regulating real estate speculation. Similar to a private finance initiative, Vanke manages the newly furbished co-working space and rents out such properties for the government. Hence, Vanke calls its new role the 'urban operator'. The redevelopment tried to avoid the costly relocation of private housing owners. Instead, through partial refurbishment and the conversion of ground space into commercial and office uses, the project hoped to inject a limited amount of investment which could be recovered by rental income from business tenants. Vanke in this case is a property developer but also a property management company.

The developer hopes to use Yongqingfang as a demonstration project for its versatile capabilities, because so far Vanke has been largely a residential developer and has no experience with business and commercial properties. It also hoped to use this opportunity to develop a good business relationship with the government for subsequent development rights in the larger regeneration area of Enning Road. Vanke aims to diversify its role of developer into broad property management, and in the future it hopes to receive service contracts from the government to manage the city.

For Yongqingfang, Vanke is not involved in neighbourhood governance. It only manages the commercial assets and business tenants of the street block. All the remaining residents, now only less than six households, are managed by the residents' committee and the street office in the area. The redevelopment of Yongqingfang literally wiped out the original residential block and turned it into a commercial and business area. It used the 'ruins' of earlier development and empty public housing, thus saving some redevelopment costs, and converted these residential buildings into retail, businesses and offices.

The neighbourhood is quite different from an ordinary Tokyo downtown neighbourhood as described by Theodore Bestor (1989), where the old middle class still live in the neighbourhood and act as community leaders to maintain social life. This incremental redevelopment project has actually completely transformed a traditional neighbourhood, despite the vernacular look of residential buildings.

The project is similar to the redevelopment of Xintiandi in Shanghai in the late 1990s and early 2000s, in that both preserved some core residential buildings but converted them into commercial and business uses. But Xintiandi was a 'property-led redevelopment', meaning that the redevelopment aimed at the residential property market. The developer, Shui On group from Hong Kong, controlled the redevelopment of the whole Taipingqiao area in which Xintiandi is a small land plot. The developer sold all the properties. The cost of redevelopment of Xintiandi was recovered from property redevelopment in the larger area. Since the Yongqingfang project has only completed its first phase, it is unclear whether the second phase in the rest of the Enning Road area will adopt a similar property redevelopment approach. But because Yongqingfang has already created an expectation of small-scale redevelopment, the business model remains questionable. From these cases it can be seen that housing rehabilitation is impossible without a substantial change of land use and residents. This deadlock is rooted in the spatiality of traditional neighbourhoods – deteriorated conditions, marginal population and the lack of financial viability.

Redevelopment of workplace neighbourhoods

For work-unit neighbourhoods, because the housing was built as five to six modern walk-up buildings, it is financially difficult to demolish and rebuild them. With the ageing population, the multi-storey buildings urgently need better accessibility with elevators. Following privatisation, residents became homeowners and have had to do their own property management. While they may be able to pay a private plumber to unblock a sewage pipe, the coordination and cost of larger renovations are challenging. As for the residents' committee that was set up after the privatisation of the work-unit housing, it does not have the capacity, as an officer at the Fifth Village comments:

> We don't have to do anything. In fact, we can do nothing. All we could do is to fix small problems here and there. [For maintaining trees and grass in the neighbourhood], this is the area where you spend money but don't see where it has gone. Trees, bushes and grass grow every year, and so you have to pay for them every year. We just spent 200,000 Yuan on the maintenance of green spaces. Whenever possible, we just had to convert grassland into hard surfaces. We had no choice.[49]

As work-unit compounds turned into 'old and dilapidated neighbourhoods' (*laojiu xiaoqu*), it became difficult to rely on residents or their administrative committee to renovate and maintain the living environment. Well-resourced work-units may contribute to the renovation of staff residential quarters, but for the compounds of multiple work-units or workers' new villages, this is more likely to be the responsibility of the municipal government. Unlike old neighbourhoods or urban villages, work-unit compounds do not disappear but either deteriorate or are upgraded. Because of their convenient locations, many are still quite stable, with only a small proportion of outsiders coming in as private renters. The need to regenerate these neighbourhoods imposes a challenge for governance, because projects like elevator installation require the consensus of existing residents – the installation of an elevator may block light and ventilation for some residents. Besides, ground floor residents do not need an elevator.

In order to proceed with such infrastructure projects, the government has to mobilise residents. Since the late 2010s, China has introduced dilapidated housing renewal. The programme was intended to expand domestic consumption demand, similar to shantytown renewal (the redevelopment of shacks and traditional neighbourhoods).[50] But there is a practical need for workplace housing renewal because of deteriorating conditions and the lack of public spaces. The programme also introduced the new practice of 'neighbourhood planners', who are local residents and volunteers for the design and renovation of dilapidated neighbourhoods.

The renewal of 'old and dilapidated neighbourhoods' in the 2010s thus extends its scope from the renewal of dilapidated housing (of traditional neighbourhoods) to modern ex-public housing microdistricts (*xiaoqu*). The renewal approach consequently changed from wholesale demolition to 'incremental redevelopment'. Because of the challenge in terms of coordination and governance, these incremental redevelopment projects are initiated and funded by the government rather than by real estate projects or residents themselves orchestrated by the government.

In Wuhan, the 'happy community campaign' was launched in 2017. A mixed neighbourhood, Huajin, managed to be selected as one of three pilots and the first case of incremental redevelopment in Wuhan (Figure 2.20). This is a large estate built since 1999, consisting of work-unit housing, affordable housing and commodity housing of several phases (hence different qualities). The neighbourhood still had a quite high density compared with traditional neighbourhoods, although as an early development project, the development still used land quite generously, leaving 35 per cent of the land as open space in the neighbourhood.

The project of redevelopment was initiated by the planning bureau and designed by a team of planners at Wuhan University. The planning process, however, involved various forms of 'neighbourhood participation' and was joined by 'neighbourhood planners' (resident volunteers). Despite the seemingly grassroots involvement, neighbourhood governance and project coordination pivoted upon the party leader who coordinated the three components of neighbourhood governance: the homeowners' association, the property management company and the residents' committee. The renewal project improved the built environment: creating parking spaces, pedestrian sidewalks to the school and public spaces – small parks for exercise and a stage for social gatherings and the performance of shows. The level of social participation and neighbourhood mobilisation in Huajin is unprecedented in Chinese ex-public housing modern neighbourhoods. The residential environment has been improved but is still modest; the neighbourhood continues to exist as a distinct generic type as per our classification in Chapter 1.

Figure 2.20 The central area of Huajin residential district in Wuhan has been renovated as a neighbourhood incremental redevelopment project. The project was designed by a team at Wuhan University and involves neighbourhood participation. Taken in 2019.

Changing neighbourhood governance: formalisation and professionalisation

The change in neighbourhood governance started with the commercialisation of 'neighbourhood services' (*shequ fuwu*). In the socialist period, the services provided to the residents in traditional neighbourhoods were quite limited. The social welfare function of the street office was mainly disaster relief and assistance to the handicapped and elderly, which was funded through the government budget of civil affairs. For residents in work-unit compounds, their welfare entitlements mainly came from their work-units as occupational benefits. As mentioned earlier, traditional neighbourhoods were quite peripheral in the system of social provision. As a result of the lack of formal state welfare provision, traditional neighbourhoods maintained some reciprocal social engagement in the form of self-help and mutual assistance. This position in the state administrative system unexpectedly preserved the features of traditionalism, which suggests that the socialist transformation of the old capitalist city was rather incomplete and less radical than commonly believed, while the 'traditional' social order was reinvented in work-unit neighbourhoods as a by-product of occupational welfare delivery under 'neo-traditionalism'.[51]

In the 1950s, the street offices of the old urban areas organised housewives and self-employed labourers into street handicraft workshops and small factories, forming the 'collective street economy'.[52] The development of the collective economy provided employment, as the formal industrialisation of state-owned enterprises was not able to absorb residents in traditional neighbourhoods, because the residents had a lower educational attainment and lacked skills. The formal channels of recruitment of new workers and staff included graduates from university and professional schools and those who completed military service. For a large number of residents, it was difficult to achieve a change of status through the formal recruitment process of state-owned enterprises. The function of employment in the collective economy was recognised to supplement the economy of state-owned enterprises.

In the 1980s, because of the return of urban youth from the countryside, the pressure of unemployment led to the revival of the collective economy and self-employment. Street offices began to organise various street cooperatives to provide services such as TV repairs, barbers and housing maintenance to absorb the returnees from the countryside. Similar to social enterprises, these small cooperatives under street offices became an important component of the collective economy, which started neighbourhood services through commercial operation.[53]

Since 1992 neighbourhood services have been officially recognised as the tertiary sector by the State Council. In the 1990s, the formal recognition of street office businesses as services rather than welfare opened the door to the commodification of public services at the grassroots. The policy of encouraging neighbourhood services (for example, tax exemption) led to the proliferation of businesses run by street offices. The street offices thus played a dual role of district government agency providing welfare and social assistance as well as the operation of tertiary businesses. Through these dual functions, street offices as the bottom level of government managed to draw additional resources.

In Shanghai, the street offices signed contracts with district governments for their amounts of fiscal budget, beyond which the offices could use their business operations to subsidise their expenditure. The practice was described as 'using (commercial) services to support (social) services' (*yi fuwu yang fuwu*). In reality, the income often was used for improving the income of street office cadres in order to maintain their staff in addition to the basic salaries of formal posts.

In traditional neighbourhoods in old urban areas, because of the history of the collective economy and socialist legacies, street offices usually have some collective assets and premises under their control and lease them to private businesses. In the Fifth Village in Nanjing, the residents' committee once developed some simple shacks to rent to rural migrants who came to the place to sell vegetables and worked in other low-end services such as cleaners.[54] This was quite different from the operation of work-unit compounds, because work-units usually subsidised services such as canteens provided to their employees. Instead, street offices treated these rentals as business operations. In this sense, the commodification of neighbourhood services can be seen as a partial retreat of the state from the neighbourhood, replaced by more business-oriented services.

Neighbourhood public space management was an important service initially offered by the street offices, while for public housing property management was carried out by municipal housing bureaus. The public housing in work-unit compounds, treated as 'enterprise housing', was financed and maintained by the respective work-units. However, housing privatisation meant that the state or work-units were no longer responsible for their maintenance. Households themselves needed to find commercial property management services for their individual properties. However, in reality, the street office still maintained the property management of 'old and dilapidated neighbourhoods' as residents were unable to afford commercial services. The facilities belonging to work-units were encouraged to open to the public and to operate on a commercial basis. Gradually, the operation of services became a separate tertiary sector. Property management, however, became more specialised and was no longer part of the street office function. Rather, the street office employed a professional property management company to carry out the maintenance.

In the 1990s, the street economy in Shanghai was encouraged by the policy to return value-added taxes generated in the place to the respective street offices. This motivated the street office which became quite entrepreneurial and tried to attract businesses. For example, in the early 1990s, the street of Liangcheng in Shanghai offered registration capital to help the registration of a transport enterprise which was actually a joint venture between the work-unit and its employees to support it registering as a private business in the territory.

The consolidation and merger of residents' committees in the 2000s removed the function of business management at the bottom level, while at the street office level, some economic functions still remain but are more regulated. To enhance administrative capacities, small residents' committees were merged into a larger administrative organisation responsible for its enlarged territory of residential community (*shequ*). The consolidation of residents' committees has also allowed the government to professionalise the previous grassroots organisations. New offices are usually built together with a 'community centre' to deal with various administrative tasks such as the allocation of minimum livelihood guarantee (*dibao*) (Figure 2.21). Many amalgamated residents' committees are too large for residents to know them personally. This relationship between residents' committees and residents thus becomes official.

The residents' committee was a 'mass organisation' (*qunzhong zuzhi*) but increasingly it has become a government organisation based in residential neighbourhoods. To 'maintain social stability' (*weiwen*), the function of the residents' committee has been strengthened since the 2000s with more funding allocated from the government. The budget of the residents' committee is now entirely allocated by the street office of the government. Faced with rising demand for social assistance and management, the residents' committee always has pressure on its budget.

Figure 2.21 The community (*shequ*) centre of the Fifth Village, Nanjing. The photo shows the gradual development of social services into a professionalised structure at the neighbourhood level. Taken in 2014.

However, it is forbidden to operate businesses to create additional income and has become a purely administrative agency. For example, previously the residents' committee developed auxiliary spaces to lease to private business or charged a fee for using public space (for example, parking charges). Now all these incomes have been transferred to the commercial property management company. This avoids the potential problems of corruption and financial irregularities.

As a neighbourhood government organisation, the residents' committee also needs to deal with requests from various government departments. The street office allocates the basic budget to cover the salaries of cadres, while additional government tasks are funded by their respective budgets. This funding mode reflects the nature of the residents' committee as an 'administrative agency on the ground' to carry out specific tasks in addition to its daily administrative duties. For example, when the bureau of statistics needs to organise a survey of urban livelihoods, it asks the residents' committee to help contact residents in the neighbourhood to book-keep their daily spending. The task has a specific fund for additional administrative costs. This practice of budget allocation on the basis of specific tasks helps to maintain the residents' committee as the agent of the government. As a governance agency, the residents' committee tends to respond to the requirement from the upper government, but at the same time the residents' committee needs to consider residents' demand. For example, residents in old neighbourhoods might not regard landscaping as a priority but since the government sets the task of removing informal development, the residents' committee strives to maintain the order of the built environment and spends its own budget on greening and landscaping rather than asking a property management company to do so as the latter would eventually charge the payment to the local residents.

Since the late 2000s a new government model, known as 'grid governance', has been implemented to combine all three levels (district, street offices and residents' committees) into territorially divided grids (*wangge*) according to geographical boundaries. According to Beibei Tang (2020), this adjustment strengthened territorial management as 'social management innovation'. For example, the Dongcheng district of Beijing divided 17 street offices and 205 residential communities into 589 'social management grids'.[55]

The officers from three levels are assigned with their responsibilities for the grids. But the aim is to encourage residents to solve their own disputes within the grids. Because grids are smaller than residential communities, the new layer of grids helps reduce the workload of residents' committees.⁵⁶ The grid thus represents the interface of the state and local society, in which volunteering is encouraged. As can be seen from grid management practice, this new model hopes to re-embed the state into the society to deal with residential disputes and the increasing workload faced by the local administration system. The new practices, however, do not alleviate the pressure on the administration system. Instead, this engagement pushes forward further professionalisation of committees and street offices.

The outbreak of the coronavirus pandemic in 2020 suddenly highlighted the critical role of neighbourhood governance, as residents' committees and neighbourhood organisations helped maintain quarantine, provided social support during enclosure and implemented social distancing. Now, the professionalisation trend continues as university graduates find management positions in street offices very attractive as they are permanent ones with good salaries.

The persistent role of the state in neighbourhood governance has been widely noted.⁵⁷ The existing interpretation tends to see the legacy of authoritarian governance or governmental tactics to maintain social stability. Community construction, on the other hand, is seen as an effort to encourage grassroots governance,⁵⁸ 'socialised governance' to reinstall face-to-face politics for the state,⁵⁹ or the responsive governance of an authoritarian state to the changing needs of Chinese society.⁶⁰ The professionalisation of neighbourhood governance can be certainly seen from this perspective.⁶¹ However, such a trend is more than the effort to penetrate local self-governance residential spaces to maintain a visible state. That well-educated university graduates rather than 'retired ladies' serve street offices and residents' committees reflects the 'normalisation' of the Chinese state in its modern meaning and a departure from a 'totalised' society rather than its continuation.

The professionalisation of the state at the grassroots level eventually destroys organic society, although the intention might not be entirely about control and could be more about providing social services in an increasingly complex, fragmented and disorganised society. But the side effect of this is the modernisation and bureaucratisation of traditional society, and as a result traditional neighbourhoods become a very different type of community.

To the working class living in industrial work-unit compounds and marginal elderly residents in traditional neighbourhoods, the dismantling of strongly bonded neighbourhoods does not mean more freedom for new lifestyles. Rather, they face alienation and social exclusion. It is true that workplace-based welfare provision created the dependence of workers on their workplaces, which allowed the state to exert more control and effectively monitor the governed.[62] However, it is more appropriate to recognise that such a dependent relationship has a double-edged effect. The interests of those who are governed cannot be ignored. The leaders of the workplace, who may live in the same residential compound, have a moral obligation to look after their colleagues and all the members of the workplace. These places bear some features of traditional society, i.e., close relations defined in a territory which is inescapable and non-deprivable.[63]

Neighbourhood life: the weakened society

After many years of neglect and lack of maintenance, traditional neighbourhoods deteriorated into overcrowded and dilapidated conditions. In the 1990s, large-scale urban renewal programmes began to demolish old and dilapidated housing. In Shanghai, the programme of 365 Old Alleyway Neighbourhood Renewal in the 1990s transformed the central city.[64] Through urban redevelopment, traditional neighbourhoods are disappearing and becoming a residual residential form in urban China. The remaining traditional neighbourhoods witness the changing social composition of residents. Better-off residents move out to suburban commodity housing estates. Some sell or rent out their street-front housing as retail premises. The houses in Beijing *hutong* or Shanghai *lilong* are extended and rented out to rural migrants. Building density in inner urban areas has increased, driving more residents to leave the overcrowded environment. The courtyard in Beijing has been turned into a 'jumble yard' (*dazayuan*) with multiple family occupation (Figure 2.22).

Surprisingly, even with co-living in a close residential environment, traditional neighbourhoods have lost their established neighbourhood ties because of tenancy changes and high residential mobility. The new generation of residents has a high employment rate – they mostly move into underdeveloped inner neighbourhoods to be closer to their jobs and often work overtime. Although neighbouring with immediate neighbours and hence reciprocal interactions exist, informal encountering is unlikely to be scaled up to neighbourhood life. Most temporary migrant tenants are the object of strengthened social administration rather than the subject of neighbourhood life. The remaining traditional neighbourhoods have seen a downward social trajectory.

Besides large-scale urban renewal, inner residential areas also see patchy and plot-based redevelopment. Smaller redevelopment projects

Figure 2.22 The courtyard housing has deteriorated into a crowded residential area with the influx of rural migrants and private rentals. The photo shows self-construction inside a courtyard in central Beijing. Taken in 2004.

may just demolish one street block, or create one or two high-rise buildings. Obviously, the social profile of residents in the redeveloped neighbourhood has been upgraded,[65] as new residents are commodity housing homeowners or renters of a commercial complex which is also used as home offices or residential rental units. As a result of these different trajectories, previous traditional residential areas become socially more stratified and fragmented. This is in fact different from so-called 'mixed communities', which are advocated in the West to encourage social interactions across different social groups.[66] Residents in these patchy redeveloped areas are unlikely to interact across these juxtaposed residential blocks.

In fact, the process of residential fragmentation was occurring before housing commodification and privatisation started. The practice of municipally organised 'comprehensive development' in the late 1980s and 1990s, which involved multiple workplaces and residents in traditional housing to build a mixed modern estate (micro-district, *xiaoqu*) did not lead to an integrated neighbourhood. At the time of construction, the policy was not intended for social mix but rather to use multiple sources of investment from workplaces and the municipal and district government.

Figure 2.23 Staff housing tenants and municipal housing residents do not have much interaction. The photo shows a resident in the inner compound of staff housing in the Fifth Village, Nanjing. Taken in 2002.

As shown in the Fifth Village in Nanjing, the modern residential estate did not overcome the residential fragmentation between work-unit based housing and municipal housing (Figure 2.23). With the development of commodity housing in traditional municipal housing areas, residential fragmentation has become even more severe.

In Shanghai, as early as the 2000s, old alleyway neighbourhoods had begun to see social fragmentation and the breaking down of social networks due to urban renewal. In the neighbourhood of Daling in the former Nanshi district, where the walled city of Shanghai was located, more than one-third of residents moved out within just three years in the late 1990s, which literally destroyed the neighbourhood life, as the director of the residents' committee lamented:

> [In this place] the old residents got along well with each other. To organise some activities, hundreds responded to a single call – you needn't ask one by one. You just tell a couple of people and they will all bring in lots of people. We have a good network because several families have their team leader and activists. Now the neighbourhood is scattered here and there; even keeping contact with residents became a difficult thing. Lots of housing land is now used for business and retail, because of large redevelopment projects in this

area like the rental of Laoximeng (the old western gate) and Xizhang Road, Zhaojiabang Road, and Zhaozhou Road redevelopment. [67]

Real estate development demolished some alleyway houses and converted them into scattered high-rise buildings of up-market apartments. Before the movement of 'community construction' in the early 2000s, the residents' committee in the traditional area was relatively weak. Unlike powerful village organisations, they could not represent or organise residents to negotiate with developers. This is because, as mentioned earlier, traditional neighbourhoods were a weaker form of residential organisation even in the socialist era. They were less organised than workplace neighbourhoods. The residents' committee often played an opposite role, assisting government-initiated demolition and redevelopment projects and persuading residents to move out of the redevelopment site.

In the late 1990s when Shanghai witnessed large-scale restructuring of state-owned industries, workers in state-owned enterprises were laid off and returned to the neighbourhood. The resident's committee played a role of social support, as re-employment advisor, for example introducing unemployed workers as security guards or nannies, as the leader of Daling listed their role:

> We introduced residents to jobs such as waitress in the restaurants, to work as cleaners and security guards in stadiums and offices, and to work as nannies and domestic helpers for the families in the 'new tall buildings'. This is welcomed because the employers feel that it is more reliable to find workers or helpers from the trusted organisation of the residents' committee. [68]

However, these neighbourhood services were soon replaced by commercial and professional organisations. The residents' committee did not evolve into a 'civil society' to represent residents' interests in urban redevelopment.

Work-unit compounds, since the late 1980s under a more unified development approach due to economic decentralisation and rising local government, have begun to join in municipal housing development projects and have obtained their residential compounds at multiple locations. The development of staff living quarters in the suburbs is also widely seen. Work-unit employees eligible for better housing are reshuffled from older to newly built residential compounds. The profiles of workplace compounds are then sorted according to their housing qualities and locational advantages.

For a less desirable location such as the Fifth Village, the retired staff are left in the residential compound, leading to a downward trajectory for the workplace compound. The construction of multiple compounds weakened location proximity between the workplace and residential compounds. Some residential compounds were built at a distance from the workplace. That is, the staff living quarter was no longer within or adjacent to the workplace. Work-unit staff were relocated and sorted in terms of their qualifications for different locations and qualities, leading to greater residential differentiation within work-unit spaces.

Later after housing privatisation, homeowners became responsible for their own housing maintenance, while neighbourhood management functions were transferred from the workplace to local administration. The estates department was no longer responsible for property maintenance. While some residential compounds still maintained their status as staff living quarters, others have seen the sale of properties to outsiders. The major changes in the work-unit residential landscape are the weakening of the linkage between workplace and residential compounds, diversification of residents in terms of workplace affiliation, and differentiation of workplace compounds in terms of employees' status.

Broadly speaking, residential changes are characterised by the subdivision and extension of internal space to receive migrant tenants or other low-income families, as well as wholesale demolition and displacement. In dilapidated old housing areas, it is impossible to initiate piecemeal infrastructure and housing renovation.

However, the super-rich may purchase large houses or villas (maybe in the form of courtyards) and hold these properties as investments or for enjoyment. The latter is hidden and *not* widespread. In most traditional neighbourhoods in inner areas, residents are disadvantaged social groups, relying on compensation from redevelopment and resettlement. The redevelopment of traditional neighbourhoods led to a change from residential to commercial and office use, and the displacement of more marginal residents by richer businesspersons or residents with a background of more powerful institutions and state-owned enterprises. Unlike informal self-build in urban villages, very few traditional-style houses have been upgraded by residents themselves. Instead, courtyard and alleyway houses have been left unattended and lack maintenance. Traditional neighbourhood areas did not see the classic form of gentrification.[69]

When describing urban changes in London, Ruth Glass (1964) actually thought 'gentrification' represented a new but important aspect of residential change: along with deindustrialisation and the rising middle class, poor working-class neighbourhoods were invaded by the new 'gentry' in service occupations such as doctors and lawyers. She regarded this latter group as the 'gentry', and therefore coined a term – gentrification – to describe the displacement of the working class as a trend in neighbourhood change. The spirit of these residential changes is displacement,[70] although the phenomenon is presented as neighbourhood upgrading. Now, demolition and displacement are included in the lexicon of gentrification.

In this expanded lexicon, traditional neighbourhoods in China have indeed seen demolition and the displacement of some original public tenants (Figure 2.24). However, more precisely, before demolition, the poorer and more dilapidated municipal housing does not see the intrusion of the new 'gentry' but instead lower-income migrants. The increasing private rental of public housing is another distinct feature of residential change in traditional and, to a lesser extent, workplace neighbourhoods. In terms of housing tenure, informal rental practices lead to greater informality *in* the built environment but not the 'informalisation' of property rights, as the tenancy of informal renting is not recognised by the state, because rights are not compensated during demolition.

Figure 2.24 The office building of Hongkou SoHo in the Hongkou district, Shanghai. The remaining alleyway housing is disappearing due to the new wave of urban redevelopment. Taken in 2016.

In contrast, the tenancy of public housing residents, no matter whether they still live in the place, is always compensated. Or, if they wish to move, they are resettled. In terms of building activities, refurbishment and physical extension are carried out at a minimum cost. Compared with urban villages, the scale of self-building is rather small and modest. Irregular construction does not turn traditional neighbourhoods into informal settlements. Before urban renewal, the traditional neighbourhood experienced a residential change in the direction opposite to gentrification. The downward social trajectory continues until the municipal government initiates a redevelopment project to remove whole blocks of traditional neighbourhoods.

Several factors may contribute to the lack of gentrification in traditional neighbourhoods. First, in traditional neighbourhoods, most residents are public housing tenants. Unlike workplace housing, municipal housing has not been privatised. Even today a significant number of residents in old areas are still public housing tenants. It is rare to 'sell' a municipal housing tenancy which is a stronger tenancy than what is understood in the market economy.[71] Public housing tenants cannot be removed without compensation, unlike rural migrant tenants in private rental housing in urban villages. Existing tenants understand well the value of their public housing tenancies and wait for redevelopment during which their tenancies are compulsorily purchased and compensated by the state. Because of this fixity of tenancy rights, traditional neighbourhoods lack an effective secondary property market.

Second, traditional neighbourhoods are quite deteriorated in terms of both housing quality and infrastructure conditions. Appropriate upgrading would be costly. Existing residents do not regard self-upgrading as cost effective, nor do they have sufficient finances to carry out a radical renewal. City planning, on the other hand, is more stringent in formal residential areas, and hence self-demolition and redevelopment of the whole building are not possible. Compared with work-unit compounds, municipal housing areas have been under-invested for a long time. Traditional neighbourhoods were inferior residential areas even in the socialist period. While living in the central city is convenient, and Chinese urban residents show a strong centripetal residential preference rather than a countryside nostalgia as in the Anglophone world, the housing in old urban areas without proper redevelopment was not a desired housing type. There is a lack of mainstream middle-class desire for alleyway housing. Middle-class homeowners do not have extra financial capacity or willingness to pay for extra private services in central areas.

Instead of gentrification, in private housing courtyards in Beijing or villa compounds in Shanghai, we may see the intrusion of the super-rich who can afford and manage to renovate these properties. This scale is less mainstream, and perhaps could be referred to as 'noblefication' or 'aristocratisation'. In most traditional neighbourhoods, residents would not be able to self-upgrade and would still need the state to assist with property management. In these old and dilapidated estates, the state failed to transfer the function of neighbourhood maintenance to property management companies. For example, in the Fifth Village of Nanjing, property management companies encountered great difficulty collecting maintenance fees.[72] Within the courtyard or alleyway housing, informal space is extended from an existing structure or through subdivision to accommodate migrants or low-income renters. The original residents move into better commodity housing. With the influx of rural migrants and the densification of population, the social composition of alleyway neighbourhoods has changed. Residents are no longer long-term acquaintances, and their interactions become reduced even when they share the same courtyard.

In workplace compounds located in central urban areas, the residential buildings were multi-storey walk-ups – not a fashionable good quality that could be renovated by individual homeowners. Despite the accessible and convenient locations, refurbishment, even with intensive renovation, is not an attractive option to meet the aspirations of the better-off residents. Remaining households have little financial capacity to renovate. In contrast to the trajectory of gentrification as seen in more developed Western market economies, workplace neighbourhoods, similar to traditional neighbourhoods, have seen a downward trajectory. These neighbourhoods, as a previously formal development, attract a different cohort of renters, for example new university graduates or younger office workers rather than rural manual migrant workers, because for the latter the rent would still be too high compared with that in urban villages.

To reduce the rental cost, landlords may subdivide and rent out their apartments to multiple renters on the basis of rooms, which is known as 'co-renting' (*qunzu*). However, this rental form creates pressure on public utilities and hazards (because of overloaded electricity usage) and is discouraged or prohibited by the government. Nevertheless, co-renting is still quite common. In the workplace neighbourhood, it would be more difficult to co-rent as workplace landlords face pressure from their workplace colleagues if they introduce many migrant renters into their neighbourhoods. In other words, regulation to prevent subdivision and the co-renting of flats within ex-workplace apartments is more effective in workplace neighbourhoods. This residential change is different from gentrification as the new residents are mostly renters and have an inferior social status to that of the original landlords. On the other hand, these workplace compounds, though facing physical deterioration, are relatively stable, and do not become 'slums'. Nor are they upgraded into gentrified neighbourhoods. In short, despite some small-scale changes, workplace compounds are quite stable.[73] Physical obstacles plus powerful work-units have made it more difficult to gentrify workplace neighbourhoods.

In both traditional and workplace neighbourhoods, there used to be relatively strong neighbourhood interactions, reciprocal and comprehensive social relations. But faced with drastic residential and neighbourhood changes, these places have seen weak social mobilisation and participation in neighbourhood affairs. Several factors may contribute to the lack of neighbourhood social participation. First, traditional neighbourhoods have been peripheral in socialist urban development. In fact, 'community leaders' disappeared. In the socialist period, private businesses were collectivised and transformed, diminishing the 'old middle class' or the petty bourgeoisie who uphold 'traditionalism', as observed by Theodore Bestor in his *Neighborhood Tokyo* (1989). Neither was there a landowning class which could play a role of community leader to boost land value as in the growth machine in the United States (Logan and Molotch 1987). These traditional neighbourhoods were maintained by less bureaucratised 'mass organisation' – the residents' committee served by retired people and housewives. Small collective workshops, inferior to state-owned enterprises in both welfare benefits and salaries, provided additional sources of quasi-employment.

In the post-reform era, the relocation of better-off and well-resourced residents to suburban estates exacerbated the weakening of potential self-governance. In short, the middle layer of governance – the community organisation – is missing, unlike in urban villages which have been strengthened by corporatisation through the establishment of 'village shareholding cooperatives' (see Chapter 3). The traditional neighbourhood lacks resources, and entrepreneurial governance is short lived. In the Fifth Village in Nanjing, the residents' committee was able to charge a parking fee for external vehicles, to collect management fees from grocery markets, to rent some shacks to migrants, and to run a 'community entertainment centre' (for computer games) for additional income. But these are now banned. In Shanghai, the old 'street collective economy' disappeared, and new street-level businesses were soon turned into commercial operations. The director of the residents' committee in the Fifth Village described how in the early 2000s they asked for 'donations' from nearby enterprises and institutes to sponsor neighbourhood social activities as if they were monks 'begging alms'.[74] But these 'entrepreneurial' activities are now rare in neighbourhood governance.

Second, workplace neighbourhoods were already part of the state system. The leaders of workplaces are state cadres, and workers and staff are state employees. Compared with traditional neighbourhoods, work-unit compounds are less dependent upon reciprocal neighbourhood relations, because the state organised collective consumption. Work-unit staff had no choice of residential location. Although the work-unit was a 'totalised society', the relation was centred more upon the workplace than the residence. Because of the politics within the workplace, residents in residential compounds, though maintaining neighbouring interactions, tended to reduce rather than intensify their social life within the neighbourhood, partly because neighbourhood social life was replaced by workplace interactions, partly because residents tried to avoid bringing politics into the neighbourhood, despite a very politicised social life. Neighbourhood cohesion was achieved through their work-units. For example, neighbourhood and residential disputes were resolved through the mediation of respective department leaders in the workplaces. The residential compound was maintained by the estates department of the workplace. Because the state also organised social activities, residents were more passive in the life of the neighbourhood. Still, because of the informal relations in workplaces, the work-unit compound itself was less bureaucratised but rather was attached to a more formal state system – work-units.

However, after housing reform and privatisation, the workplace no longer looked after the estate and became just a form of employment. It is an employer in the sense of modern capitalism which has limited liability rather than a social manager. The workplace has 'retreated' from residential life. The social function has been transferred to the territorial government – now subdistrict street offices and residents' committees. But the development of territorial governance does not strengthen reciprocal social relations but rather exerts more pressure on the state to establish a more bureaucratic administrative management. It is in this sense that the state 'returns' to neighbourhood life – a return with a territorial administration (a professionalised neighbourhood organisation pivotal upon the residents' committee).[75]

In the context of East Asian culture, we might expect a lingering traditionalism in China. However, even in urban Japan, the extent to which such a picture of traditionalism exists is still questionable. Despite the claim for preservation or creation of traditionalism in the downtown Tokyo neighbourhood, Theodore Bestor (1989) admits that:

> [W]ritten for an audience in the United States not terribly familiar with Japan, it concentrated on the 'Japaneseness' daily life.... In writing for an American audience, I had necessarily stressed those details of life that Americans would find different from their own. (p. 257)

However, Bart Wissink and Arjan Hazelzet (2012) suggest that in their studies of neighbourhoods in Tokyo, not all neighbourhood social networks include all residential groups and functions all the time. In urban Japan, residents 'without local social networks are still socially bonded but their bonds just have taken on new spatial forms' which go beyond neighbourhood ties (p. 1546). They find that the Japanese neighbourhood now has a more symbolic role, which suggests that on the ground the Japanese city might see similar declining neighbourhood-based social solidarity. The Chinese city may be in the same trend of weakening its traditional social bond.

The picture of self-mobilisation and inclusive neighbourhood society does not seem to exist in post-reform urban China. Unlike the old merchant class or the little bourgeoisie whose business was rooted in the neighbourhood in Japan, the more professionalised residents' committee is a quasi-government agency. While residents are encouraged to participate in organised social activities, they do not set the agenda and are not responsible for decision making.

The creation of a much larger residential community (*shequ*) which consists of different natural residential blocks, has led to a more heterogeneous administrative area.[76] These neighbourhoods have different social groups and perhaps housing tenures. In Wuhan, the Huajin community includes different housing tenures – affordable housing and commodity housing – while community leaders are externally appointed. Residents have different demands for neighbourhood social life. While the community organisation tries to mobilise residents in social activities, residents have different preferences and are more passive. Residents need to make a living first and, even when they have time, they may not find neighbourhood activities attractive. Interaction between immediate neighbours is reduced too, under a new social norm of greater privacy along with the changing composition of residents. They are more likely to participate in entertainment activities than in the organisation to claim their political and social rights. The community service centre has been set up by a more professionalised state to deal with social claims.

In short, if the term 'gentrification', in its strict meaning of residential change, does not adequately capture the *major* change in traditional and workplace neighbourhoods, as Ruth Glass saw in inner London, then what might be the more appropriate description? For remaining traditional and workplace neighbourhoods, one important aspect of change might be the end of traditionalism and 'neo-traditionalism', accompanied by individualisation, immobilisation, alienation, diversification and peripheralisation. Despite a strengthened and professionalised administrative form created in these neighbourhoods, efforts to organise residents territorially do not reverse this trend of dismantling traditionalism, although this does not necessarily mean that neighbouring – social interaction between immediate neighbours – has entirely disappeared. Professionalising neighbourhood governance eventually creates a 'disorganised' society of more individualised residents, based on formal rules and relations rather than the differential mode of association.

The end of (neo-)traditionalism

This chapter describes residential changes in traditional and workplace neighbourhoods. Before market reform, these were state-organised residential spaces supported by state collective consumption to a variegated extent. Traditional neighbourhoods were more marginal in state-led industrialisation, and hence had weaker formal state organisation and preserved stronger reciprocal features. In these earth-bounded societies, the social order was established through internalised norms, self-regulation and mutual observation. The neighbourhoods were 'self-governed' by the residents' committee served by retired people and housewives. They received very little financial allocation from the government. But because residents lived in an intimate environment, the relationship between those who govern and those who are governed was close and engaged, bearing the features of the society 'from the soil'. Work-unit neighbourhoods replicated some traditional features, and may be described as places of neo-traditionalism.[77] Compared with traditional neighbourhoods, workplace neighbourhoods were more formal. The state work-unit played a significant role in the construction of social space, while the role of the residents' committee was more peripheral.

In both traditional and workplace neighbourhoods, the state management of grassroots society has been strengthened in comparison with the pre-socialist period. However, both maintained a high degree of informality and close social engagement. The residents' committee in traditional neighbourhoods was a voluntary organisation, despite the guidance from the government street office. In workplace neighbourhoods, the social space overlapped with workplace institutional space, and hence the state was more embedded within social space and governed the neighbourhood as an internal manager rather than an outsider controller.

In this sense, the notion of the 'authoritarian state' is not entirely appropriate and accurate for China before market reform, which was in fact a more 'totalised society' as the Chinese sociologist Liping Sun (2004) argues. In this totalised society, the interests of the governed could hardly be entirely ignored, because information transmission was much easier with lower costs (as shown in the spread of 'gossip'). Despite a modern industrial organisation, the work-unit shares some feature of the totalised society. The leader in the workplace community had a moral obligation to look after all the members of the work-unit. This embedded relationship lays down the relatively transparent and egalitarian allocation of resources such as public housing provision within the work-unit. For those who are in charge of allocation, it is a duty to do so in a socially acceptable way rather than conducting it as a bureaucratised professional task according to some externally defined standard and performance evaluation.

The end of collective consumption has led to the decline of social interaction and social integration. For dilapidated residential areas, many residents left – physically and socially – after urban redevelopment. There may be nostalgia for the close social relations of the past. On the other hand, inner city dwellers clearly have a longing for a better-quality living environment. Some residents moved out along with their children or the younger generation. Some were relocated during demolition and urban renewal. There might not even be a trade-off between a better physical environment and closer neighbourhood relations, considering that the social environment in traditional neighbourhoods is also changing and that residents do not really wish to engage in intense neighbouring. The old neighbourhood has been socially 'deserted' by its residents. Demolition and forced relocation are only *one* aspect of residential change. Together with the rising middle-class desire for modernity and better living environments, the *key* aspect of urban changes in China is 'leaving the soil'. This notion describes not only leaving the countryside to become urban but also leaving a totalised society of traditional and workplace neighbourhoods, the legacy of socialism, which are becoming more marginal and residual.

As residents leave old neighbourhoods for gated communities in the suburbs (see Chapter 4), these old neighbourhoods are no longer 'earth-bounded'. The movement of 'community construction' in the 2000s, aiming to recreate territorial governance through establishing a professional neighbourhood organisation, ironically speeded up the destruction of organic neighbourhoods. Despite residents becoming homeowners, it is difficult to establish a self-governance mechanism (e.g., homeowners' association) in these neighbourhoods. For these traditional neighbourhoods, what we have seen is not the 'retreat' of the state after marketisation (neoliberalisation), neither was it a 'return' of the state to strengthen its control through the movement of community construction. The notions of 'retreat' and 'return' implicitly assume that there was a modern state outside the society before market reform. As argued previously, this was not the case as traditional and workplace neighbourhoods were totalised societies in which the state and society were embedded. What we have seen here is the separation of the state from its previous embedded position, the formalisation of the state and the professionalisation of social service delivery. Here there was no pre-existing dualistic state–society relation. It is in this sense that neoliberalism is not an entirely accurate description because it represents a more modern view ahead of the time of Chinese traditionalism.[78]

Thinking about the role of the state, one may argue that state presence has always been strong and has never truly retreated from these neighbourhoods. However, neighbourhood control was a side-effect of a totalised society rather than being performed by a bureaucratic system on a territorial base. Now, there is a significant difference. The omnipresent state is no longer embedded into dense territorial relations. The new state–society relation is more administratively oriented. The change is a reaction of these traditional neighbourhoods to market development – a social protection mechanism. But this mechanism of social self-protection has eventually transformed society itself – beginning with the restoration of some state redistributive functions.

In order to redistribute social welfare, the nature of 'the society from the soil' has been transformed. Reciprocal relations declined in the post-reform era, and this is quite different from the change from redistributive to reciprocal relations in other post-socialist economies where the lack of state capacities led to residents' self-help. In post-reform China, administrative and social expenditure increased. The strengthening of neighbourhood governance is not only about the intention to extend the state's authority but also stems from a practical need to deliver services to local communities. We should not regard governance change simply as the establishment and strengthening of social control (the continuation of authoritarianism) but also as a process of building up capacities for the redistributive functions of the state. Along with the task of dealing with the problems created by marketisation, the state apparatus has been formed, improved and upgraded at the neighbourhood level.

In sum, we have witnessed the second 'revolution' since 1979, which has created profound implications for Chinese society. The first socialist revolution earmarked in 1949, aiming to strengthen industrial capacities, left traditional neighbourhoods untouched, despite transforming their housing from private to public ownership. In the state redistribution system, alleyway housing neighbourhoods occupied a relatively marginal position. There were lingering reciprocal relations due to shared communal spaces. These neighbourhoods were self-organised through residents' committees served by retired people and housewives. For new industrial development, the state reproduced traditional society in work-unit compounds and embedded itself into everyday life. But constant political movements did break up some aspects of family- and lineage-based traditionalism, creating a social mentality of individualism through a process of 'individualisation' which has been materialised through neighbourhood changes in the post-reform era.[79]

Now, old fashioned services provided by the residents' committee are no longer needed and have been replaced by commercial services. We see a more procedural and bureaucratic state apparatus in a Weberian sense. Compared with the revival of reciprocal relations in post-socialist cities in Europe, where the state's capacities declined after shock therapy and residents' self-help became necessary,[80] and with the remaining or reviving traditionalism in East Asian economies where the middle class and bourgeoisie play a role of community leader,[81] Chinese (neo-)traditionalism has come to an end. The residents' committee has been transformed and formalised. In the management of residential social space, the work-unit has been replaced by the government organisation in neighbourhoods. Faced with difficulties, conflicts and problems created by marketisation, the state has had to resort to a more professionalised apparatus, which is 'squeezing' the state out of organic society. Now, the state directly faces individual citizens at the interface of the neighbourhood. The territory is no longer self-mobilised, and there is no alternative way to restore traditionalism or the differential mode of association.

Notes

1. See Wu, 2015.
2. See Gibert-Flutre and Imai (2020) for alleyway housing form in Asia as an urban vernacular.
3. There is an extensive literature on urban demolition in China. See Shao, 2013; Shih, 2010, 2017; Ren, 2014; Shin, 2016; Zhang, 2018.
4. There is a huge body of literature on gentrification. See Lees et al., 2016; Shin, 2016, Hamnett, 2021. For gentrification in China, see He, 2007; Wu et al., 2018. But the precise meaning of gentrification in China is debatable: see Wu, 2020b.
5. See He, 2010. But we did not see the classic form of residential upgrading accompanied by the return of the middle class from the suburbs to traditional neighbourhoods. Perhaps Chinese suburbanisation has been less complete and many better-off residents still live in the central city.
6. Wu, 2018a.
7. See Liu and Wu, 2006; Wu Webster et al., 2010.
8. Wu, Zhang, and Liu, 2022. Wang, Zhang, and Wu, 2022.
9. See also Lü and Perry (1997) for Chinese work-units and Frazier (2002) for Chinese industrial workplace in particular.
10. Lu, 1999.
11. Pan, 2005.
12. Honig, 1992.
13. Liang, 2014.
14. Wu, 1996.
15. See Zhang (2013) for a comprehensive study of courtyard housing.
16. Zhang, 2013.
17. Abramson, 2007; Fang and Zhang, 2003; Shin, 2009.
18. Li, 2015: 29; see original discussion on profit making by real estate developers in colonial Shanghai, Lu, 1999.
19. Zhao, 2004.
20. Scheen, 2015: 176.
21. See discussion in Zhang, 2008; Visser 2010: 208.
22. Li, 2015: 149.
23. There is a similar argument about rural migrants who introduced traditionalism into the cities, see Wu and Logan, 2016.
24. This is similar to what Walder (1986) discovered in workplace neighbourhoods.
25. See Lu, 2020.
26. Wu, 2015.
27. Thanks to one of the reviewers for reminding me of Walder's points and offering these insights.
28. Thanks to one of the reviewers for this insight.
29. Wu, 2015.
30. Frazier, 2022.
31. Frazier, 2022.
32. For more information, see Wu, 2018a.
33. The figure was from an interview in 2002.
34. See Wu, 2016d.
35. See Fang and Zhang, 2003; Shin, 2009.
36. See He, 2012.
37. The project was led by Professor Wu Liangyong at Tsinghua University; see Wu, 1999. Also, Zhang, 2013: 159–62. The project received several awards, including the *World Habitat Awards* 1992.
38. Zhang, 2013: 156.
39. Zhang, 2013.
40. See Shin, 2010.
41. For poor inner-city neighbourhoods, see Wu, 2004a; Wu, Webster et al., 2010. For Dashalar, see Evans, 2014.
42. Arkaraprasertkul (2018) described this process of self-gentrification in a neighbourhood in Shanghai.
43. Arkaraprasertkul, 2018.

44. There are extensive studies on Xintiandi redevelopment; see He and Wu, 2005; Liang, 2014: 199–204; Yang and Chang, 2007; Ren, 2008.
45. Yu et al., 2015.
46. Interview in Guangzhou, April 2019. See also, Wu, Zhang and Liu, 2022.
47. The Enning Road area is perhaps the most studied area in Guangzhou. See He, 2012; Tan and Altrock, 2016; Wang et al., 2022; Wu et al., 2022.
48. Yongqingfang has become a popular site for policy learners. Among my many visits to the neighbourhood, one trip in April 2019 was organised by the Urban Renewal Association of Guangdong province, for the training workshop at which I was a keynote speaker and teacher. When leaving Yongqingfang, we returned to our van parked at the roadside. Our group mistakenly got into another identical white van which was being used by another group of visitors. At the same time, I counted four or five groups of visitors touring the neighbourhood.
49. Interview, November 2014; see Wu, 2018a: 1184.
50. He et al., 2020.
51. Walder, 1986.
52. Lu, 2020.
53. Wu, 2018a.
54. See a full description of the case, Wu, 2018a.
55. Tang, 2020.
56. Tang, 2020.
57. For example, Read, 2012; Tang, 2018; 2020; Tomba, 2014; Yip, 2014; Wu, 2002a; 2018a.
58. Tang, 2020.
59. Woodman, 2016.
60. Tang, 2016.
61. Wu, 2018a.
62. Walder, 1986.
63. Wu, 2010c.
64. Wu, 2016d.
65. In the literature of gentrification, this is called new-built gentrification. See He, 2010, and Arkaraprasertkul, 2018.
66. See Blokland and Nast, 2014.
67. Interview and fieldwork in July 2000.
68. Interview and fieldwork in July 2000.
69. The concept of gentrification has been greatly expanded and now includes almost every form of neighbourhood changes. Here we stick to the classic version. For the debate, see Wu, 2020b.
70. Slater, 2006.
71. Marcuse, 1996.
72. Wu, 2018a.
73. Wu, He and Webster, 2010.
74. Wu, 2018a.
75. Wu, 2018a.
76. Administratively *shequ* probably bears some resemblance to the ward in the UK.
77. Walder, 1986.
78. However, if we regard neoliberalism as a rising market mechanism without implying state absence, the term captures some aspect of the political economic change in China.
79. For 'individualisation', see Yan, 2010.
80. Stenning et al., 2011.
81. Bestor, 1989.

3
Transient space with a new moral order

Landing on a socialist urban topography

The influx of rural migrants into Chinese cities has created a ubiquitous landscape of 'urban villages' (*chengzhongcun*). These are former rural villages encroached upon by urban expansion, which have evolved into enclaves of informal rental housing for rural migrants. Therefore, urban villages are rural villages left over during state land appropriation which became semi-urbanised during urbanisation. They are not like squatter areas in the global South because these urban villages are not created by outsiders on common land. In other words, Chinese rural areas are encroached upon by the expansion of formal urban land uses rather than squatters. But the encroachment of rural agricultural land has led to informalisation of the residential space. Urban villages are self-upgraded rural villages. Residents' housing tenure has changed, but the original governance structure of rural villages remains.[1] To understand this difference, it is useful to imagine how the situation has changed from squatting in the treaty-port cities in the semi-colonial era to land encroachment in post-reform cities in late socialism.

In the 1920s and 1930s, to escape constant wars, richer rural migrants came to Shanghai to buy purpose-built semi-detached or terraced housing built by developers (particularly foreign companies in the French Concession Area and the International Settlements but later extended to the entire urban areas). Some owners later became landlords and rented out spare rooms in their buildings, leading to the densification of some areas (for example, creating the landscape of the so-called '72 tenants under the same roof').[2] The tenants living in these new houses were 'little urbanites' or the middle class at that time. Many of them were migrants themselves in the earlier waves of migration but had settled down and became little urbanites. However, migrant refugees from poorer rural areas such as northern Jiangsu (*subei*) landed in the area along open sewage courses or creeks in the fringe areas, living in shacks and straw huts.[3] They were informal labourers and did not have formal industrial jobs.[4] In short, they were 'urban outcasts' who 'were forced by desperate circumstances in their rural homes to flee to the city in search of sheer survival'.[5] Hanchao Lu (1995) observed:

> Unlike the slums of twentieth-century America, which were clearly associated with the inner city, slums in Shanghai were all peripheral, often located along the boundary of the city's foreign settlements. The peripheral location of Shanghai's slums reveals what we might call the superfluous nature of the slums and their occupants. (p. 264)

When rural migrants came to the cities initially in the 1990s or in greater numbers in the 2000s, most had a clear purpose to work in industry or lower social services. The residential status of the population was formalised by *hukou*. Similarly, it was difficult to find accommodation in central areas. Industrial workers were either in a factory dormitory or in peripheral villages near the industrial area. Through socialist transformation, Chinese cities became more formally organised than before through work-units and residents' committees inside traditional neighbourhoods. There was literally no spare room in extremely densified old neighbourhoods or work-unit compounds because of housing shortage. Only after some residents moved to suburban areas for better commodity housing did some old flats become vacant and then rented to migrants. It was not practically possible to occupy space along railways, rivers, sewage pipes or other 'commons', as these spaces were all 'occupied' and managed by state work-units or farmer collectives. The capacity of the state to prevent these squatting activities was much stronger than in the semi-colonial era.

However, this strong capacity was not due to city planning or the enforcement of development control, as in modern capitalist cities. Actually, the Chinese socialist state could not thoroughly plan its city – there was great autonomy in land use and discretion over subdivisions.[6] The work-units managed their built environment as a 'totalised society' and suburban lands were occupied by either industrial work-units or production brigades. Maintaining the residual space between work-units, the local municipal government could quickly detect illegal constructions, if no work-unit claimed that they were responsible for the development. While work-units had discretion over how to use their land, they would not allow others to use their land freely. Perhaps also influenced by the propaganda of slum clearance in the past, migrants did not even think that it was possible to build shacks in the city. In other words, when a migrant landed on the socialist urban topography, it was a landscape of a totalised society, seemingly cellular but not unorganised. The state was pervasive and maintained the overall order of the built environment through decentralised responsibilities. To stay in the city, rural migrants nowadays have to pay rent to existing urban or rural owners who have the right to the city.

Except in peripheral Beijing, where land management was ironically lax (see the development of Zhejiang village and large compounds later in this chapter), the urban village was built based on rural villages. In this way, it was similar to terrace housing (*shikumen*) in old Shanghai, where more tenants were accommodated in smaller rooms rather than through substantial new construction. These residential buildings had already been built by real estate developers. While entirely new reconstruction based on individual plots was possible in Guangzhou and other cities in southern China, places in Shanghai only saw partial extension and internal subdivision (see the example of Gaojiabang later). With the concentration of rural migrants, urban villages were poor neighbourhoods.[7] More successful migrant entrepreneurs could later move to commodity housing or into central areas, but most were stuck in their peripheral location of urban villages. Their upward social mobility across classes was halted. In fact, their fate was almost pre-determined when they landed on the socialist urban topography. In the 1920s and 1930s, richer migrants from Jiangsu and Zhejiang moved into *shikumen* in Shanghai and became landlords. Rural refugees remained urban outcasts in peri-urban areas, while industrial workers and office clerks managed to settle down as 'little urbanites'. Similarly, rural migrants now find it difficult to cross the class line. The first-generation migrants mostly returned to their hometowns, perhaps not the original rural villages but small towns and county seats in their place of origin.

While not providing housing to rural migrants, the Chinese state maintains an overall order of the built environment and attempts to remove informally built urban villages whenever possible. The state's capacity is much greater than its counterpart in the republican era. As can be seen from the cases later in this chapter, urban village clearance is driven by multiple motivations, not necessarily middle-class pressure as seen in slum clearance in India.[8] Often it is the responsibility of the state, or a response to the governance challenge created by the demise of a totalised society. Government initiatives may not be profit-oriented, although a profit needs to be made by real estate projects in order to involve them in urban renewal. These real estate projects are often treated more as an instrument or means to achieve a political mission such as maintaining a social order.[9]

Housing and tenants in urban villages

In the global South, 'self-help housing' in squatter areas provides a popular form of cheaper housing.[10] However, informal housing is characterised by dilapidated physical conditions as well as insecure residential tenure. Self-help housing is built informally, but informality is not unusual as middle-class construction can also breach building codes under a more privatised and 'neoliberal' approach.[11] Urban development in the global South has seen widespread informality, not confined to self-help housing. However, the housing in China's urban villages is not a type of 'self-help housing'.[12] Villagers have their ownership certificates issued only by the township government as self-used housing non-tradable in the housing markets in the cities. Some additional spaces built through extension may not be recognised, and this is often used as informal rental housing. But the majority of residents living in urban villages are migrant tenants who did not build or own any housing. Thus, the village housing is informal rental housing.

A survey in 60 urban villages in Beijing, Shanghai and Guangzhou in 2010 reveals the overall characteristics of urban village housing, besides some general observations of 'kissing buildings' (referring to buildings that are very close to each other) and narrow alleyways in urban villages.[13] The sample was randomly drawn from urban villages and thus reflects the overall composition of housing in them. Only 17.4 per cent of households lived in owner-occupied housing, namely their own village houses. A large proportion of this owner group were in fact landlords, unless some village housing had been bought by migrants, which was unlikely. Nearly 70 per cent of households were in informal rental housing – they were migrants. In other words, these tenants in informal housing had nothing to do with housing development. This village housing was actually an informally developed form of cheaper rental housing by its owner. In some areas in Beijing, villagers went even further to sell purpose-built apartments to urban residents. But often these newly built estates of owner-occupied housing were not regarded as part of the village.[14]

The housing conditions in urban villages were dilapidated and inadequate,[15] as rental housing in urban villages suits the specific demand for low-cost housing. The standard of village housing was variegated but modest. Housing units were much smaller, especially in Shanghai where the constraint on housing development in urban villages was stronger. The average per capita housing space per unit in the three cities was only 16.5 square metres. But for Shanghai the figure was as low as 7.9 square metres, far below the average of 17.5 square metres in the city at that time. Very few rental housing units had more than two rooms, indicating that the rental was based on rooms rather than apartments.

In urban villages in Shanghai, over 80 per cent of housing units had only one room, and over 80 per cent had no reception room. In Beijing, the percentage of rental units with one room was 75 per cent. The figure was lower in Guangzhou, at 59 per cent. That is, about 41 per cent of rental units in Guangzhou had two or more rooms. About 73 per cent of rental housing had one reception room in Guangzhou, indicating that urban villages in Guangzhou were more developed and had evolved into studios or self-contained flats. Considering that most tenants in urban villages were married, the living conditions in urban villages were indeed crowded. Especially in Shanghai, about 47 per cent of rental housing had an average per capita space of less than 5 square metres. According to the standard of minimum living space in Shanghai, nearly half of rental housing breached this basic requirement. The tight space was due to strict control over self-build and extension of village housing in Shanghai. Because of the poor structure of old farmers' houses, it was difficult to create additional space without demolition.[16]

While the rental cost of village housing was low, measured in terms of housing space village housing was actually more expensive than ordinary private rental housing. The average monthly rent was 544 Yuan per housing unit and 36 Yuan per square metre in the sample of three cities in 2010. More units were at the lower end. For example, in Guangzhou, 66.7 per cent of housing units in urban villages had a rent between 251 and 500 Yuan per month per unit. While cheaper housing was available in Beijing and Guangzhou, in Shanghai it was very difficult to find rental housing below 250 Yuan per month, which resulted in a much more expensive rental housing sector in Shanghai, with an average rent per square metre as high as 49 Yuan per month. Owing to the abundance of urban villages in Guangzhou, migrants found cheaper housing there. The relatively higher rents prevented the lower end of migrants from living in Shanghai.

It is ironic that village rental housing was more expensive than ordinary private rental housing, measured in terms of rent per square metre.

Because commodity housing was larger, rural migrants could not afford the price of the rental unit. Some apartments in the central areas were subdivided and rented out to migrants to co-live in apartments originally designed for a single family. This co-renting (*qunzu*) is prohibited. It is easier to manage co-renting in formal housing than in informal village housing. The average size of a village rental is only 10 square metres, while the smallest commodity housing apartments according to the government regulation for affordable housing is over 90 square metres. Low-income migrant families had to live in more expensive rental housing in urban villages. The only way to save costs was to reduce the size of the living space – many rented on the basis of number of rooms and sacrificed housing quality.

Compared with housing in slums, Chinese village rental housing generally has better conditions. In terms of location, urban villages were developed from former rural villages in 'normal' and physically safe places, unlike Brazilian favelas on steep slopes or Indian slums near deserted land alongside railways, sewage and water pipes. In fact, only rural villages at a convenient location near job markets in the urban fringe had a chance of being selected by migrant renters. Although the residential choice was constrained, rural migrant workers did exert consumer demand on the rental housing market. The housing in urban villages thus has been upgraded along with the arrival of migrants working in better-paid jobs. Hence village rental housing has evolved in response to changing demand, as can be seen from the urban villages in Guangzhou, which presents a more established rental market.

The level of facilities in urban villages in Beijing, Shanghai and Guangzhou varied (Table 3.1). Almost all rental housing units in the samples of the survey had connections to electric and water supply. As rural villages did before, rental housing lacked inside toilets and separate kitchens. Internet connections were also increasingly available. But some rental units had air conditioners, especially in Guangzhou due to the hot weather, while in Beijing because of the cold weather heating was installed in over half the housing units. In Guangzhou about 77 per cent of households had an independent kitchen, while in Beijing the rate was lower at 29 per cent. In Shanghai, the figure was the lowest at 21 per cent. Without a separate kitchen, urban village dwellers have to use a gas or electric cooker in the corridor or outside the house to cook. Because space is extremely cramped and electric wiring is overloaded and outdated, cooking and boiling hot water can lead to potential fire hazards.

In general, Guangzhou had better conditions of urban village housing than Beijing and Shanghai. In Guangzhou, about 89 per cent of village rental housing had an indoor toilet. Landlords built toilets inside

Table 3.1 Facilities in urban villages in Beijing, Shanghai and Guangzhou (in percentages)

Facilities	Beijing	Shanghai	Guangzhou	Total
Kitchen	28.9	20.8	77.2	42.2
Toilet	21.4	17.5	88.7	42.5
Shower	17.2	13.6	79.4	36.7
Liquid gas	46.8	77.0	86.0	69.9
Piped gas	5.7	7.3	5.8	6.3
Air conditioning	24.4	23.8	33.8	27.3
Heating	52.9	0.8	3.5	19.1
Internet	42.6	21.5	47.9	37.3

Source: adapted from Wu, 2016c: 862.

apartments to suit the needs of tenants in a more developed rental housing market and because many of these rental housing buildings have been rebuilt, whereas in Shanghai the rental market in urban villages was more constrained by external development controls. As a result, landlords in Shanghai could only incrementally extend housing space or more often subdivide it into smaller rental rooms. It is difficult to install an indoor toilet. The dwellers in Beijing and Shanghai have to use public toilets. In Shanghai, urine containers are still used.

Because of the lack of a shower or bathroom inside the house, dwellers in Beijing and Shanghai had to go to commercially operated bathrooms in the winter. The charge was usually very low. These bathrooms used large boilers to provide hot water. In Shanghai, because of the lack of a kitchen and more expensive fuel for individual families, residents were encouraged to buy hot water from the central boiler shop installed in urban villages because the central boiler could be more appropriately maintained to reduce the fire hazard. Thus individual households could avoid using electricity to heat water and overloading the capacity of the electric wiring in the summer. The conditions of housing in urban villages were still poor, as can be seen from the low percentage of air conditioners. Because of extremely hot weather in the summer, air conditioning is now a necessity for ordinary urban residents. The rate of having an air conditioner in urban villages varied from 34 per cent in Guangzhou to about 23 to 24 per cent in Shanghai and Beijing. Because of lower voltage due to overloaded use, the constraint on electricity capacity meant air conditioners could not be widely installed in urban villages without upgrading the infrastructure.

Rural migrants choose to live in urban villages because for migrant families who work for social services or informal labour markets, factory dormitories are not available or not preferable for family life. For some working in low-end services such as foot massage parlours and restaurants, the employer might provide accommodation in shared rental apartments. But most are not able to rent formal private housing. Migrants who come to urban villages have no intention of settling down because this would not be a realistic plan. Therefore, urban village dwellers show low place attachment and low social participation. They come mainly for economic reasons and select urban villages for cheaper rent and an accessible location to their work (for example, Tangjialing village near the Zhongguancun Software Park in Beijing; see later).

The occupational distribution of the dwellers in the surveyed villages in Beijing, Shanghai and Guangzhou shows a concentration in commerce (retail and wholesale), social services and catering.[17] In 2014, the National Health Commission of China conducted a nationwide survey of migrants in eight cities.[18] The total sample of 16,000 migrants shows the residential patterns of migrants. In term of residential form, the concentration of migrants is quite obvious, because over 43.4 per cent of migrants lived in neighbourhoods mostly composed of migrants themselves.[19] In terms of the distribution of their housing tenure, the largest was 'rent in village housing' at 56.5 per cent. The next group was 14.8 per cent 'rent in commodity housing', which was followed by the third category, 'rent in old inner-city housing', at 14.4 per cent. Housing ownership accounted for less than 10 per cent, indicating that the road to home ownership was still for a minority of migrants.[20]

Governance means 'business'

The adoption of the household responsibilities system in rural China decentralised agricultural production decision making to individual households. The growing urban population increased demand for agricultural products and created other market opportunities. Capable villagers, very likely cadres, used the opportunity to develop village-based enterprises or later private businesses. Hanchunhe, a village of 910 families in southern Beijing, managed to tap into the lucrative construction material market and soon developed a village collective enterprise with over 50,000 construction workers across Beijing.[21] The villagers built not only 518 villas for themselves but also roads, parks, schools, hotels, a high-tech market garden and a village tourism business centre

Figure 3.1 The urbanised village of Hancunhe in southern Beijing. The villagers built not only their villas but also a central square for tourism. They captured the opportunities of the construction materials business and informal housing markets in Beijing. Taken in 2004.

(Figure 3.1). This development in the 1990s was led by then party head, Tian Xiong. Near the original village, over 5,500 apartments had been built by 2004, and over 80 per cent were sold to Beijing residents. These apartments were built upon village land and thus did not have property certificates (Figure 3.2). They were so-called 'small property rights housing'. Although Chris Webster and his colleagues (2006) regarded this case as a 'village condominium' – a continuing collective institution surviving at the end of socialism – the small property right housing developed by villages reflect the rise of the corporatist city which is governed by a different set of rules, beyond family or lineage oriented particularism.[22] Although a small group of people controlled the business, the operation of village 'collective' assets reflects privatism rather than collectivism.

In southern Jiangsu, the boom in township and village enterprises (TVEs) in the 1980s and 1990s maintained the strength of village organisations. But the bankruptcy of TVEs in the 2000s meant a total transformation of village governance – into the hands of business elites. In southern China, the transfer of TVEs into private corporations was even more apparent. In fact, many enterprises started as private companies. The privatisation of rural industries does not necessarily suggest that market development must lead to atomised individuals. Some could

Figure 3.2 'Small property rights housing' in Hancunhe village, Beijing. Without a property deed from the government, these properties only have village-certified ownership documents. The informal housing, however, cannot be detected from its appearance. Taken in 2004.

become family-run businesses or 'village shareholding cooperatives' (see later). Some 'local heroes' of village-based economies were able to play a role of community leader and distribute the benefits over a village's social welfare, while village resources supported these village-based enterprises. But the form of governance in essence means 'business'.

In terms of consumption, villagers manage their properties and look for new opportunities to refurbish and redevelop their houses into private rental housing to earn rental income. Rural collectivism no longer works. The village cannot even coordinate rampant redevelopment and ensure basic health conditions in the built environment – the village's public goods. This is not a 'tragedy of the commons' because of ambiguous property rights but rather because of disappearing collectivism – a moral order on which the commons were sustained for thousands of years throughout imperial and into socialist China.

Even just before the coming of market development, traditionalism had been seriously impaired. Rising 'individualism' started much earlier under state socialism, as a transfer from 'family' to the individual self.[23] The ripples of the differential mode of association stopped at the boundary of nuclear households. The boundary was clarified as households became property controllers. With their assets, households formed an economic unit, while the extended family (for example, between brothers) no longer held together, let alone lineages and clans. However, privatisation of the rural economy and later urbanisation of villages created unprecedented changes.

The most significant change in village governance has been the adoption of shareholding cooperatives (*gufen hezuoshe*) at the level of former production teams, and several shareholding cooperatives jointly forming an 'association of shareholding cooperatives' or joint shareholding cooperatives (in short, *jinglianshe*) at the level of the former production brigade and now the administrative village.[24] These economic entities are also referred to as 'village collectives'. While You-tien Hsing (2010) emphasises the legacy of lineage landholdings and collective organisations in what she calls 'village corporatism' – a strategy against an extractive state,[25] Karita Kan (2019b) observed that:

> Despite clarifying villagers' rights of control, income and transfer in collective property and thereby enhancing their access to power, shareholding still leaves the actual exercise of such power in the hands of intermediaries who may or may not be effectively constrained in their capacity as managers of collective wealth. That few institutionalised means are provided for villagers to hold these agents accountable creates an environment prone to arbitrary uses of power in which the dominant elite could control property rights and adjust distributive relations in its own favour. (pp. 147–8)

The reform of collective asset management into the corporatist form of shareholding companies did not lead to greater collectivism. Instead, the reform clarified and delineated the property rights of individuals, generating more individual- (or family-) based interests, which are no longer possibly reigned over by the internal social order or differential mode of association. It is this generative process that later demanded greater state intervention.

Different from being entirely dispossessed, villagers can gain benefits from land redevelopment. The role of collectives presents a new form rather than continuing rural collectivism. It is a 'club' of property-rights owners, which helps villagers negotiate and gain benefits from land appropriation.[26] Indeed, the process of corporatisation of the village economy, eventually in the hands of political-converted business elites, is not too dissimilar to the grabbing of state assets in post-socialist economies. The 'club' form of governance is regarded as 'private governance' rather than a revival of the collective economy. There is a temptation to regard the club as a community. But the shareholding cooperative is in essence an economic organisation built upon the legacy of collective relations and does not mean that members follow traditional norms and cultures.

The urban village thus becomes a private residential space. But, different from middle-class gated communities, to which the attention of private governance research has mainly been paid, not all residents in semi-urbanised villages are club members. Migrant residents are not shareholders. The concentration of migrants does not scale up their rights of residency to their entitlements or to claiming their right to the city. The club owners of rental businesses do not pay tax to the municipal government, although indirectly their rental economies raise land values in the area, from which land development initiated by the local state manages to draw a land income. The economic activities in urban villages are not a source of municipal revenue. Neither migrants nor their landlords enjoy public facilities and so remain outside the public sphere. Further, with fewer and fewer villagers living in the original village, or rental income being increasingly drawn from the corporatist development of rental housing, the situation is not too dissimilar to the financialisation of rental housing in recent Western economies,[27] as villager landlords are shareholders and thus purely investors in these assets.

This transformation has led to disappearing traditional village collectivism. The villagers' committee is becoming a mere administrative tool. The only form is the shareholding economy, which manages assets but is not able to run the village as a whole or as a totalised society. The capacity of these shareholding cooperatives is limited not only because they are businesses but also because actual control is fragmented in the hands of individual households.[28]

'Private governance' might sometimes be an efficient way of handling village business, but it is not an effective way of coordinating the 'public' interests in the village. First, it lacks legitimacy over negotiation and conflict resolution outside property rights. Second, the cost of negotiation would be enormous, just like homeowners' associations pursuing litigation for the governance of gated communities.[29] In most cases, city planning has not been developed within urban villages. Without a social infrastructure underneath its governance – e.g., a moral order of collectivism to support city planning (collective action and collective coordination) – the cost of private governance is too high. Even faced with the threats and requirements of the government, in places like Tangjialing the village could not become self-disciplined and failed to act collectively to improve its 'chaotic' and under-serviced informal development before the state stepped in to remove the 'disorder'.

How is the urban village different from the traditional village of Fei Xiaotong? The urban village is not an organically organised 'natural' rural village but rather an urbanised village in which urbanisation triggers a distinctive mode of governance. While rural villages have already experienced profound governance changes,[30] urban villages located in peri-urban areas experience the most significant transformation.

Inspired by post-colonial critiques, we should not regard this process as 'neoliberal' transition of governance, because 'rurality' prior to urbanisation persistently affects these villages. For urban villages as an enclave of migrants, conventional village organisations as well as 'community affairs' are based on clans but are irrelevant to migrants. They are renters, even though the rental economy is not formalised. They brought with them social relations with other fellow migrants from the same place of origin (*laoxiang guanxi*; see the discussion about the social interaction later), knowing and helping each other. But in terms of governance, they could not build a community of their own – unlike a club of the middle class in a gated community. It is indeed a *legacy* of how both rural and urban populations were governed by *hukou*, but the governance feature is not solely created by the state or its *hukou*. The governance of urban villages is derived from but not defined by *hukou*. The original farmer villagers had a rural *hukou* and still became shareholders. They did not give up their rights from rural *hukou* even when they became urban residents; and many nowadays refuse to join urban *hukou*. What we have seen in the urban village is the end of a totalised society. The totalised society of rural village, different from a society under the surveillance of an external totalitarian state, had a total integration of, rather than a separation between, state and society. It was a pre-modern place 'from the soil'.[31] But urban villages are the society 'leaving the soil'.

The urban village is both a production site and a rental market. Based on these functions, 'translocal' relations and a community of shareholders were created.[32] It is not a place of their own. Landlords may be away or separated from the everyday life of residents, as they are 'cultivating houses'. In terms of how urban villages were built, there was a great deal of informality as irregular and under-regulated development breached the formal rules. This is 'informalisation', not according to a predefined set of rules, which is part of urbanisation processes. However, urbanisation together with property development necessarily led to the delineation of rights, creating such structures as shareholding cooperatives – a clearly modern concept – and the redefinition of the rural 'informal' – its associated relationship – needing to follow the market operation. In short, the urban village is no longer a rural village; it is a village leaving the soil.

Now leaving the soil, the governance of the urban village unavoidably invokes state intervention. Even though urban villages provide cheap and affordable housing to migrant workers, they cannot be romanticised as 'ideal communities'. Subject to a wider agenda, not necessarily profit-making, they are constantly under the pressure of rebuilding or modification. Some initiatives even introduced 'enclosed management' just like gated communities (see Chapter 4), with the security features of physical gating, surveillance and village social order control centres.[33]

Even for ordinary rural villages, there has been dire need for the provision of basic welfare. In Dongguan, the base of China's global factory, the welfare of villagers almost completely relied on the rental economy.[34] Village 'public finance' was funded by collective shares in the village shareholding companies, which even self-funded the local police station.[35]

In Jiangsu, a well-developed coastal province, deteriorating public hygiene in the village living environment prompted the provincial government to initiate a 'village improvement programme' to maintain the water-course, encourage waste collection and transfer, recycle animal manure, and ensure the safety of drinking water.[36] However, the provincial government was unable to fund the substantial cost of redevelopment, while the village public finances were weak. The scheme only selected some pilot villages. The programme was driven neither by neoliberal 'place promotion' nor by a real estate 'growth machine'. Trying to find a business model to combine rural tourism with village improvement, the Jiangsu provincial government indeed intended to showcase its welfare intervention.[37]

Perhaps more importantly, naming the village improvement programme as 'beautiful Jiangsu's countryside' reveals its intention to align its work with the central government's initiative 'Beautiful China'.[38] No matter whether it was a case of an initiative of security enhancement, improvement of the living environment, 'face-lifting', or land revenue generation, when collectivism retreated, a new 'process of state building' began.[39] Understanding the governance of urban villages as a matter of 'business' – a version of entrepreneurialism or village corporatism,[40] suggests that informal development and informalisation are only one side of the process. The other side is accompanying 'formalisation', the creation of urbanism, and an imposed order from outside, revealing a departure from the soil.

New space of production, translocal network and deterritorialisation

Faced with rapid urbanisation and rising demand for construction, some villagers not only individually expand their rental properties but also jointly set up businesses or enterprises. In the Pearl River Delta in the 1980s and 1990s, household-based and then village-based workshops developed material processing industries. Some developed further into real estate businesses such as 'small property rights housing' which is sold to urban residents. Conversion from rural to urban residential properties is not permitted, but some villages subverted the controls, or the controls were not effectively enforced.[41] The villages then developed their own real estate projects and sold the properties directly to homebuyers. However, these properties cannot receive a certificate from the municipal government. They have only a certificate of rural property from the township, which is not equivalent to the deeds. Because the land is cheaper, so is 'small property rights housing'. Some younger urban families who need accommodation but lack affordability still choose this type of housing. Some projects are quite large in scale, and the residential buildings of small property rights housing can hardly be distinguished from other commodity housing by their appearance (Figure 3.3). As a result, urban villages now take on various new functionalities. Some become production sites, while others may be converted into formal economies. The remainder of this section discusses an example that takes on the new function of production.

In southern Guangzhou, Dongfeng village in Haizhu District has been transformed from a rural village to a cluster of garment businesses. It has also attracted a large number of migrants from Hubei province and thus gained a nickname, 'Little Hubei' (*xiaohubei*). Former villager houses were enlarged to accommodate migrant workers and garment workshops and became 'three in one' (*sanheyi*) – a rudimentary building form that combines workshop, residence and warehouse functions. Little Hubei is in fact a large urban village. In 2010, there were 4,200 local villagers and another 800 local residents from urban areas in Guangzhou, but 120,000 rural migrants.[42] Most migrants had come from the same town of Tianmen and nearby counties in Hubei and worked for garment industries. More than 2,000 garment factories had been set up (Figure 3.4). Most were small producers, employing about 10 workers. About 70 to 80 per cent of garment workshops were owned by Hubei people. The concentration of Hubei migrants brought about new opportunities for small restaurants and hawkers' food stalls to serve Hubei-flavour

Figure 3.3 'Small property rights housing' in the northern outskirts of Beijing. The photo shows the scale and formal appearance of the informal housing built by villagers. The standard, judged from the style, is lower and more modest compared with 'commodity housing'. Informal housing construction has been widespread. Taken in 2010.

Figure 3.4 Garment workshops in 'Little Hubei', Guangzhou. The ground floor of village buildings is usually used by workshops and warehouses, while migrant workers may live on the upper floors. The photo shows a production function of urban villages. Taken in 2010.

food. Like Gaojiabang in Shanghai – nicknamed 'Little Hong Kong' (see later in this chapter) – and many other urban villages, Little Hubei has bustling streets.

As a migrant enclave and a production base for migrant entrepreneurs, Little Hubei is, however, different from the earlier famous Zhejiang village in Beijing, in which businessmen from Wenzhou, Zhejiang province, managed to build their own large housing compounds for fellow migrants. The migrant entrepreneurs in Little Hubei could only rent individual houses self-built by original villagers. In other words, they rented not only accommodation but also spaces for workshops and businesses. Zhigang Li and his team studied this village. The landscape of Little Hubei reveals an enclave of migrants and their businesses:

> In response to the growing rental market, indigenous villagers of the Dongfeng Village renovated their own buildings and built more floors to maximise rental income. Most of these self-built houses are mixed use: the ground floor accommodates either commercial activities (e.g. restaurants and grocery stores) or producer service activities (e.g. machine repairing and wholesaling); the rest of the building is either garment workshop or worker dormitory. The dormitory is often quite small: about five to ten workers live in a room of about 10–20 m². It is very common for garment manufacturers to provide free food and accommodation to their employees. Migrants working for the same employer generally eat, work and sleep in the same place. Consequently, the little Hubei is not only a place of working but also a place of living. (Liu et al. 2015, 3094)

This combined form of residential, industrial and warehouse uses, although rudimentary and sometimes hazardous, proved to be very cost effective. They are 'sweatshops' requiring long working hours on the basis of piecework. But through the network of fellow villagers, Hubei entrepreneurs were able to quickly recruit their Hubei migrants. Through the social network, business owners can effectively find subcontractors to outsource production.[43]

In Little Hubei, there are symbiotic relationships between the original villager landlords, migrant entrepreneurs and migrant workers. The landlords protect the garment workshops: 'Once the authority is about to inspect garment factories, the village cadres will let our landlords know immediately',[44] while migrant workers 'confronted the local policy and fought against the confiscation of their machines by government agents'.[45] Migrant workers were also looked after by their workshop owners, as 'it is easier for migrant workers to accumulate business and management skills by working for their *laoxiang*' than by working for large factories.[46] However, their symbiotic relationships are essentially built upon obtaining rent, making a profit and earning a salary. As a result, although these relationships were built within the same place (urban village) or place-based social network, they are more fluid than in traditional villages.

Businesses are subject to competition. Like a nanny in a large city, migrant workers were able to walk away for other jobs or work for other workshops. They have their job choices and show higher residential mobility. Based on this space of production, migrant entrepreneurs built up a translocal network, linking garment traders to migrant workers. The workshops in Little Hubei produced low-priced clothes but with 'fashionable design', which suited the rising demand from Chinese rural areas in the 2000s.

Unlike the ethnic community in suburbs, known as 'ethnoburbs' in the US,[47] migrant enclaves like Little Hubei are not communities of migrants themselves. The relationships originating from the same place are grafted onto the business network and operate within a confined living and working environment. Both workshop owners and migrant workers live in rental spaces. These communities are different from work-unit compounds because work-unit membership was almost non-deprivable and permanent, which gave the workers a basic right or bottom line when they engaged with the employer. In other words, the workplace membership is a local citizenship. This permanent membership is the 'weapon of the weak'. In other words, the work-unit community is the community of workers. For urban villages, the territorial relationships are 'transplanted' but territorial relationships cannot faithfully replicate a rural village – the relationship has lost the territory in which it operated. For example, there was no village social and moral order to condemn unacceptable behaviour. Migrants could protest, as a 'labour movement', but it is difficult for migrant workers to resort to village support as a member of the community. Migrant workers have to simply walk away or resort to state authority.[48] It is this urbanised environment that makes them 'free'.[49] The origin of the same place is used to recruit and retain workers, to make it more cost-effective in a flexible labour regime. The relationship also brings some social support to the workers and solidarity as in the case of protesting against local police confiscating factory machines. But overall this solidarity is weak and limited.

The development of Little Hubei may reflect the agency of migrants, especially entrepreneurs, in adapting and extending the territorially originated network. However, it is regarded more as a relation (*guanxi*),[50] which can be seen from the expression *laoxiang guanxi*, which is derived from the traditional root – differential mode of association – but adapted in a modern context because relation (*guanxi*) as an exchange and the 'back door' to the formal procedure. The social network is informally built up on the trust of the same place origin but its purpose is more utilitarian rather than kinship or the membership of the village. Migrants' agency is not based on their citizenship or entitlement to a political community. This is not to suggest that their everyday practices are irrelevant; on the contrary, these practices are part of the new *urban* landscape in China today, rather than a revival of the rural society of differential mode of association in modern business.

While Laurence Ma and Biao Xiang (1998) show that the 'traditional' relation does not disappear in urban villages, the territory in which the state and society were closely embedded into each other is 'leaving the soil' and becoming urban. The social network originated from the same village in Little Hubei, just like other cultural proximity between traders and producers in garment industries facilitates business flexibility and lends advantages to production. But it is not an order or structure (*geju*) that provides guidelines and stability. Confronted with the village shareholding company and the administrative residents' committee, the migrant 'leaders' of Hubei origin could hardly intervene in neighbourhood (village) affairs in Guangzhou, even though they were residents there. Similarly, although they formed a symbiotic relationship with Hubei investors, the Guangzhou local villagers could hardly coordinate themselves with the impact of resources coming from outside the village. The deteriorating built environment reflects a declining order of traditionalism. Indeed, an unprecedented morality challenge[51] happens not only in urban villages but also in a vast number of rural villages, as the dismantling of traditional bounded territory continues. The translocal network is a new relation, derived from traditionalism. But like a gift, the relation lubricates transactions, indicating the demise rather than the replication of differential mode of association.

The state is not absent from Little Hubei. Law enforcement by the state provides an overall safe and stable policed environment in which business operations and rentals are possible. However, state intervention in terms of social provision and governance is ineffective because of the tradition of village self-governance. Rural villages, even in the suburbs, have not been 'municipalised' or 'incorporated' into the state system. The state does not have sufficient resources to absorb rural villages into its governance, as villagers, even after they have become entrepreneurs and possess millions of Yuan in rental assets, have not paid taxes. In the landscape of business, they are 'extraterritorial'. The village governance is privately operated, showing similarity to enclosed estates (*fengbi xiaoqu*), in which residents pay for their own property management and maintain their estate through property management companies. At most, what the state can do is execute the 'policing right' – of which city planning is one kind, to maintain safety and prevent fire hazards.

Transient places: changes, demolition and transformation

Urban villages are transient places. They are created and then disappear. One example is the famous Zhejiang village in Beijing, studied by Laurence Ma and Biao Xiang (1998) and Li Zhang (2001), which eventually disappeared. In the late 1990s, large compounds that combined residential and workshop functions were demolished. New wholesale markets and industrial districts were set up by the government in the 2000s. Similarly, Tangjialing in north-western Beijing was replaced by a new town comprised of resettlement and affordable housing. In contrast, Little Hubei in Guangzhou survived and continued to maintain its garment business, despite several attempts by the local state to clear up the urban village.

Why were there such different fates? Both Zhejiang village and Tangjialing village were large-scale extensions by external investors. The scale of development indicates the weakness of the local villagers because they could not develop the workshops or housing themselves and hence had to lend the land to private developers, many from Wenzhou in Zhejiang province. Wenzhou entrepreneurs and their employees, as outsiders, were not able to establish their own communities. Their informal economies were eventually formalised by the government. The business leaders were absorbed into the formal administrative organisation and the party. In contrast, Little Hubei was built by villagers themselves. They own the assets and hence were able to resist state intervention. The clan organisation initially supported the village's collective action which was later codified through the village shareholding company. The tradition of more flexible governance in southern China is another reason for a relatively more autonomous village society.

Tangjialing: from 'ant tribe' enclave to new town

Tangjialing village is located in the town of Xibeiwang outside the fifth ring road of north-west Beijing. It is near the aerospace town of Dengzhuangzi on the periphery of Beijing. Before 2000, the area still presented a typical rural landscape. Around 2000, the Zhongguancun Science Park created a new park – Zhongguancun Software Park – in this area. Meanwhile, Shangdi IT industrial base was set up near Tangjialing (Figure 3.5). Just west of Tangjialing, a private college – the China Software Management College – was set up. The students of the college became the first group of tenants in Tangjialing.

These developments attracted migrant workers in the IT sector. The total population of local villagers was about 3,000, while the migrant population reached as much as 50,000. The ratio of migrants to local population was very high. The outstanding feature of Tangjialing was the profile of migrant tenants, as there was a large proportion of new graduates and new migrants to Beijing. There were 17,000 new graduates. Many of them worked in the IT sector with a tertiary education but earned a modest wage of 2,000 to 3,000 Yuan per month. These IT workers, just like their counterparts in industrial assembly lines, worked in routine coding jobs as low-income 'white-collars'. However, they could not afford the middle-class lifestyle and sarcastically called themselves 'IT migrants', indicating their working-class status. They mostly lived in small rooms

Figure 3.5 The entrance of Tangjialing village, Beijing. The photo shows a booming village at the time of demolition. The area had many markets and restaurants, due to the agglomeration of IT migrants. Taken in 2010.

Figure 3.6 The alleyway of Tangjialing village, Beijing, before its demolition. The photo shows that the residential density is generally lower than in self-extended urban villages in southern China. Taken in 2010.

in shared rental apartments converted or extended from crowded village housing. They became known as the 'ant tribe' (*yizu*) in Chinese because they could not afford formal housing and lived like 'ants'.

Spontaneous construction started in 2000 (Figure 3.6). Villagers began to extend their houses from two floors to four or five floors to provide more rental housing. In 2005, the villagers' committee tried to control the speed of self-built rental housing and required villagers to stop further extension. However, rampant housing development occurred in 2006 and 2007. Besides spontaneous self-building on individual housing plots, large-scale development occurred on collective land. The villagers rented out land for private developers to build standard rental apartments in the form of residential compounds which were managed commercially.

Unlike villages in southern China where large-scale multi-rise buildings based on the land plots of individual households were constructed by the villagers themselves, but more like the earlier Zhejiang village in southern Beijing, villagers tended to lease collectively owned land to private builders who developed large residential compounds, in addition to constructing their own rental properties. Some residential compounds were managed by property management companies and offered standard

Figure 3.7 Purpose-built rental housing in Tangjialing, Beijing. The village lent the land to small developers to construct standard rental housing which appeared quite popular owing to the low cost and better conditions. Taken in 2010.

packages with a more formal contract to tenants. These residential buildings in large compounds were secured with electronic codes or swipe cards. The rental housing was better than in other places because of the slightly higher socioeconomic status of the tenants. The rental units in residential compounds were purpose-built and of a generally good quality.

The building density in Tangjialing was high, leading to narrow alleyways and potential fire hazards. Nevertheless, there were plenty of small restaurants, eating places, shops and stores, barbers and hair salons in the village. It was a very convenient place to live. In terms of transport, Tangjialing was also very convenient with several lines connecting to the Zhongguancun Science Park and central areas, although in peak hours they were congested because many workers commuted to their workplaces near Tangjialing.

The scale of rental apartment buildings was thus much larger than that of individually extended villagers' houses. In other words, these apartment buildings were purpose-built for migrant workers who required better housing conditions, facilities and security (Figure 3.7). These residential buildings were managed commercially by private companies and were sometimes known as 'student apartments' or 'white-collar apartments'. Thus, in Tangjialing as well as in other urban villages in Beijing, while these apartments were informal in terms of their building process (without formal planning approval, for example), the housing showed a trajectory towards greater formality in terms of its 'professional' management by private companies. The quality of these apartments was much better than in self-built blocks. However, this type of rental housing was still regarded as informal because the rental companies were not registered as formal businesses that should pay taxes to the local government. Instead, they paid a fee to the rural villagers who lent them land. The development also contravened land-use regulations because of the illegal conversion of agricultural land into urban uses.

The rent in Tangjialing village was very low, in 2010 ranging from 300 Yuan per month for a low-quality room of around 10 square metres to 700 Yuan per month for a relatively better quality 20 square metre studio with kitchen and toilet. Most rental housing had an internet connection, because it was deemed necessary for migrants in the IT sector and young students. Because the rental housing market was quite competitive, the landlords of residential compounds strove to improve housing conditions and facilities with an affordable price. These improvements and solutions were quite innovative and cost-effective, as the landlords ultimately depended on their customers paying. For example, in some buildings, the corridors of the second floor and above used transparent panels to allow light to pass through to lower floors (Figure 3.8). When we visited the

Figure 3.8 The decent living conditions of purpose-built apartments constructed by small developers in Tangjialing, Beijing. The photo shows how natural light is introduced into the corridors. Taken in 2010.

site in 2010, an architect accompanying our research trip acclaimed it, saying, 'This is really marvellous; we could not do this because we simply do not know what the tenants need'. Another example of market-driven innovation was the provision of transport connections. The landlord of Dongjia compound provided a small shuttle bus for the tenants to the bus station at the entrance of Tangjialing. It became a selling point to attract tenants, and thus other landlords soon followed. The management was rather informal but efficient and responsive to market demand. The informal practices of white-collar housing were thus welcomed by tenants who seemed to be fairly satisfied, considering the low rental cost.

The wide spread of informally built residential compounds in Tangjialing triggered concerns. The publication of a Chinese book, *China's Ant Tribe*, in 2009 brought wide attention to the living conditions of non-traditional low-income migrants. Tangjialing as the major residential area of the 'ant tribe' received much media attention, which led the government to redevelop this village. In March 2010, the Tangjialing redevelopment project officially started. Rather than 'demolition and relocation' (*chai qian*), the new policy adopted the approach of 'vacating' (*teng tui*), which was *in situ* redevelopment to retain the original villagers (Figure 3.9). The approach was similar to the policy applied to other villages in the green belt of Beijing. To release the land

Figure 3.9 The main road leading to Tangjialing village, Beijing, at the time of demolition. Banners show the campaign to 'vacate' the urban village, as villagers affected were mostly accommodated in nearby Tangjialing new town. Taken in 2010.

for green space, these low-density villages were removed while high-rise resettlement housing was built to accommodate villagers. The purpose was to vacate space through village consolidation. According to the Tangjialing redevelopment plan, the original villagers were temporarily vacating their old homes and then returning to the same places after the project was completed. In other words, the redevelopment aimed to rebuild a resettlement neighbourhood at the original place; this was the planned Tangjialing new town. However, the original tenants were simply dispersed during redevelopment and never returned to the new town.

By late 2010, two land parcels had been sold through auction. Vanke, one of the largest real estate developers in China, and Wukuang, a state-owned enterprise under the central government, gained the development rights. In total, 5.2 billion Yuan were bid for the land of Tangjialing new town, with 29 high-rise residential buildings. The new town, mainly made of resettlement housing, was completed in 2012. The relocation housing amounted to 350,000 square metres. The redevelopment project relocated 2,099 households and 4,816 residents. On average each villager household received a compensation space of 174 square metres, which was quite high in terms of per capita floor space, or two to three housing units as compensation. But compared with Liede in Guangzhou, the 'windfall' benefits for Tangjialing villagers were very modest.

The villagers of Tangjialing continued to use these apartments as rental housing to bring in additional income. About 188,000 square metres of additional space were used for office and public rental housing. Some public rental housing was returned to the village as their collective assets. The villagers received the rental income from these collective assets. Instead of using private companies to manage them, the public rental housing was managed by the government office of rental housing. In total 260,000 square metres of building were constructed. The relocated housing buildings, located at the south side of the aerospace town near the village, were dense and 15 floors high. However, after redevelopment, the rent immediately increased significantly from about 600 Yuan per room to over 2,000 Yuan per unit (studio), which was equivalent to a two to three times increase. The commercial rental housing targeted a different cohort of tenants in the region, equivalent to the entry wage of IT workers at that time.

Tangjialing represents a new model of rural village redevelopment – relocation of rural farmers into a concentrated resettlement housing area; at the same time, the state used real estate projects to build public rental housing. The state still acquired the land in Tangjialing and released it to the land market for these projects. The municipal government of Beijing made a huge commitment, as the redevelopment project was not profit-making. In essence, the project converted private rental (even in large-scale residential compounds) into public rental housing. This is quite different from 'three olds' (*sanjiu*) redevelopment in Guangdong, where village redevelopment was not organised by the municipal government. The villagers in Liede in Guangzhou negotiated directly with developers to release the land (see later).

The postcolonial description of informal development in the global South points out the persistence of informality during urbanisation and redevelopment as a result of a more flexible and even deregulated approach to urban redevelopment, due to colonial histories, complex social structures and local politics. For a long time, the villagers' committee served a dual function as the arm of the state in the local area but also as the representative of villagers' interests. The village even managed to lend collective land to small developers for informal housing, which was also a response to market demand as seen in the evolution of facilities and services (e.g., mini-shuttle bus).

But the large-scale redevelopment begun in 2010 has completely transformed the nature of this quasi-organic rural society (Figure 3.10).

Figure 3.10 The demolition of Tangjialing village, Beijing. The demolition and redevelopment were rather swiftly completed owing to the programme of affordable housing provision in Beijing, which is largely for registered Beijing residents. Taken in 2010.

Through this large-scale, state-led redevelopment project, informality disappeared. The project was initiated as a response to a 'chaotic' self-rebuilt village in the city's peri-urban areas. The state intervened through the large state-owned enterprise and real estate developer. The case of Tangjialing demonstrates strong state intervention and the transition of an informal urban village to a 'modern' housing estate.

Through 'village construction', Tangjialing village disappeared, and was replaced by Tangjialing new town. The once (in)famous Tangjialing also faded away from media attention. The new community (*shequ*) is just an ordinary resettlement housing estate, officially covering two residential areas of 4,000 people. The resettled villagers still do not have their property certificates, which means that they can own the use rights or rent out the properties but cannot resell them. This is very similar to 'small property rights housing'. However, 'illegal' transactions still exist, creating a market price of 40,000 Yuan per square metre, lower than the price of equivalent housing at 60,000 Yuan per square metre in the town of Xibeiwang. A flat with two rooms and one reception with a floor space of 80 square metres rented at 6,000 Yuan per month in 2019. But the area still lacks supermarkets and other facilities. The original 50,000 renters moved away. With fewer consumers, it is difficult to maintain a bustling street.

Within the 'new town', an affordable housing estate of 100,000 square metres is operated by Haidian district. Tangjialing was one of the first experiments in building public rental housing on rural collective land. In fact, it was built using trusted builders by the district government for Tangjialing villagers. The government then rented 1,980 units from villagers at a price of 39 Yuan per square metre per month in 2013. This was exactly the same or slightly higher than the price of villagers' private rental! The government now plays the role of secondary landlord. But the villagers no longer rent out properties themselves. In other words, the housing management bureau of the district government has replaced the private developer in operating the rental housing, which is now much formalised. The renters are only low-income urban residents of Haidian, excluding rural migrants. In 2017, the bureau, through a random draw, allocated 927 flats of 35, 45, or 60 square metres to eligible households at a rent of 35 Yuan per square metre per month for a three-year contract. Most original renters would not even have qualified.

What we have seen in Tangjialing is not 'displacement' of original rural farmers – they still have their 'collective assets', that is, public rental housing under their names. But they do not even participate in the operation of their assets. Indeed, without a clan organisation like Liede in Guangzhou or the support of a village shareholding company, it is unimaginable for villagers to continue to manage their assets. Tangjialing as an urban village has been thoroughly eliminated. The status of peasants came to an end in Tangjialing. Former villagers may have two or three spare apartments to rent out and collectively possess some assets from which to draw another source of stable income. They are a special rentier class without having to rent out properties themselves. Some may adapt with new skills. For example, one young lady is celebrated for her successful adaptation, now working for the residents' committee. But this is an exceptional case. Many villagers perhaps no longer live in this area and have been absorbed into restless urbanism.

Gaojiabang: vanishing into a business park

Gaojiabang was hidden away behind a clean street in the prosperous district of Xuhui, a well-developed central district in Shanghai. Opposite Guilin Park, across the Caobao Road, is the very modest entrance gate to this former village (Figure 3.11), unexpectedly leading to a high-density, congested, low-quality housing area with bustling narrow alleyways full of small shops and stores. The registered population of Gaojiabang was 1,373 local residents, but the migrant population added about 3,000 in

Figure 3.11 The small entrance leading to a large urbanised informal housing area in Gaojiabang, Shanghai. Taken in 2010.

2008. Most former residents had moved out to the suburbs for better housing. Only about 20 per cent of local residents lived there just before redevelopment.[52] Divided by main roads, the block where Gaojiabang was located included another dilapidated neighbourhood called Qiaojiatang. The names *bang* (waterside) and *tang* (pond) indicate that this place might have been low land or wetland before – perhaps similar to those squatter settlements in peripheral Shanghai prior to 1949.[53] In total, this block is about 100 *mu* (6.67 hectares), while Gaojiabang occupied land of 60 *mu* (4 hectares).

The modern history of Gaojiabang was associated with the rise and fall of Shanghai's colour TV industry. Before the 1980s, the place was at the edge of the built-up area of Shanghai. The agricultural land of Gaojiabang was acquired by the factory of Shanghai Electronic Meters. In 1980, Shanghai Jinxin (Golden Star) TV factory was set up to develop a joint production line with Japanese investors and thus acquired 60 *mu* of land in this area, and recruited 99 rural labourers into the TV production industry. About half of the rural labourers were absorbed by industrial development. According to the regulation of the time, two rural labourers were entitled to be recruited for every one *mu* of land acquired.[54] In 1984, the second phase of development absorbed 20 more rural labourers. Because working for the state industrial sector was more advantageous than farming in socialist times, rural elites and cadres managed to become state workers who, as 'insiders of the system' (*tizhinei*), enjoyed lifelong welfare entitlement.

In the 1980s and 1990s, farmers in Gaojiabang sold their spare houses to workers in small enterprises which could not provide 'workplace (*danwei*) housing' to their employees. These small enterprises included factories such as Shanghai Carpet Factory, Shanghai Plant of Electric Resistance and Shanghai Panel Plant in this area. As a result, the composition of residents in Gaojiabang was more complicated than in a rural village, compared with Tangjialing in Beijing or Liede in Guangzhou. Through early industrialisation, Gaojiabang had been partially urbanised, as its residents included those with urban *hukou* and worked for industrial sectors. However, the process of urbanisation of Gaojiabang was halted.

Since the late 1990s, Shanghai has experienced large-scale industrial restructuring. Industrial workers of state-owned enterprises were laid off.[55] The workers recruited from rural areas suffered most. The colour television factory began to experience difficulties from 1992, because more production lines were introduced from overseas to Beijing and Fujian province and competition became severe. In 2002, the factory was

Figure 3.12 The low-rise informal housing of Gaojiabang, Shanghai. The photo shows rather modest self-built housing and redevelopment. Most houses had only two floors in the place where the former village was partially absorbed into the urban fabric and institutions. Taken in 2010.

merged into the Shanghai Broadcast and Television Corporation. Many workers of the factory were made redundant and returned to Gaojiabang.

Around that time, the Caohejin Economic and Technological Development Zone (ETDZ) was set up. Its development was driven by a state-owned development corporation; local people called it the 'Cao developer' (Cao *kaifa*). Soon, a large supermarket was opened in this region and recruited about 1,000 shop workers. It was not clear how many came from laid-off workers or from new rural migrants. But the demand for private rental housing increased. Many Gaojiabang residents began to subdivide their 'spare' space to rent it out (Figure 3.12).

On the other hand, compared with the more lax situation in southern China and, ironically, casual management in peri-urban Beijing, Shanghai was able to maintain a relatively stronger development control. Under such control, existing owners were not able to demolish a whole building to build multi-floor rental housing apartments, as they did in southern China, or to build large residential buildings and compounds in places like Tangjialing in Beijing. Instead, existing residents could

Figure 3.13 After many informal houses were demolished, some original self-extension became visible. The building was dangerously increased to four and a half floors. The original ground floor house was still visible and had a rather weak foundation and structure.
Taken in 2013.

only subdivide rooms and append more layers. Residential buildings in Gaojiabang were dangerously extended and modified (Figure 3.13). As a result, private rental housing in Gaojiabang was further subdivided into smaller units, with deteriorating housing conditions and a crowded living environment.

The rental economy in Gaojiabang was more modest in scale compared with that in Tangjialing in Beijing, Liede in Guangzhou or other urban villages in southern China. This was due to the stronger capacity of local government to enforce land use control in Shanghai. The extension of village housing required the approval of the district planning office. Illegal constructions were in general stopped and demolished.[56] The rental housing in Gaojiabang, as a semi-urbanised village for a long time, was mainly formed through the subdivision of existing rooms and internal space of buildings and densification within the neighbourhood rather than expansion and new build in urban villages.

The history of development reveals why Gaojiabang remained an urban village for a long time. In 1997, owing to administrative boundary changes, the agricultural production team of Gaojiabang was temporarily under the management of Hongmei town in Minhang district, a suburban district outside central Shanghai. In 2002, Hongmei was converted from the status of rural administration (town) to an urban administration – 'street office' (*jiedao*), or sometimes called the sub-district office. However, the production unit of Gaojiabang remained as a rural administrative unit – a village under sub-district office. Its jurisdiction was later returned to Xuhui district. During the temporary management (*tuoguan*) under a suburban town, the control of housing construction was relatively lax, because of a management vacuum. In this fringe area, farmers' requests for additional housing plots (*zaijidi*) were quickly approved and building permits issued, laying the foundation of the rental economy. As mentioned, nearby the village site, some former agricultural land acquired by the factory was transferred to the 'Cao developer' in 2009 when the enterprise finally went bankrupt. This created a juxtaposition of industrial land owned by the development zone and the village site of Gaojiabang administratively managed by the urban district government.

The 'Cao developer', however, was not a traditional government organisation. Compared with other development zones such as Zhangjiang High-tech Park, it was more market oriented. The development of Caohejin was led by the development corporation rather than a quasi-government agency – the management committee (*guanweihui*).[57] It was less concerned about comprehensive urban renewal and adopted a more pragmatic approach. It also lacked the financial capacity to carry out large-scale urban redevelopment. This characteristic of the Cao developer meant that an incremental land acquisition approach was adopted. Rather than acquiring the whole area, the Cao developer acquired the land gradually to meet its needs. The development was carried out in phases.

This incremental approach created a complexity of land ownership, in addition to the mix of rural and urban landlords. These complexities made large-scale redevelopment even more difficult. The Cao developer had not been willing or planning to acquire the village site until 2008 when Shanghai started large-scale urban renewal for Shanghai Expo in 2010 (Figure 3.14a and b). Here the development process is described painstakingly in detail in order to comprehend how a rural village was transformed and village traditionalism disappeared step by step, not just at the point of once-and-for-all demolition. This broad process is better described as formalisation rather than specifically gentrification.[58]

Figure 3.14 Two images from Google show the disappearance of Gaojiabang, Shanghai. The central area of the photo shows Gaojiabang. In the 2021 image the site still appears vacant, while a nearby informal housing area was transformed into commodity housing estates (left corner). (a) captured in 2011; (b) captured in 2021.

Liede: corporatisation and massive redevelopment

Liede village is located in the southern part of 'Pearl River New Town' – the new central business district (CBD) of Guangzhou. This central location means that Liede is exceptionally important for the image of Guangzhou.

This rural village had been long established before it lost its farmland in the early 1990s and became a place of informal rental housing. But village housing remained. The villager population has been stable, with a total population of 7,800 villagers (about 3,000 households) since the 1990s. However, the migrant population reached 8,000 in 2007, just before redevelopment. The total floor space of buildings prior to reconstruction was 653,000 square metres, of which over 90 per cent received formal property certificates as village housing (equivalent to 595,000 square metres) from the draft development plan, obtained in 2009. The large percentage of legally recognised properties meant a significant cost of compensation for redevelopment projects.

The municipal government of Guangzhou had striven to redevelop the village for some time but failed because of the formidable cost of land requisition and compensation. The cost of redevelopment has risen considerably over time in Guangzhou. For a single village, the cost of redevelopment could amount to several billion Yuan.[59] Under the office of Lin Shusheng, the former mayor of Guangzhou in the 1990s, private developers were excluded from village redevelopment.[60] The municipal government monopolised land supply through the compulsory purchase of village land. Only land leased from the municipal government was allowed to be used by real estate developers for commodity housing development. This helped the municipal government to capture the differentiated land rent. However, none of the 139 urban villages managed to be redeveloped, because the relocation and redevelopment cost was too high. Faced with rising costs, the municipal government of Guangzhou made virtually no progress in the 1990s.

Before village redevelopment, Liede had already experienced changes in village governance. The adoption of a household responsibility system in the 1980s weakened the power of village leaders and the overall collective capacities of the village. The abolition of agricultural tax further reduced the capacity of the village for social organisation and mobilisation. However, the clan organisation persists in southern China, and this strengthened the village's bargaining power to resist land acquisition and redevelopment. In the mid-1990s, the village received 'economic development land' which was reserved for the village during land acquisition. The land became the collective asset of the village.

To manage the asset, the village shareholding company was set up. The shareholding company later fixed its share structure according to the village membership of residents.[61] It jointly developed a shopping mall with an external developer and realised its asset value appreciation. The shareholding company also distributed dividends to the villagers, which became an additional source of income. Through the development of collective assets, the village accumulated experience and capital and came to a better position to negotiate with the government. The establishment of the shareholding company complemented the weakened village governance. In other words, the village became 'corporatised'. But the operation was still limited to the collective asset. Individual villagers still maintained their private rentals. The village site remained as informal housing for migrants till the 2000s.

The redevelopment of Liede was proposed as early as 2002. But substantial redevelopment only started in 2007. Its redevelopment pioneered a new approach to village redevelopment. Liede was an experiment for the later policy of so-called 'three olds redevelopment' (*sanjiu gaizhao*). For *sanjiu*, the government provided quite a generous deal which allowed the village to negotiate directly with developers without converting their land into state ownership. In other words, the resettlement housing was built on the collective land without paying a market land price to the government. In the new phase of redevelopment starting in 2008, the municipal government of Guangzhou considered the forthcoming Asian Games in 2010 and adopted a more pragmatic approach to allow villagers to participate in redevelopment and share the benefits. In Guangzhou, the government was willing to negotiate with individual villages and adopted 'one village, one policy' (*yicun yice*). In the case of Liede, it received a good deal from the government to get a full compensation package, regardless of the property rights status of buildings in the village. That is, all the floor space of farmhouses, even non-certified floor space, was eligible for compensation. The government also kept the practice of 'returning' the development rights and ownership of collective land, which was the pool of village assets. To create more resettlement units, the government also lifted the building height restriction; the plot ratio was raised from 2.4 to 5.2 in the rehousing area, well exceeding the norm for residential development in Guangzhou.

In 2006 the proposed Liede Bridge cut through the village. This time, the village had accumulated sufficient experience and capital for redevelopment. By the mid 1990s the village had already been 'corporatised' because the village shareholding company had been set up to manage the village's collective asset – the 'economic development land' reserved for the village during land acquisition. The development of Liede Bridge acquired more village land and thus returned more 'discretionary' land to the village. More assets were injected into the village just before village redevelopment.

Besides the support of the clan, the corporatised Liede village thus had a stronger capacity for social mobilisation and negotiation. It had more capability than before to lead and operate its own redevelopment project. Liede proposed to the municipal government that it would not require an external investor and that the village wished to redevelop informal housing as a whole package by itself, meaning that the village itself should find finance and builders. The whole area was divided into three parts: a high-rise resettlement area, a business area to develop a five-star hotel, and an area of commodity housing properties for sale which was used to finance the project. The proposal sounded attractive to the government at the time when Guangzhou was going to organise the Asian Games in 2010. The government wished to improve the image of Guangzhou. The village was located on the pathway to the sites of the Asian Games and thus needed to be redeveloped. Without incurring additional investment, the government was willing to forgo the land premium from redevelopment projects. In addition, the government offered tax exemption and returned the income from the auction of a land plot in the village site to start up the redevelopment project.[62]

The redevelopment of Liede proceeded swiftly and was completed in 2009, before the Asian Games. The resettlement buildings are as high as 15 floors, creating the densest urban village in China. To Liede villagers, the redevelopment was a success. On the day of the opening of the new re-housing buildings to residents, the villagers' committee decided to arrange a banquet of 808 tables to celebrate the success.[63] Through village redevelopment, the collective asset was not dismantled but rather enlarged. The annual rental income alone increased from 50 million Yuan to 500 million Yuan.[64] According to some villagers, they deliberately chose collective ownership for their resettlement housing in order to prevent their children from irresponsibly selling assets, as the collective asset would be their source of livelihood. Through this redevelopment, the villagers realised that it was important to remain as a collective entity to be able to negotiate with the government. In addition to the historical tradition, they consciously preserved their clan organisation and customs and have rebuilt their ancestor hall (Figure 3.15).

After redevelopment, the profile of renters changed owing to the rent increase. The rent increased on average from 10–15 Yuan per month per square metre to 30–50 Yuan per month per square metre.[65] Former rural migrants in low-service jobs and manufacturing industries were replaced by new office workers in the CBD, new migrants to Guangzhou from other cities and white-collar university graduates. The estate was

Figure 3.15 Reconstructed ancestor hall in Liede village, Guangzhou. The redevelopment of the village has been extensively studied, owing to its exceedingly high plot ratio after reconstruction and its central location along the Pearl River. Taken in 2010.

built with a modern style of buildings, with a higher density but greater privacy. By its nature, residents in high-rise buildings have fewer social interactions. Social interaction between renter and landlord was almost minimal. It is difficult to detect the history of an urban village from its physical appearance or community atmosphere, as the neighbourhood is mostly for white-collar middle-class renters.

The only trace remains in land ownership which is still under the collective control of villager landlords. But that legal matter does not need to be comprehended by ordinary renters or visitors. Millionaire landlords were created by redevelopment; they became less 'entrepreneurial', as small increases of rental income did not matter much. The real wealth creation is through property value appreciation. There is no homeowners' association as in other gated communities of commodity housing, because villagers had already formed their shareholding company. The shareholding company operates in a more effective way to maintain the properties, as in China the homeowners' association has no corporate legal status and usually does not possess a bank account. The shareholding company is a business entity and is able to organise development jointly with builders or partners. Instead of working on property and estate maintenance themselves, landlords are now richer and prefer property management companies. The villagers' committee (actually now residents' committee) helps to sort out rental-related matters if these issues matter to the neighbourhood.

One may detect some traditional practices and village 'heritage' and argue that traditionalism has not disappeared in Liede. Indeed, Chinese festivals such as the 'dragon boat game' are maintained and celebrated; the ancestor hall has been rebuilt; and the lineage and clan strengthened. Liede has become an urban community with a distinctive history and cultural tradition. But neighbourhood governance and property management are now subject to greater economic rationality. It is a neighbourhood but also more like a community of owners of the same shareholding company.

From the perspective of governance, Liede village disappeared in the mid-1990s, long before its final demolition and reconstruction in the late 2000s. During its redevelopment, Liede as well as other urban villages demonstrated a greater 'informality' in terms of exceptions made for density and height control and the participation of villagers (actually their shareholding company) in the redevelopment process. The 'collectively' owned land was regarded as land of ambiguous property rights. It is widely noted in the literature that the property rights were not clearly defined and were ambiguous[66] – because while they were owned by villagers in name, actual control was in the hands of villager cadres. However, the village assets were under a more formal structure of corporative governance.

In terms of property rights, there was no ambiguity as to who could get what benefit from the collective asset – the property rights are clearly defined through shares. While attention has been paid to informal governance and the 'ambiguous' property rights of urban villages in China, here we stress that economic governance has supplemented, strengthened, and even to some extent replaced administrative capacities. When the villagers of Liede lost their land in the mid-1990s, they were converted into residents with urban *hukou*; the villagers' committee also changed to the residents' committee. But unlike other residents' committees, Liede still has its collective asset, and its villagers became shareholders to gain dividends. The 'village' organisation still organises cultural, leisure and social activities. In other words, the villagers did not lose their identity; on the contrary, they recognised the benefits of the old-fashioned practices.

Despite prolonged cultural practices in Liede village, the new governance demonstrates some features. First, it has a more formal administrative structure as an urban community, just like other residents' committees which have undergone 'professionalisation' (see Chapter 2). Second, in contrast to a purely administratively managed neighbourhood like the Fifth Village in Nanjing, which struggles for resources to maintain its estate, the property owners of Liede are entitled to the shareholding companies. Economic governance has been supported by the traditional organisation such as the clan. The key decision making is made by the village shareholding company rather than residents' committees. Third, the village neighbourhood became a rental estate, although a large number of original residents still live in this place. The changing profile of renters suggests that more urbanites than rural migrant workers are dwellers.

The impact of residents from other places has already weakened a socially self-contained village, but new urbanites bring in more urbanism rather than traditionalism. Renters feel that this place is not very different from other rental estates, despite the slightly cheaper rents. In terms of ownership, Liede has turned into a 'vertical urban village' from a village of self-built and self-lent private rental housing, with extremely high building coverage.[67]

In terms of neighbourhood governance, we witness the changing form from differential mode of association to one based on economic rationality, delineation of property rights and market transactions. We witness informality in the redevelopment of urban villages and governance. However, prolonged informality does not mean the preservation of traditionalism. Instead, it may be a symptom of disappearing traditionalism. The traditional social structure such as the clan helped gain a real estate business. But the latter inserts a new rationality which has destroyed traditionalism – village affairs mean a business.

Much attention has been paid to informality as a mode of governance in the global South – 'regulation by exception'.[68] New market developments have to be understood through operations and practices embedded in local politics and social cultures. Flexibility is thus a salient feature. However, such flexibility is not confined within traditional society or poor neighbourhoods; as argued by Ananya Roy (2005), 'informality, once associated with poor squatter settlements, is now seen as a generalised mode of metropolitan urbanisation' (p. 147). The massive 'informal' redevelopment of Liede has been achieved through flexible governance brought about by the municipal government of Guangzhou and the 'corporatisation' of former rural villages into a modern shareholding estate. The three cases illustrate that these urban villages are transient spaces. Tangjialing shows that the state strived to cope with the 'problem' of informal development and remove village-based development with an affordable housing project managed by the municipal housing authority. Gaojiabang reflects state entrepreneurialism in that the state used a development corporation to convert the site into an office park for the municipal economy. Liede demonstrates 'village corporativism' as the state tolerated and even encouraged the village shareholding cooperatives to develop high-rise residential buildings, a hotel and a shopping mall for an aesthetic environment. They all reveal the profound impacts of marketisation on Chinese society.

A new moral order based on property rights and surveillance

Urban villages have been informally built as rural migrant rental enclaves. The concentration of migrant tenants has led to an overwhelming majority migrant population in these villages. The proportion of local versus migrant population has changed – so many urban villages are called 'villages with inverted population' (*daoguacun*), meaning a larger migrant population than local. However, urban villages are neither alien places of renters who are isolated from society and each other, nor are they places of disorder or social chaos.

So what are the forces underlying the social and moral order? This was a profound question asked by Robert Park and the Chicago School when the city of Chicago experienced immigration and urbanisation.[69] As can be seen from earlier descriptions, the traditional differential mode of association has receded from rural villages in China. Why were villager landlords confident to rent out their properties in the environment where the majority were outsiders? What if renters refused to pay the rent? As can be seen in a later section, rural migrants have brought their social relations with them into the urban villages – many are from the same town or village and are acquaintances. However, social order in the rental business is not maintained on the basis of territorially based trust, but rather on the basis of property rights, even if the property rights are only partially backed by the state.[70]

From the human ecological perspective, the city was recognised by Park as a new institution built upon a set of social relations with different characteristics from traditional settlements, a moral order.[71] Louis Wirth characterised the order further as urbanism,[72] in which the industrial organisation of the city and impersonal relations defined by law and money replaced the traditional neighbourhood social structure, which resonates here in urban villages and migrants' interactions with the city.[73]

Migrants maintain social interactions in urban villages and in the city in general. In fact, because migrants work in low-level services and need to survive in an unfamiliar environment, they are more willing to interact with the locals than the locals with the migrant population.[74] Hence the traditional relations did not disappear.[75]

However, the external influence from the state is important, in the form of the 'police right', for the social order. In response to 'chaotic' construction and the problems often generated, as can be seen from earlier discussion on village demolition, the state has strengthened its role. New practices have been introduced. First, address identification is achieved through giving an identifiable address to each unit of accommodation. Second, increasing surveillance and local police capacities are introduced. In Beijing, 'enclosed management' (*fengbishi guanli*) has been developed since 2010.[76] Although most urban villages nowadays in China remain open access, identity registration at the local police station and the routinisation of patrolling are more widespread. Although the level of security might be lower than in gated communities, village governance has been greatly strengthened. In comparison, migrants are less mobilised. Migrant NGOs, if there are any, are either set up by non-migrants or face difficulties operating. Migrants can rarely claim their rights based on residency.

To discover the nature of tenancy, a survey of 60 urban villages in Beijing, Shanghai and Guangzhou was conducted in 2010. It was found that a large proportion of rental housing had no formal tenancy contracts.[77] The percentage of written contracts in Guangzhou was 56.3 per cent, while the figure was as low as 15.8 per cent in Shanghai and slightly higher at 27.8 per cent in Beijing. The majority of rental housing in urban villages without a written contract may be due to the fact that informal housing in Shanghai was of much lower quality, mainly through self-extension rather than new build as in Guangzhou. The latter had a customised rental market.

What was the source of tenancy informality? In fact, this informality was not due to the high job mobility of migrant tenants. Residents in urban villages generally had quite stable job histories, in contrast to the common perception that most migrants are very mobile. More than 65 per cent of the migrant population had not changed jobs in the last three years before the survey. Very few had changed more than three times. Job mobility does not reduce the probability of signing a contract. On the contrary, more frequent job changes gave movers more experience in protecting themselves through a tenancy contract. For the majority, job stability and job contracts did not have a significant effect on tenancy contracts. Compared with other non-local residents who came from the city, rural migrants were less likely to sign a tenancy contract. Other demographic factors, such as marriage and the presence of children, the age of household head or educational levels, did not affect tenancy contracts.

Tenancy contracts were related more to the value of rent and the length of residence. The more expensive the rental, the more likely was there to be a tenancy contract. This is because both landlords and tenants wished to protect their investment in the better rental housing. However, longer residence actually reduced the chances of having a written contract. This is probably because those who intended to rent longer and indeed stayed longer might have been introduced by trusted fellow tenants. In other words, long-term tenants were not even initially anonymous to the village landlord. As can be seen from the informal tenancy which is the norm rather than exception, life in urban villages does involve traditional relationships and intense social interactions (see the next section). For cheaper rental housing and the informal job market, rental housing without a written contract is a way of life, providing much flexibility. But such a rental market has evolved. The conditions of Guangzhou village rental housing were much better than those in Beijing and Shanghai. Informal rental housing in Guangzhou is becoming mainstream housing for new migrants, including those from other cities or new graduates who cannot afford the price of commodity housing. Consequently, the chances of signing a written contract were higher in Guangzhou than in the other two cities. In short, household attributes did not matter much in the formality of tenancy contracts.

The comparison of three cities even suggests that the status of migrants was irrelevant in the sample. Tenancy informality is essentially a feature of the cheaper rental market in urban villages, which provided cheaper and more flexible accommodation to migrants. When cheaper rental housing is upgraded to mainstream housing even in the location of urban villages, the relation between landlords and tenants is necessarily becoming less traditional and more formal.

Informal tenancy arrangements do not prohibit landlords from developing their houses into rental housing, because the landlords are confident that tenants would leave if they failed to pay the rent, partly because the property to rent has little value and new tenants may be introduced through existing tenants who have developed trust with the landlord. In contrast, many apartments of commodity housing are left vacant because the owners bought the properties for investment and value appreciation. The owners are often reluctant to rent out the property due to concerns about legal complications and taxation. Private rentals of commodity housing or ex-public formal housing generally require a formal contract, often through estate agents. The landlords of village housing, however, do not have full property rights. The lack of formal full property rights does not prevent the development of a buoyant informal rental market. Informal tenancy with only a verbal agreement or without agreement at all is widespread. The lack of formal tenancy contracts may be because there is a lack of tenancy protection in general in China and informal tenancy is not recognised by the state.

But the 'informal' ownership of villagers is endorsed by the state through its redevelopment and compensation practices. In other words, the ownership of village rental housing, including rental housing developed on the land plots of individual households (*zaijidi*), mainly for rental purposes and housing that is developed by shareholding cooperatives, is not ambiguous.[78] When informal housing is redeveloped, tenants are simply displaced without compensation, regardless of whether there is a tenancy contract. In this sense, a rental contract does not guarantee the 'tenure security' of tenancy for migrant renters.[79] But for villagers as *de facto* owners, their right to compensation is fully recognised, even for some 'illegally' extended spaces. Actual redevelopment often takes a pragmatic approach to compensating for unauthorised spaces. Often, villagers rush into building some temporary structures or unfinished housing skeletons before imminent redevelopment schemes. This perceived security of tenure gives villages the confidence to develop informal rental housing. However, this security of tenure is not 'perceived' or recognised by a local community as a 'customised' right. The moral order is not derived from a tradition or differential mode of association, but rather endorsed by the state and backed up by its redevelopment practices.

Social relations and neighbourhood interaction

Rural migrants in Chinese cities are not a 'floating population' (*liudong renkou*) in the sense of neighbourhood social relations, despite the term being used in the official population census. In terms of residential status, they are 'sojourners'.[80] However, they form social relations and interact with neighbours in urban villages. But compared with urban locals, despite higher residential mobility, they interact more frequently with neighbours than with others.[81] They left the countryside where they had a dense social network but at the same time they bring with them a social network transcending locality. They rebuild their networks in the urban villages. In this sense, urban villages are not an alienated social space.

It is therefore useful to contrast migrant renters with urban homeowners.[82] Compared with an average length of residents for Beijing locals as long as 19 years, migrants had 9.6 years – but still, this was not a short period. Migrants have indeed stayed in the city for some time. Neighbouring social relations can be seen from casual visiting, many forms of helping, and sentiment. Neighbouring is a form of social interaction, as shown in visiting and the exchange of help. First, visiting refers to casual interactions (*chuanmen* – literally dropping off at a neighbour's house), a phenomenon often seen in traditional neighbourhoods where neighbours visit without making an appointment.

Second, help in the survey refers to actions with a modest level of commitment and without financial obligation, such as 'looking after each other's children'. Compared with more casual visiting, helping neighbours through looking after children is a stronger commitment.

Third, neighbourhood sentiment (*qingqiegan*) emphasises slightly more affectionate feeling or feeling at home. This is different from earlier studies, which measured the attachment (*guishugan*) towards the sense of belonging and association, or more about place attachment.[83] Neighbourhood sentiment (*qingqiegan*) is also an attachment, derived from neighbourhood social relations rather than a sense of citizenship from formal membership.

Compared with urban locales, after controlling for educational attainment, income and other demographic factors, rural migrants are more likely to visit neighbours. In the informal living environment, rural migrants are more likely to help neighbours. Longer residence increases the likelihood of helping neighbours, while higher education or income either reduces it or does not have a significant effect. In other words, rural migrants are not socially disengaged in their immediate life circles in urban villages.

Neighbouring enhances sentiment towards the neighbourhood. Rural migrants did not regard their urban villages as a terrible place to live; on the contrary, many still felt them to be satisfactory.[84] Stronger sentiment is associated with more frequent visiting. Fulong Wu and John Logan (2016) observed that:

> Compared with those who never visit their neighbours, those who often visit their neighbours are 29.5 times more likely to strongly express a positive feeling (versus holding a neutral view), and

occasional visits to neighbours would raise the equivalent propensity by 7.7 times. Rural migrants have more frequent neighbouring activities and in this sense demonstrate more connection to the neighbourhood. (p. 2985)

In fact, rural migrants among other social groups are more likely to have the highest level of neighbourhood sentiment. Education, income and employment status do not have a significant effect on neighbourhood sentiment. Rather, they may present a countervailing effect – being more highly educated, having a higher income and being in formal employment mean more chances of connections outside the neighbourhood.

To understand an overall picture of social interaction, the Beijing survey presented four statements to interviewees to generate a composite measurement: neighbours are friendly with each other; neighbours look after each other; neighbours trust each other; neighbours are familiar with each other.[85] These four statements measure friendliness, trustworthiness, acquaintance and social support. From the composite neighbourhood social relations, the survey from Beijing did not find that rural migrants were significantly different from urban locals. Length of residence enhanced neighbourhood socialising. In other words, despite being a renter and having higher mobility, a rural migrant did not reduce socialising with other residents in the neighbourhood, in this case the urban village, because of their migrant or renter status.

This is remarkable, countervailing the common perception that rural migrants are 'floaters' yet reconfirming the thesis of translocal migrant enclaves such as Zhejiang village and Little Hubei.[86] Wu and Logan (2016) argued that:

> Or at least, renters can have a stronger neighbourhood interaction and sentiment. Rural migrants are able to develop new neighbouring and reciprocal relations in their place of living. They do not need to become homeowners in order to develop their sentiment. Based on neighbouring, the affectionate attachment towards the neighbourhood is under formation. (p. 2987)

Rethinking social life in urban villages, rural migrants are actually a factor countering the process of 'modernisation'. They bring a traditional relation into their enclaves. They interact with fellow migrant neighbours and try to carve out a social space of their own – managed socially through everyday life but not in terms of governance. Neighbouring and helping neighbours leads to a better evaluation of their place – at least with affectionate feeling. This is against a general trend of declining neighbouring and increasing privacy as in middle-class commodity housing in present-day China.[87]

Migrants' involvement in neighbouring is a result of the mechanism of both self-selection into affordable rental housing in urban villages and external constraints on their locational choice. In short, urban villages are places with good sociability and neighbourhood help. Migrants are more likely to engage in socialising and the exchange of help with neighbours, and consequently strengthen their sentiment towards these places. As a generic neighbourhood type still bearing some traditional imprints in contemporary China, is the urban village a pathway for migrants' integration into urban society? Does the differential mode of association work in this place where such a socially engaged though differentiated (*chaxu*) relation can lead to an integrated social order or 'cohesion' (*geju*)?

Implications for social integration

Despite being a sociable living space, the urban village fails to be a space for social integration. In a traditional rural village, residents were socially integrated through extended family, lineage, clan and dense but differential social relations. The influx of rural migrants changed the social composition of these villages. The legacies of collective structures shaped both local villager landlords and migrant tenants. Informal practices are pervasive in urban villages in terms of construction activities and social relations.

However, these collective relations do not re-establish the mechanism of social integration in urban villages. Richer migrants – private business owners – simply choose to buy commodity housing in gated communities; some manage to convert into urban *hukou*. Often, the lack of urban *hukou* and access to state welfare do not hinder their integration with urban society. Their integration is achieved through the market mechanism.[88] For migrant workers, their reciprocal relations do help them cope with the challenge of living in the city. But because of low affordability, they cannot achieve integration through the market. Although they are associated with the more formal economy, their links are fragile.

Inside the urban village, their participation in neighbourhood affairs is excluded by a rising property rights-based regime. As mentioned earlier, property rights occupy a central position in village economic and social life. The collective land is controlled by the shareholding cooperative. The villagers' committee often becomes the board of directors of the cooperative, through informal village corporatism. Because of the lack of transparency and checks and balances, property rights are actually controlled by a minority of village cadres.[89] It is in this sense that village collective ownership has some 'ambiguity', because individual villagers cannot take an action to deal with their properties but the governance structure of collective ownership has some informality. Yet the fixation on shares and clarification of entitlements in shareholding reform have actually defined the boundaries of rights. Rights are determined by property rights rather than community membership or residency, even in the case of *hukou*. Membership is not universal and has nothing to do with the length of residence.

In this sense, the notion of a 'club', which describes the phenomenon of gated communities in the Western societies, is probably an appropriate characterisation.[90] But this club does not mean collectivism. The club membership based on property rights excludes those who actually live in the community. In other words, the actual residency does not matter – meaning the end of territorially based cohesion. Besides regulation through property rights (landlords and tenants, both are rural population), the limited rights of migrants are further reinforced by the practices of village redevelopment and security management. Migrants do not live under reciprocal relations with local residents. They survive through market exchange – as informal workers and tenants for housing. But they are still associated with the state apparatus, as seen in the residency or territorial management.

To strengthen the management of the floating population, a territorial management (*shudihua guanli*) penetrates the urban villages in addition to property rights (in this sense, migrants are not 'anonymous' tenants known only to the landlords, and they are subjects of the professionalised state). In particular, rental addresses are defined and migrant tenants have to register, matching these addresses. This sounds rather draconian, but in reality except in some campaigns for migrant clearance (such as reducing the total size of the residential population in Beijing), there is great discretionary space for the operation of property rights. Informality still exists and is replicated, despite the demolition of villages.

The urban village is a low-end, informal, largely self-governed 'private community'. From Beijing's Zhejiang village to Little Hubei in Guangzhou, there have been over 20 years during which the nature of rented space for production has not changed. We need to understand this particular feature of the urban village in order to understand the implications for migrant social integration. The collectiveness of the village as shown in its shareholding organisation imposes an obstacle to the integration of the fellow rural population, which is endorsed by the state as a modern way of governance.

In a way, rural migrants nowadays might feel it was even more difficult to integrate into the host urban society than it was for their counterparts in the 1920s and 1930s, because the latter started a long process to become 'little urbanites'. With the disappearing traditionalism of differential mode of association and the establishment of shareholding economies, urban villages are more 'codified' and exclude the right to the city. I argue that the obstacle is not purely due to *hukou*, as easily stressed by most studies. It is due to the commodification which at the same time fails to integrate rural migrants in its own market way, or the problem of the 'market society'.

This obstacle to migrant social integration suggests that urban villages as migrant enclaves are different from immigrant enclaves or the ethnic suburbs known as 'ethnoburbs'.[91] There, the accumulation of social capital by ethnic entrepreneurs identifies a new pathway to assimilation, not necessarily confined through spatial proximity and co-living with the majority residents. Assimilation can be achieved through different spatial and social segments, hence known as 'segmented assimilation'.[92] In the North American situation, residential segregation arguably does not halt the process of assimilation.[93] Market-based segmented assimilation is possible for ethnic entrepreneurs who manage to exchange their capital for the right to the city, and integrate (assimilate) through market exchange. As residents of their communities, they are also included in the state system of redistribution. Chinese migrants, however, with their low incomes, cannot follow this path. They experience 'entitlement failure'[94] as they leave the countryside where they had survived on reciprocal relations but only manage to obtain limited rights through market exchange – as rent payers staying in villages. Even rural villagers who are not well organised through lineages and clans and capable cadres playing a dual role to mediate with the state can also experience entitlement failure and become landless farmers.[95]

The urban village is also different from the Paris working-class *banlieue* in that the latter is a public housing estate, that is, a formal residential area, according to Loïc Wacquant (2008). While accommodating a large proportion of immigrants as well as French nationals, the second-generation immigrants there have already established 'integration' earlier through state redistribution. Their entitlement failure in the *banlieue* as so-called 'advanced marginality' is largely attributed to 'the uneven development of capitalist economies and the recoiling welfare states'

(p. 2). The two forces work together to create an impact on 'the segments of the working class and the ethnoracial categories dwelling in the nether regions of social and physical space [of the *banlieue*]'. (p. 2) These are 'structural' explanations, which are relevant to Chinese cities.[96]

However, residents in Chinese urban villages face difficulty in integration, largely unrelated to the retreat of the welfare state. These villages used to be a form of 'traditional society' in which the state role was not obvious but was embedded. Since Chinese villagers and migrants are associated with China's global workshop, they are not excluded simply by economic forces such as deindustrialisation. In fact, Chinese migrants have been created by China's new industrialisation in the post-reform era. Although urban villages are characterised as 'dirty, chaotic, and backward' rather than a nice living environment, and indeed many are the 'neighbourhood of poverty', the concentration of migrants in urban villages did not create a stigma for these places or a label as 'no-go areas'.[97]

The inspiration for the 'structural' change is the 'breaking up' of an organic and 'totalised society' in China, as the rural village leaves the soil to become the 'urban'. Traditionalism no longer governs, and differential mode of association no longer prevails. In this sense, urban villages are not the successors of rural villages. The development of a renter–rentier class relation plus the overall oversight of the state of a social order create new conditions for social integration. In the late 1990s and 2000s, migrant entrepreneurs in Zhejiang village were very keen to play a public role, to join the party and even become officials.[98] After demolition, Zhejiang village was no longer a migrant base for production. For migrant workers, urban villages are not the pathway towards social integration.

Finally, to understand the social disintegration of rural migrants in urban villages, we need to go beyond the scope of neighbouring, neighbourhood interaction and social capital. We also need to go beyond policy issues such as the 'equalisation of social services', changing *hukou* regulation, and 'transforming migrants into urban citizens' (*shiminghua*). The social integration of migrants needs to be examined in the context of urbanisation, social transition and the creation of urbanism. The general trend of dismantling a totalised society and a rising modern state operation defines the situation faced by rural migrants in urban villages. Their disintegration is due not to the loss or 'recoiling' of the state but rather to a new, different governance mechanism, indirectly endorsed by the state, through limited rather than totalised or comprehensive social relations. Social disintegration demonstrates the negative impact of marketisation on China's society which is becoming 'urban'.

Conclusion

Urban villages as a transient type of neighbourhood still preserve many traditional features. This is often described through the notion of 'informality', indicating the persistence of traditional social and cultural structures.[99] Hence, the urban needs to be understood not only with attention to new development processes but also through the effect of these historical legacies. However, referring to the traditional social feature does not mean that the place remains static and the same as rural China. The purpose of understanding the residual traditional feature is to bring up a contrast with what is new in urban villages. The feature of informality can be explained with the development process.

In urban villages, informal practices are created from several sources. First, they are caused by fragmented land ownership. Land acquisition converts farmland into state ownership, while the housing plots remain in the hands of individual households – a *de facto* private ownership, albeit with sale restriction. During redevelopment, the state has even 'returned' some developable land to villages as their 'collective assets', which are not permitted to be sold in the land market. This paved the way to village 'corporatisation'. But these restrictions are imposed by the state; and the regulations are executed by the state. However, as a traditional village the operation relies on local cadres. Villagers extend their houses into private rentals; often the elite leaders themselves rent out the collective land to developers for informal housing and real estate projects. Informality associated with collective ownership remains salient in urban villages.

Second, land management was lax and development controls as in modern city planning were entirely absent in rural villages. Villagers lacked the capacity to develop large-scale housing projects. In rural areas, land for housing was allocated to farmers according to their family size. But since the late 1980s new land allocation has been replaced by self-extension due to land shortages. Therefore, self-build is the norm rather than the exception in rural areas. Villagers build more housing spaces and increase building densities, subject to a usual limit such as 'two floors and a half [loft space]' (a space between 240 to 280 square metres). Urban villages are characterised by high building coverage. Third, villages are outside the municipal provision of public services. Limited welfare is supplied by the village collectives themselves. On the other hand, village landlords do not pay tax to the municipal government. Roads, ditches and public spaces are maintained by villagers themselves. In other words, there is a tradition of 'private governance'. Fourth, actual constructions are organised by villagers themselves or occasionally, for ancestor halls and public facilities; the development is contributed by villagers.

All these informal practices of self-build and governance continue and even increase in urban villages. The practice of returning development rights to villagers for some of their land, known as 'economic development land' or 'economic reserved land',[100] strengthened informal development practices. Even the village shareholding cooperatives may not pursue profit maximisation and thus are different from a modern private enterprise as they are still a collective economy.[101]

However, despite these informal features of urban villages, traditionalism disappeared even before they were physically destroyed. In Tangjialing, the state's swift action transformed Tangjialing village into a rehousing community (*shequ*). Their tenants have been dispersed, while new tenants 'qualified' for public rental housing, presumably for the nearby software park, are accommodated in a newly built living quarter. Tangjialing villagers thus have no relations with these public housing tenants, despite retaining the status of landlords and receiving rentals. In Gaojiabang, the state developer removed the entire neighbourhood and converted it into a business park. The original residents were relocated to large resettlement estates in peri-urban Shanghai. In Liede, villagers managed to persuade the government of Guangzhou to allow them to demolish their village themselves to rebuild at a massive scale and to create collective assets controlled by a corporate structure. The strength of the clan brought them economic benefits as they became the owners of multiple apartments. Hence, they tried to keep the clan as much as possible and preserve traditional practices and festivals. However, the power of decision making lay more in the shareholding company than with the seniority of the community. All these neighbourhoods, if they remain, are converted into urban neighbourhoods in terms of their administrative status.

This chapter reveals disappearing traditionalism and the dismantling of the 'totalised society', in particular in the case of rural villages in peri-urban areas. The detailed development process and social changes in these villages are examined. From rural villages to urban villages, we try to understand precisely what remains. Collective control over assets may be achieved if the village has a strong clan structure. If the village was weak during early industrialisation and late socialism, it is likely to totally disappear. If there are mounting concerns for the lack of social order (the 'chaotic' environment) or village self-build activities, the local government may strongly intervene to rebuild the urban village.

For example, Zhejiang village has been turned into a modern wholesale market, and Tangjialing has been rebuilt into a new town. The village is physically transformed and disappears.

There is a temptation to interpret the change as a result of Chinese authoritarianism – strong state authority and a weak society under socialism. According to this modernist view, market development has created diverse interests outside the state sphere, perhaps a potentially 'civil society' (in these former villages), leading to the loosening of the state's grip over rural areas. In response, the state still wishes to control and hence strengthens its institution of control through village management. This interpretation attributes urban villages to a discriminatory institution (*hukou*), land management practices and the role of the state.

However, the main problem with this view is the inappropriate assumption about state and society relations in the past. There is a need for a more spatialised view to understand the Chinese residential landscape.[102] We need to understand both broad urban changes and how the state and society co-evolve under the impact of marketisation, generating significant impacts on the traditionalism of rural society. Urban villages represent not only residential differentiation but also the process of differentiation between the state and society, through which the state is separated from the society in the process of urbanisation. In other words, the state has been 'forced' out of its embedded position in a totalised society and then takes over new functionality – partly as a social protection mechanism to respond to the threat of a marketised society. The urban village is an exemplar of disappearing traditionalism that remained strong due to urban–rural dualism under state socialism until the Chinese urban revolution. The prolonged informality in the urban village reflects a new mode of social relation, resulting from the impact of commodification on traditional societies.

Notes

1. In other words, these urban villages have not been converted into the neighbourhoods under urban administration.
2. See Lu, 1999; Li, 2015.
3. See Lu, 1995; Honig, 1992.
4. Honig, 1992. For a long time, even after socialism, they were subject to discrimination.
5. Lu, 1995: 589.
6. Wu, 2015.
7. Li and Wu, 2006.
8. Ghertner, 2015; also Myers, 2020.
9. Wu, 2018b. See also Wu et al., 2022, for various state political considerations for urban renewal.
10. Turner, 1976.
11. Roy, 2009b.

12. Although earlier studies recognised that this type of housing was built by villagers themselves rather than the state and hence a sort of 'self-help' (Zhang et al., 2003).
13. See Wu, 2016c for more information about the survey.
14. This type of housing is called 'small property rights housing'; see later in this chapter and also Liu et al., 2012; He et al., 2019.
15. See previous studies on migrant housing in general, Tian, 2008; Wu, 2016c; Zheng et al., 2009.
16. See the case of Gaojiabang later in this chapter.
17. Wu, 2016c.
18. See Lin et al., 2020; Lin et al., 2021; Liu et al., 2022; Xu et al., 2022.
19. This is a subjective measure, from the statements of migrants (hence their judgement of the composition as 'mostly migrants').
20. Lin et al., 2020.
21. Webster et al., 2006.
22. Sa and Haila (2021) provided another example of village development in Northeast China. They explain how villagers have become real estate developers.
23. Yan, 2010.
24. Po, 2008; Kan, 2019a, 2019b; Smith, 2021; Sa, 2021.
25. Hsing, 2010; see also Smith, 2021.
26. Zhao and Webster, 2011.
27. For financialisation of rental housing, see Fields and Uffer, 2016; Aalbers et al., 2017; Wijburg et al., 2018.
28. Kan, 2019b.
29. McKenzie, 2005.
30. See Tang, 2015.
31. Fei, 1947/1992.
32. Liu et al., 2015.
33. See Kan and Wong, 2019.
34. Xue and Wu, 2015.
35. Po, 2012.
36. See Wu and Zhou, 2013.
37. Wu et al., 2022.
38. Wu, 2018b.
39. Wong, 2015.
40. Hsing, 2010.
41. Kan, 2019b.
42. Liu et al., 2015.
43. Liu et al., 2015.
44. Liu et al., 2015: 3097.
45. Liu et al., 2015: 3094.
46. Liu et al., 2015: 3099. See Zhan (2021) for village housing upgrading programmes promoted by the state in Shenzhen; Siu Wai Wong et al. (2018) for village redevelopment in Guangzhou; Liu et al. (2017) for the social impact of village redevelopment in Guangzhou.
47. Li, 2009.
48. Like the land dispute related to married-out women villagers in the Pearl River Delta, Po, 2020.
49. Wu and Wang, 2019.
50. Two recent books have thoroughly examined *guanxi*: a more universal social relation derived from the differential mode of association (Bian, 2019), and *guanxi* as a social relation embedded in Chinese social culture (Barbalet, 2021b).
51. As deterioration of morality (*shifeng bugu*).
52. Interview, June 2010.
53. See Lu, 1995.
54. Interview, street officer, June 2010.
55. See Giles et al. (2006), Wu, Webster et al. (2010), and Frazier (2019) for informalisation and urban poverty.
56. Interview, the district planner, September 2010.
57. For the role of the management committee in development zones, see Wu and Phelps, 2011; Shen et al., 2020.
58. See Wu 2016d; Wu, 2020b.
59. Interview, September 2010.

60. Tian, 2008.
61. Po, 2008; Po, 2012.
62. Guo et al., 2018: 1430.
63. News from sina.com.cn on 28 November 2010.
64. Guo et al., 2018: 1431.
65. Guo et al., 2018.
66. Zhu, 2002.
67. Wu et al., 2013.
68. Ong, 2006; Roy, 2005.
69. See Wu and Wang, 2019.
70. Because these properties could not be sold in the urban market.
71. Park, 1915.
72. Wirth, 1938.
73. Wu and Wang, 2019.
74. See Wang et al., 2016; 2020.
75. Wu and Logan, 2016.
76. Kan and Wong, 2019.
77. For a full statistical analysis, see Wu, 2016c.
78. Even though capable village cadres may hold more shares and have more power over their uses; see Kan, 2019b.
79. 'Tenure security' is mainly discussed under informal housing ownership rather than tenancy. Tenure security has been promoted through titling programmes in the regulation of informal housing in developing countries, under the influence of de Soto's (2000) work. But it has been suggested that perceived tenure security is more important than *de jure* property rights (Gelder, 2009; Varley, 2002).
80. Solinger, 1999.
81. Wu and Logan, 2016.
82. For more detailed information about the survey in Beijing, see Wu and Logan 2016.
83. See Wu, 2012.
84. Li and Wu, 2013.
85. The measurement is similar to the sense of community index (SCI) used in the USA, which includes elements of membership, influence, meeting needs and a shared emotional connection (McMillan and Chavis, 1986).
86. Liu et al., 2015.
87. There are extensive observations on declining neighbouring; see Wu and He, 2005; Forrest and Yip, 2007; Wu and Wang, 2019.
88. Here, we are thinking along the Polanyian mode of integration, and the inevitable emergence of state 'redistribution' (control).
89. Kan, 2019b.
90. Webster et al., 2002.
91. Li, 2009.
92. Portes and Zhou, 1993.
93. Known as 'segmented assimilation', see Portes and Zhou, 1993.
94. Wu and Webster, 2010.
95. He et al., 2009.
96. Wu, 2009b.
97. Liu and Wu, 2006.
98. In a Chinese paper, Xiang (2017) discusses the formalisation of social relations in Zhejiang village.
99. Wu et al., 2013.
100. Tian, 2008; Wu et al., 2013.
101. See Sa, 2021.
102. Hsing (2010) notes the territorialisation of the state as a process of urbanisation, or urbanisation of the state.

4
Residential enclosure without private governance

The ubiquitous landscape of residential enclosure

Residential enclosure is nowadays a ubiquitous landscape of Chinese cities. In China, there has been a long tradition of building the walled city with gates. Individual compounds of courtyard housing also had walls and gates. But the residential neighbourhood of alleyway housing usually does not have walls or gates, except occasionally modest doors at the entrance. In the imperial period, rural villages and neighbourhoods in the cities were rarely sealed off, except for some defensive reason. The physical enclosure at the neighbourhood level was more widely developed in the socialist period through walled work-units together with their residential quarters.[1] Walls and gates have been extensively constructed in 'commodity housing' estates after the economic reform. These commodity housing estates are called 'sealed micro-districts' (*fengbi xiaoqu*).[2]

These sealed micro-districts are sometimes also referred to as 'gated communities' in the academic literature.[3] However, in China, the gated communities are not deliberately built as a product for governance choice. Some governance features of gated communities are derived from gates. The sealed micro-district is perhaps the most accurate way to describe those commodity housing estates (hence private housing) with security features and with some degree of actual control through services delivered by property management companies. First, micro-district (*xiaoqu*) indicates that this neighbourhood must be a planned and designed product. Hence, the gated traditional area or sealed village areas would not be referred to as gated communities. Second, 'sealed-off' (*fengbi*) suggests a higher degree of security which is largely impossible for everyday life in alleyway housing areas, workplace housing areas or informal rental housing areas in villages. High security is unique to more exclusive upper-end housing estates but also exists to a lesser extent in mainstream middle-class housing.

This chapter is about residential estates built after the economic reform, especially housing commodification.[4] Because in the post-reform period residential estates are rarely built into open residential areas without gates and security fences, gated communities represent a mainstream and ubiquitous built form. As the name sealed (*fengbi*) suggests, these estates must contain some degree of security control, imposed at the neighbourhood level. This criterion is in fact not difficult to satisfy as most estates are enclosed to some extent.

The second criterion is that they are usually owner-occupied housing estates. Again, most commodity housing estates are built for homeownership, although some buyers have the purpose of investment and may rent out unoccupied housing. These properties may be used as a second or third home, or simply be left vacant for many years. Therefore, tenants in commodity housing estates living with other homeowners are not the majority group of residents. Although some estates built predominantly for rental – for example, social rental housing – may have some security features, these communities are mainly managed by the state and do not constitute the majority of gated communities. In this study, *fengbi xiaoqu* is different from the notion of 'gated communities' in that the former does not necessarily require 'private governance'. In this way, *fengbi xiaoqu* excludes metaphorical 'gated' communities that have only institutional restrictions (such as urban villages under shareholding management, as mentioned in the previous chapter).

Although it is claimed that gated communities are globally widespread, even in the US where the concept of gated communities originated the gated community does not occupy a mainstream status. Hence the novelty of gating has attracted the attention of researchers. Whereas in the US the suburban division of single-family homes with front lawns and white picket fences is the mainstream landscape,[5] in China gated communities are now the mainstream form of housing for the 'middle class' and even for relocated residents from traditional neighbourhoods.[6] Because the majority of housing has been developed since 1979, gated communities are therefore a standard built environment.

Chinese gated communities are generally built with a population density that is lower than that of traditional neighbourhoods or often as a mix of high-rise residential buildings and large detached houses, which are called villas in China. Such a mixture of high-rises and single houses is intended to target different housing markets and to increase the overall plot ratio so as to increase profitability. In order to attract homebuyers, real estate developers indeed try to introduce a lot of product innovations in the way of design style, communal gardens and green spaces. One such innovation is the style of the 'townhouse' and villas in gated compounds surrounded with a gate and walls. The neighbourhood provides various property services, for example, gardening and landscaping, security and private guards.

Residents in these neighbourhoods do not seek collectivism but rather greater personal privacy in gated communities. It is in this sense that Chinese gated communities are 'private communities' for homeowners, not public housing tenants. Housing consumption fosters a new consumer identity of the middle class.[7] The advertisement of commodity housing in gated communities together with the design creates and reinforces such an identity. The experience of living in gated communities is a process of what Li Zhang (2010, 107) called 'spatialising class'. The varying standards of commodity housing and estates begin to define residents' social strata (*jieceng*). These residential compounds provide 'a class milieu' in which the new middle class is created.[8] By choosing these places, residents are more aware of their social strata and act accordingly.

The class refers to a wider 'imagined' community of similar people, although they do not interact with each other and have no personal relations except common interests in property ownership. It is not a sphere defined by relations (*guanxi*) but by common attributes (income, socioeconomic status, consumption preference and lifestyle). Second, related to consumer identity is a rising awareness of 'self' and 'private life' in China to supersede collectivism.[9] Therefore, it is actually difficult to 'build a community' in the context in which Chinese society is experiencing individualisation.[10]

The emergence of social strata in the territory of gated communities indicates that the gated community is a very different society – a space moving away from the totalised society. Thinking about social strata instead of territorial relations, the society is growing out of the differential mode of association. This does not suggest that the state is absent in these residential compounds. Nor are gated communities necessarily an anonymous and socially isolated neighbourhood. But the relations between residents are based on their common attributes as homebuyers in a particular place. Residents keep a comfortable social distance from each other.

The concept of gated communities in its anglophone context contains two defining features: physical enclosure and security, and private governance. The two features match in typical gated communities in the United States. However, as can be seen from the above discussion, it is impossible or inappropriate to apply these two criteria simultaneously to Chinese neighbourhoods. First, physical security has been widely featured and has a long cultural tradition, and hence it is not unique to the gated community.[11] Walls and gates alone are not the defining features of gated communities. If physical gating is stressed but private governance not so much, then a variety of Chinese neighbourhoods nowadays would be regarded as gated communities. Although gating is ubiquitous in China, the form of gating and the degree of security in fact vary significantly. Only urban villages are generally open access neighbourhoods, although some recent experiments have introduced new village-level security (but in practice this is too costly economically to enforce).[12] The Chinese gated community is only an upgraded version of neighbourhood security and enclosure for economically better-off residents. It is a built environment product with a higher quality of housing and security rather than a particular or distinct governance form, although in these gated communities social relation and governance have been transformed.

Second, as will be seen later, the degree of private governance in Chinese gated communities is not equivalent to governance by market contract in the United States (for example, covenants, contracts and restrictions, CC&Rs), which is a key mechanism for managing the estate. In other words, these communities in the United States are governed by 'private agreements', oversight by private organisations through 'private enforcement', which replace zoning or city planning.[13] Such a private mechanism serves as an intermediary institution so 'residents do not have to talk to their neighbours'.[14] This avoids direct moral judgement and intervention by residents. CC&R is thus a 'moral minimalism'.[15] The gated community maintains 'self-control' through the market mechanism (contracts with the homeowners' association). The market is regarded as a 'private' force.

If the criterion of private (market) governance was followed, then the urban village residences and estates developed by village shareholding cooperatives could be regarded as gated communities, but they are generally open access. In Chinese gated communities, homeowners' associations are set up to manage properties or intervene in the affairs of property management, for example, to manage the semi-public spaces inside the estate or appoint a property management company. But their relations with residents are less enforceable, because the homeowners' association has a limited right to represent residents. In part, the homeowners' association lacks an independent legal identity and consequently a bank account,[16] and therefore cannot fully assert the property rights of owners. On the other hand, the state formalises the registration procedure to make them 'legible and governable'.[17] Maintenance funds are controlled either by the housing bureau or by the property developers. In other words, the gated community is not governed by CC&Rs or 'agreement' which can be enforced through the legal system. Residents do not sign a contract with the homeowners' association when they move into a commodity housing estate. Perhaps in most cases, in a newly built commodity housing estate, the homeowners' association would not have been set up when the properties were sold.

Third, there is another conceptual complication which concerns 'self-governance' or control at a scale smaller than the public as private governance or 'club governance'.[18] If this view of governance is adopted, then a variety of public housing estates organised by workplaces could be regarded as a special kind of gated community,[19] as they have both some degree of security features and control at a scale smaller than the municipal public organisation. But calling workplace neighbourhoods as 'gated communities' in its usual anglophone usage would mask their huge differences – as shown in an earlier chapter, the workplace neighbourhoods is a neo-traditionalism society 'from the soil'. Now, the Chinese gated communities of commodity housing are different from the work-unit compound,[20] even though both are controlled, to some extent, by a smaller group than the general public.[21] For most residents in Chinese 'gated communities', the market means of neighbourhood property management and services does not represent 'self-governance' through homeowners' associations.[22] The residents prefer or actually choose these services provided by companies rather than government agencies which are either unavailable or of lower quality. Residents' satisfaction with homeowners' associations is generally low, reflecting the reality that these neighbourhoods have not achieved a good degree of self-governance or legitimacy of governance from the residents' point of view. Despite market provision, neighbourhood governance still requires state intervention.[23]

So what is the major change in the process of the declining work-unit compound and rising gated communities? Or, what are the precise implications for governance, urban life and mentality? This book does not presume private governance as the defining feature of gated communities but rather examines a concrete and material product of the built environment in order to understand social transformation. As will be shown in this book, urbanisation, as manifested in the concrete form of gated communities, reveals the change of social life and mentality.

As can be seen in other chapters, there is a general trend toward building a society that is 'leaving the soil'. Chinese gated communities indicate departure from rather than continuation of collectivism. They are not a distinctive governance category but, together with other neighbourhoods, they demonstrate the beginning of the end of collectivism.

Because the state continues to play an important role in gated communities and also in the general governance of neighbourhoods in China, it is tempting to regard the gated community as an invention by the state to strengthen its control over society, albeit giving residents more autonomous rights to choose their place of living. However, this understanding does not conform to the historical development process of gated communities. It is thus more appropriate to investigate how Chinese gated communities are actually formed to understand their logic and consequences in a historical context.

Development process

The Chinese gated community is first and foremost a consumer product invention. After years of political movements, Chinese residents feel fatigue in the public sphere and require more privacy at home. They also demand a higher quality of housing and the residential environment. Because of strong *de facto* ownership in traditional neighbourhoods and the cost of demolition, commodity housing development has largely occurred in suburban or peripheral areas. These places lacked basic infrastructure, facilities and amenities.

The Chinese model of land development gives municipal or district development corporations – state-owned enterprises – the right to conduct 'primary' development. By 'primary' is meant that the corporation monopolises the land supply through converting non-state rural land into 'saleable' land in the urban land market. These corporations usually develop initial infrastructure such as roads and electricity and water pipelines, while leaving other facilities such as sports facilities, parks, supermarkets and shopping malls to the 'secondary' developers who buy or obtain the land plots from the municipal corporation. The secondary developers may also build nurseries, schools and hospitals, which may later be operated by the government. The construction of these facilities is regarded as a contribution to their obligations regarding land rights.[24] But sometimes, just as with the construction of the magnificent gate of Beijing Sun City (see later), developers are also willing to build these basic facilities such as nurseries and schools, groceries and supermarkets as a marketing strategy, as these suburban places lack an urban atmosphere and convenience. The construction of these facilities is deemed necessary by developers, because the development of commodity housing needs to lure customers into these unknown places.

Several factors contribute to the adoption of a walled compound form for new residential estates. First, there is a strong demand for privacy by new property buyers. Second, the suburban location is often in the midst of large rural land tracts and lacks character. Magnificent gates present a good image to attract customers. Third, there is a long-standing tradition of the walled city in the imperial era and work-unit housing compounds in the socialist period. Fourth, in low density suburban areas, residents require enhanced security to such an extent that the installation of security may go beyond the practical need to form a gated estate. Fifth, in these formerly rural areas, land is divided into large plots for developers. These estates are built on large plots and built plot by plot, at a much larger scale than 'plotting urbanism' in African cities.[25] But China adopts a massive scale of plots which evolve into separate large housing estates. The huge land plot is assigned to each developer to construct a brand of estate for the company, which means that the gated community rather than open streets can delineate a clear boundary. Sixth, the super block is the most cost-effective way to develop the commodity housing estate, as it saves the government development corporation the cost of developing dense minor roads. The secondary developer usually reduces the road networks inside their estates. Seventh, to assure buyers that these estates are properly managed, the developer may boast professional property management. The development of magnificent and highly decorative gates and clubhouses is symbolic to indicate the quality of property and property management. For the government, it is practical to leave developers to decide the actual built form and treat these as product inventions. Just like gated communities in the United States, if homeowners are able to provide some amenities for themselves (in fact through the developer), the government can save the cost.[26]

In China, developer-centred property management is also regarded by the government as the most effective approach to meet consumer demand. However, this approach also makes possible later conflicts between developers and homeowners. The homeowners' association was created later to deal with such conflicts. Because these property-based or property-derived disputes and controversies are 'private' matters, the government and its agencies – the street office or community (*shequ*) organisation and residents' committees – are not sufficiently developed in these suburban areas. It is also believed that government agencies should not be involved in these property management matters. In short, the form of gated communities is a supply-side invention, not because residents as consumers are irrelevant, but because it is indeed created by the developer as a product with enhanced consumption features.

From the view of actual development processes, some degree of 'private' control is derived from the practical need to represent buyers' rights, just like a 'consumer rights association'. The contractual relation between the entity of gated community – represented by the homeowners' association – and residents is loose and not well developed. Even where there are residents' behaviour codes, they are more like general social standards promoted by the government as 'social civilisation'[27] rather a specific set of CC&Rs in different estates. In other words, there is not a specific set of rules that residents could 'choose' when buying into an estate.

As gated communities are a mainstream product, albeit with variations, residents do not have the choice between enclosed or open microdistrict (*xiaoqu*), because the latter is deemed non-viable. Homebuyers do choose the variety of gated communities according to 'grade' (*dangci*) or taste, but these variations are more product differences rather than specific governance forms. In general, although gated communities are developed through the property market, they are not outside the state provision of services such as police, education and health. Private guards are employed by the property management company as a feature of property management. However, only the most exclusive upper-market neighbourhoods can afford their own social services. These mainstream estates still rely on government-provided services such as local schools.

In other words, the residents do not have a choice between municipal residential areas and 'unincorporated estates' outside the municipality.[28] In terms of tax status, residents in gated communities are no different from residents in other types of neighbourhoods. Similar to the 'consumer rights association' which is a public agent to listen to the complaints of consumers, the homeowners' association helps consumers with their rights but cannot represent homeowners in legal matters with the developers, nor can the homeowners' association dispute with their members through legal means. When homeowners buy their properties, these consumers do not have the intention to form such a body of governance either to exert their legal rights or to discipline their fellow residents.

In the remainder of this section two examples are described to illustrate the development process of gated communities. The first example is an estate in peripheral Beijing. Despite an ostentatious square at the entrance, a magnificent gate and a man-made lake of two hectares inside

Figure 4.1 The magnificent decorative gate of Beijing Sun City, Beijing, mimicking neoclassical styles. This neighbourhood, however, is a rather 'ordinary' commodity housing estate. Taken in 2004.

the estate, Beijing Sun City is not in fact a luxury commodity housing neighbourhood (Figure 4.1). The estate occupies 42 hectares, consisting of 1,800 residential units in total, a mixture of villas, apartments and elderly care homes. It is located in the northern suburb near the six ring road and thus can afford to use the land quite lavishly.

Behind the gate is a retirement estate, bought into by wealthier residents for their parents. What is unusual is its combination of commodity housing with elderly care. The selling point of the estate was its provision of age-friendly facilities and services, which was rare in China at the time when the project started in 2000. The project is therefore often mentioned as a model for retirement properties for residents in inner cities to relocate to the suburbs when they are retired. Some apartments inside the neighbourhood offer long-term leases as care homes. Although the project uses Western architectural motifs, it was developed by a domestic developer who claimed to boost the Chinese culture of filiality. In fact, the gate at the entrance is merely decorative without security guards. However, each block of apartments has security guards. The residents need to join the club in order to enjoy the facilities. Both the neoclassical style of the gate and the claim for the traditional culture of 'filial piety, benevolent moral integrity, and sincerity' are project marketing tactics to attract visibility. The developer also operated a hospital, inside which

Figure 4.2 An upper-market gated community, Garden of Kindred Spirits, Wenzhou. This gated estate mainly consists of villas and was once the most expensive area in Wenzhou. Taken in 2014 by Tingting Lu.

there were also Chinese medical and therapy clinics. However, the hospital went bankrupt around 2015, creating difficulties for the elderly who had bought properties or lived in care homes.

The second example is the Garden of Kindred Spirits (Figure 4.2), which is located in a suburb of Wenzhou, a city known for its diaspora entrepreneurs and private enterprise. For many years, Wenzhou lacked a real upper-market estate, despite its reputation for creating rich local businessmen. A real estate developer under the provincial government, which is responsible for constructing government buildings, found a development opportunity in Wenzhou in 2000, shortly after China started large-scale housing reform. Borrowing capital from the provincial government and with a mortgage based on the collateral of a government hotel,[29] the developer negotiated a good land deal with the city government of Wenzhou, because of its status as a state-owned enterprise directly controlled by the provincial government and thus having extensive social capital. In fact, the expectation of the provincial government was to create a profit of 80 million Yuan.[30] At that time, Wenzhou also wished to clear up eight 'urban' villages in the suburb near the airport and build a large new residential district of 150,000 residents.[31]

The project therefore became a flagship development in this area. The government of Wenzhou reduced the land premium to 190 million Yuan and allowed the developer to pay the land premium by instalments, which greatly eased the financial pressure. At the same time, the developer managed to raise the plot ratio from 0.9 to 1.6, creating a large profit margin.[32] The project, however, still maintains coverage of green space as high as 54 per cent.[33] The developer invested another 190 million Yuan for roads and other infrastructure associated with the development project.[34] The government was responsible for the removal of urban villages, resettlement and site clearance. The project later became the largest business taxpayer in the city of Wenzhou.

The neighbourhood is a mix of high-rise apartments and villas. When the first phase was completed in 2004, the project broke the record for housing prices in Wenzhou. Similar to the housing boom elsewhere in China but much more dramatically here in Wenzhou, the price of the Garden of Kindred Spirits increased by ten times in just five years. The developer insisted that the quality of the estate was the priority. As in all upper-market gated residential estates, the developer employed a property management company from Xiamen and provided a private kindergarten and clubhouses. The two major services include security guards and estate maintenance. Although a homeowners' association was set up later, management has been centred on the property management company appointed by the developer.

The election for the homeowners' association has been difficult, not only because residents are busy but also because the residents' committee has intervened in the process. In other words, homeowners are able to exert hardly any influence over the property management company, even though some homeowners have felt that the maintenance charge was too high and the performance of the company was not entirely satisfactory. In short, residents chose this neighbourhood not for potential self-governance but rather for its status as an upper-market estate that suits richer local entrepreneurs: larger properties, good housing quality, greener landscaping and professional property management services.[35]

This detailed description of project development processes reveals that the project represents a mainstream approach to commodity housing development in China, despite its upper-market position. It is the outcome of a joint venture or growth coalition between the local state of Wenzhou and a 'government' developer that directly serves the provincial government of Zhejiang. This is a governance innovation in development approach rather than a shift in neighbourhood governance. Indeed, gating and walls – not a new feature in China – are used together with other enhanced property management services.

Although the development and property management have been led by a real estate developer, the degree of self-governance, even in this more exclusive and highly secured upper-market gated community, is quite limited. The scope of private provision is still limited to property-related services. The state has reinstated its governance role through the usual mechanism – the residents' committee – applied to all neighbourhoods and constraining the homeowners' association to the sphere of property management. But the homeowners' association could not even exert much influence as the whole process has been led by the developer. As will be shown later, disputes between homeowners and developers in commodity housing estates are a driver for the establishment of homeowners' associations as the government is unwilling to be involved in property matters, now a 'private' sphere. Due to the dysfunction of its homeowners' association, the Garden of Kindred Spirits cannot be claimed as a 'privately governed' community. The role of the state is still visible in its administration.[36]

Not all gated communities are exclusive upper-market housing estates like the Garden of Kindred Spirits. In fact, even though there are villas at an average price of 40 to 60 million Yuan within this neighbourhood, the apartments have a price range of 4 to 5 million Yuan which is a quite standard price in Wenzhou. The quality of gated communities varies, covering a wide range of residential estates. In Wenzhou, they include affordable housing estates and resettlement estates, all built in gated forms. In an affordable housing estate 28 kilometres away from the city centre of Wenzhou, 70 per cent of residents are former rural households who were converted into urban residents because of land appropriation.[37]

Another resettlement estate is located in the central area of Wenzhou to accommodate households relocated by urban renewal. A state-owned enterprise developed the commercial area and used the income from shopping malls to pay for resettlement housing. Strangely, both adopted the style of gated communities. The latter even created a neoclassical arch and named itself European Town, which served the purpose of creating a new urban image of high taste, matching the commercial properties developed by the company rather than the residential preference of its residents. In other words, the gate and architectural design is for property buyers in the whole renewal project rather than the relocated residents. As we already observed, in traditional neighbourhoods residents have low affordability and were not able to sustain the charges for property management, even though the developer of this neighbourhood reduced the fee to one-third of its original cost.[38] In both neighbourhoods of affordable housing and resettlement, residents were not satisfied with the property management and did not manage to set up a homeowners' association. In fact, the constraint of affordability means that these fee-paying schemes are not feasible, as residents coming from traditional neighbourhoods and rural villages did not need to pay for maintenance in the past.

A built environment product

The gated community is a mainstream built environment product with variegated standards and quality. It is now a more 'ordinary' residential form in both central and suburban areas, although the more expensive upper-market gated estate presents more salient and sometimes ostentatious features of gated communities. In essence, Chinese cities are now built through residential plots by different developers. Figure 4.3 shows an area near Hongkou Football Stadium in Shanghai, along the inner ring road. The place is hence a quite centrally located mature urban area, although not in an upper-market location. The largest estate is City Garden redeveloped on the site of the former Mr Lincoln's Lane.[39] The smallest estate, Liulin Court, consists of only two towers but has its own security-guarded gate (Figure 4.4). These gated estates have different design qualities and sizes and have created a patchy landscape in Chinese cities.

The design of the upper-market gated community pays more attention to landscaping, green space and communal gardens. Youqin Huang (2006) observed that:

> The developer of Purple Jade Villas, an upscale gated community with multimillion-dollar villas in central Beijing, created a luxury but heavenly peaceful oasis amidst the chaotic urban environment. In addition to modern amenities such as swimming pools, a fitness centre, spa, and an ice rink, there are two artificial lakes decorated with lotuses and weeping willows, a hiking trail along an artificial mountain with several waterfalls, a grand central lawn, and numerous exotic animals such as peacocks, swans, and pheasants wandering around the Purple Jade Villa, offering the rich a nature retreat and an idealised Chinese country life without leaving the heart of Beijing. (p. 519)

Figure 4.3 Housing estates near Hongkou Football Stadium, Shanghai. The photo shows the high-rise buildings of the City Garden estate built in the mid 2000s. Taken in 2017.

Figure 4.4 A small-gated estate, Liulin Court, among many large gated communities near Hongkou Football Stadium, Shanghai. The photo together with the overview of the City Garden estate shows a quite spatially subdivided residential structure in Chinese cities. Taken in 2009.

Because of the emphasis on a high standard of design, the gated community often adopts Western architectural motifs. This practice of 'transplanting' landscapes reflects local imagineering rather than a change imposed by globalisation.[40]

In other words, the adoption of Western built forms is a result of place promotion during housing commodification through the use of imagined and claimed globalisation. Such a borrowing tactic suits local instead of global demand. For example, the so-called 'townhouse' style, basically terraced or semi-detached housing, is adopted in the suburbs as a lower-density development compared with five- to six-storey buildings in inner cities, and this suits the local desire for a more exclusive suburban life but at the same time the requirement to maintain the profitability of real estate.

According to the explanation of a real estate consultant, the townhouse is designed for those 'who want to own a plot of land under the feet and a piece of sky overhead', and the ownership of the townhouse will bring them 'land, sky, garden, and garage'.[41] In the North American private neighbourhood, because of the imperative of the building industry to suit the needs of consumers who want style and distinctiveness, as Paul Knox (1991) described, developers packaged 'community amenities and expensive-looking materials, dramatic master bedroom/bathroom suites, and integrated but distinctive design based on traditional and vernacular styling' (p. 187).

Similarly, the Chinese gated community represents the pursuit of commodity aesthetics by the 'new bourgeoisie'.[42] But instead of seeing this demand as arising out of postmodernism, this book depicts the process of general urbanisation – moving away from collectivism and rurality to individualisation and greater urbanity. Here, we do not see the creation of Chinese gated communities as the globalisation of gated communities. The development of Chinese gated communities does occur in the context of globalisation. They are connected with globalisation through general political economic processes: rising personal wealth and greater social inequalities as the Chinese economy has become a global factory and major cities are globalising – making possible the utilisation of architects from the West and with overseas travel bringing awareness of alternative built styles. However, property buyers are mainly local Chinese purchasing for their own living or investment. The local Chinese are landlords, while the expatriates are only renters.[43]

Hence, the transplanted landscape is not a product imported from the West, influenced by Western ideas, or replicated from actual Western gated communities. The Chinese gated community is an indigenous local

Figure 4.5 A rather exotic style as seen in China, but quite 'ordinary' detached houses in North America, in the 'Orange County' estate, Beijing. Taken in 2004.

product, as both developers and consumers are local people, although housing sales have boasted that they are 'alien' and 'exotic' Western products. But to a Western eye, the landscape is of quite ordinary suburban subdivisions with large detached houses (Figure 4.5).

The authenticity of ostentatious and decorative 'Western'-style landscape is questionable. Various packaging and branding practices attempt to create an aesthetically appealing environment, which is bound to be a melange of different classic, continental, European and North American styles. Chinese gated communities are thus dressed up with de-contextualised and diverse built forms. No matter what genre it is, an 'exotic' and 'stylish' style is important to fulfil the quest for the good life (Figure 4.6). The purpose is to signify quality by design, to showcase luxury, especially in the upper housing market in which the discourse of 'luxury' is often deployed to differentiate lifestyles.[44] This is deeply associated with the perhaps unconscious Chinese mentality that the Western represents 'civilised modernity'.[45]

In fact, the authenticity of architectural genre does not need to be interrogated. It does not matter whether they are designed as French castles for the nobility or American subdivisions for the

Figure 4.6 The highly decorative gate of 'Orange County', Beijing. The gated community strives to use the gate to symbolise its high-quality housing and residential environment. Taken in 2004.

middle class. Rebutting criticism about fake styles, a senior real estate consultant argues:

> People's desire for exotic styles is unstoppable! Who can have the authority to claim what is authentic? You British eat Chinese takeaway. If you say it is Chinese [cuisine], it is Chinese [cuisine]. [46]

The Chinese gated community is a fake replica, even if a defined architectural style is used (Figure 4.7). The mainstream Western open-access neighbourhood does not suit the Chinese context. From the actual development process and underlying urbanisation, we can appreciate why gating is a natural built form.

Throughout history, Chinese residential compounds have had various forms of modest and practical gating, but only recently have these gates evolved into a highly decorative style (see also the gate of Beijing Sun City, Figure 4.1). In the American context, gating is more exotic and problematic. In the UK, gating is largely absent or modest as the roads inside estates are adopted by the local council and have public access. On the contrary, gating is not itself exotic in China. While new urbanism design aims

Figure 4.7 The gated housing estate in Thames Town, near Songjiang in Shanghai. The estate together with the 'new town' aims to follow the style of a British market town. Taken in 2010.

to promote a community atmosphere in otherwise low-density suburbs, traditional neighbourhoods in China do not lack such a closely engaged residential community. Rather, the exotic impression is largely created by design styles as a new built environment product.[47]

New concepts are borrowed to develop the gated community as a product innovation. For example, 'new urbanism' and 'transit-oriented development', both originating in the United States, are used to build gated neighbourhoods and the new towns in which these gated neighbourhoods are located. Neo-traditionalist urban design stresses a higher density and a more compact form of neighbourhood in the suburbs. These neighbourhoods are open access without gates. However, they are built as gated estates in China. The new urbanism neighbourhood in North America aims to promote neighbouring and social interaction, while Chinese gated communities stress residential privacy and security.

In the Chinese context, developers copy the morphology of neo-traditionalist design while ignoring the communitarian discourse of new urbanism. In fact, many gated communities boasted as Chinese 'new urbanism' are car-based neighbourhoods for the affluent rather than the whole populace (Figure 4.8). The developers of these gated communities

Figure 4.8 The gated community is often associated with new town development. Many are built into high-rise form rather than detached or semi-detached houses, owing to the land cost. The photo shows one in Jiading new town, northern Shanghai. Taken in 2013.

understand new urbanism as an urbanity with interesting landscapes which is quite different from the standard and boring socialist industrial suburb. These new residential areas have two kinds of novelty. First, they have 'transplanted landscapes', and second they have new private service provision. That is, these places are not only owner-occupied commodity housing but also privately serviced estates.

These places are often given foreign place names such as Orange County, Yosemite, Fontainebleau, Napa Valley, Thames Town and McAllen.[48] Figure 4.7 shows that the whole residential area – literally a small new town in the Thames Town of Shanghai suburb – copies an English market town. European and North American motifs are particularly popular. Observing a project called Fontainebleau, Guillaume Giroir (2005) described:

> [S]ymbols of the France of the Ancien Régime are particularly visible in the scenery of the housing enclaves, notably a replica of the equestrian bronze statue of Louis XIV, and there is another bronze sculpture representing a group of stags, while a wrought-iron entry

gate separates the two parts of the villa area. The monumental entry reminds one of the impressive horseshoe stairs in the Chateau de Fontainebleau. (p. 214)

Developers often boast that they recruited a foreign design team. In fact, the involvement of global architectural design is nominal or supplies only a concept. Ironically the alien design styles are created for those who have no overseas experience. Because they are unfamiliar with these design styles, the new gated community becomes even more fascinating. The simulated landscape is thus more like a fantasy. To homebuyers, they seem to sell authentic lifestyles from Western societies. Many projects are indeed built into gated communities with exotic landscapes. This satisfies the desire of the new rich or rising middle class for an alternative good life after socialism – different from matchbox multi-storey walk-ups in workplace neighbourhoods.

The design gives the residents in a gated community a new status symbol.[49] Translating landscapes, it suits diverse preferences and individual choices, distinguishing the new private life from the socialist utopia based on collective consumption (Figure 4.9). The attractiveness of

Figure 4.9 Neoclassical decoration in the compound of a gated community in Guangzhou. The compound is also carefully landscaped. This, however, is not at ground level but is a platform. Underneath are two floors of shopping and car parking spaces. Taken in 2000.

Figure 4.10 The highly decorated lobby of an apartment building in the gated community in Guangzhou shown in the previous photo. Taken in 2000.

gated communities lies in its purified space, interesting landscape and high residential privacy, which is different from the intertwined social relations in traditional neighbourhoods (Figure 4.10). The provision of property services through professional management companies reduces unnecessary mutual help among neighbours. The communal neighbourhood life is less relevant as residents have social resources unbounded by the territory.

Another salient feature of the gated community, in addition to its decorative design, is an emphasis on security. In the gated community literature, gated communities are argued as a club form of governance to prevent service free-riding.[50] However, such prevention could be easily achieved through other mechanisms such as membership rather than physical gates and walls. In suburban areas, because of the distance between residential areas, access to green space inside each estate is difficult and impractical. Because there is no property tax in China, services are more universally distributed through the fiscal system across jurisdictions. Therefore, moving into suburban gated communities is not about retaining taxes for local services.

Enclosure is a practical and efficient way to maintain security. While enclosure inevitably imposes an effect of 'exclusion' (gated communities in the same area generally representing a similar profile of residents), it is less about excluding a particular social group from service provision. These estates adopt enclosure because open access would impose a security challenge. A resident in the upper-market housing estate in Shanghai explains:

> [For the theft case], we did report to the police. But eventually they didn't catch the thief. The previous security guard team was not so good. But we could not go to [live in] open communities. For open communities, how many policemen would you need? The cost would be too high. The government would say your community is not secured enough – there are too many 'leakages'! For these individual houses, the government would have to send ten policemen. But when these policemen come, they would tell themselves, ok today you two should be on duties, the other eight go to sleep. You see, this would be quite low efficient. That is why it would be ineffective! However, homeowners' association has also difficulties, because all board members are volunteers. But they don't even have to use legal means. They just come to force you – do you really want to live here any longer? [51]

In short, the gated community in China is a built environment product rather than a special form of governance. Gated communities reflect some consumer preferences and also practical requirements during the building of these estates. Building estate by estate is a practical way to organise residential development by developers. Residents do not seek self-governance, or to escape municipal governance and service provision. Because of the taxation mechanism in China, it is difficult for residents to self-fund infrastructure such as roads and schools. But gated community building does bring in some changes in neighbourhood governance. The next section will discuss the implications for governance in detail.

Neighbourhood governance

The novelty of Chinese gated communities is not private governance – governed by market contracts. Despite the appearance of gating, the gated community resembles an ordinary modern Western neighbourhood. Its novelty can only be understood in the specific Chinese context, in comparison with its predecessors in alleyway and workplace areas. The gated community is now becoming a mainstream residential form, indicating the end of traditionalism and 'neo-traditionalism' (often associated with collectivism), or more precisely, disappearing differential mode of association in which individuals are organically but differentially associated. The gated community is a community of homeowners who are presented as individuals with less comprehensive social relationships.

What distinguishes 'gated communities' in the United States from open access neighbourhoods is their unique mode of governance – private governance. The 'private community' in that context is not just an estate of owner-occupied housing (private housing) but also a community of 'private governance', which creates a specific sense of identity and security. As Setha Low (2003) explains:

> The 'privateness' refers to its development as a common interest development with rules, regulations, and fees for maintaining the collectively owned bay beach, hiking trail, and reserve areas. (p. 173)

> Homeowners associations (as well as property-owners associations or landowners associations) are a special kind of residential association created by the covenants, conditions, and restrictions of a common interest development. Elected boards oversee the common property, and each home is purchased with the CC&Rs as part of the deed.... In an overwhelming number of cases, particularly when racial discrimination is not an issue, covenants are treated as private agreements that need not comply with the constitutional standards that apply to the laws adopted by public local governments. (pp. 174–5)

Since the introduction of new market-based housing development and property management in China, the developer and often the subsidiary property management company have become leading actors in neighbourhood governance. However, instead of seeing gated communities as a form of private governance, Youqin Huang (2006) argues that they represent a tradition of collectivism and political control:

> [D]ominant Western-based theories such as the discourse of fear and private provision of public services are less applicable, even though they are becoming increasingly important in the new gated private housing. Gating and neighbourhood enclosure in China help to define a sense of collectivism and foster social solidarity. (p. 507)

Youqin Huang and Setha Low (2008) further stress the 'collectivist tradition' in China, which 'points to a very different social construction of gating from those in the West, which is centred on individualism, privatisation, social segregation, and exclusion' (p. 184). They explain that:

> China has a long history of using gates and walls in residential development, and is now experiencing a new wave of gating as its socialist housing system privatises... .
>
> In the context of China, the term of 'enclosed neighbourhoods' is used for residential developments with gates and surrounding walls or fences. The entrances may be guarded by security personnel and/or card activated gates, or by the watchful eyes of senior members in the neighbourhood. While some enclosed neighbourhoods include amenities such as swimming pools and legal agreements among residents, others may have only a small patch of green land and no legal agreement. In other words, an enclosed neighbourhood in China is a broader concept than a gated community in the US, and it emphasises the physical form of enclosure, not the legal and social aspect, of the housing development. (pp. 185–6)

They rightly cast doubts on the applicability of 'private governance' to China because in Chinese enclosed neighbourhoods state control over residential communities is still strong. Arguing for a cross-cultural analysis, Setha Low (2006) reminds us that 'the Chinese example gives "private" and "public" different meanings that also must be considered'. (p. 8). Private governance or the theory of the club realm (see later) represents the supply-side explanation, while a demand-side explanation is needed. She sees the fear of crime and others (or the 'perceived crime' and the 'discourse of fear') as a cross-cultural explanation.

The result is a new type of 'enclave urbanism' in which 'cities transform into networks of physically, legally and/or socially bounded enclaves, each home to selected groups or activities'.[52] This notion of enclave urbanism emphasises the nature of splintering and fragmented residential landscapes without endorsing the idea that the gated community is a cause or outcome of 'private governance'.

This book similarly explores the demand-side explanation in addition to the supply-side cause of housing marketisation and real estate development. But instead of seeing specifically the fear of crime, this book understands the overall trend of individualisation, prevailing across all kinds of neighbourhood, as a major driving force from the demand side. While the earlier explanation combines the fear of crime and continuing collectivism in the gated community,[53] this book suggests that the changing residential landscape indicates the departure from a social order based on collectivism. Residents do not intentionally seek collectivism or to maintain their collective identity by building an enclosed neighbourhood of their own, nor is the gated community an outcome of collective action.

The Chinese gated community is not a disappearing community.[54] Residents have strengthened 'social solidarity' based on property rights and hence strong 'place attachment'.[55] On the other hand, in the private housing neighbourhood, the state maintains its visibility. The 'rights-defending activities' in the neighbourhood often require the state to intervene against the malpractices of developers and irresponsible homeowners' associations.[56] The gated community is a product of neither deliberate action nor the policy of the state. The state does not intentionally use the form of gated communities to maintain or strengthen its control. Instead, the state may even wish to 'govern from afar', creating self-governed subjects as described by government studies.[57] But the consequence of neighbourhood development has created a new form of neighbourhood governance which reinforces the imperative of direct governance by the state, in both traditional and workplace neighbourhoods and gated communities.[58] In contrast to this collectivism-maintained argument,[59] this book argues that it is exactly by the end of collectivism in gated communities as well as in all other generic types that such an imperative has been created.

The gated community is not a top-down authoritarian state-controlled society. The neighbourhood is formed by a group of residents or the 'community', smaller than the 'public'. According to Chris Webster (2002), this is a club form between the private and the public. This small group, property-based social form is often called the 'private' in the Western context, and the role of the individual or the private sector is recognised, leading to the notion of the 'private city'.[60] Thus, the gated community ceases to be a distinctive category of public estates, as shown, for example, in the construction of Hancunhe, by a retired businessman; Baibuting in Wuhan, where a mass suburban housing estate was constructed by an ambitious developer with a party background;[61] or Tianmian village in Shenzhen by entrepreneurial villagers.[62] Other studies support this view that the gated community is a club form of governance.[63] The club governance indicates the potential civil society arising from such a privatised provision. This would be a profound implication for governance.

However, Fei Xiaotong (1947/92) warned that the distinction between private and public is understood quite differently in Chinese society:

> Sacrificing the family for one's own interests, or the lineage for the interests of one's household, is in reality a formula. With this formula, it is impossible to prove that someone is acting selfishly. The person concerned would likely deny it. He might contend that a person who sacrifices his lineage for the sake of his family is performing a public duty. When he sacrifices his country in struggling for the interests and rights of his own small group, he is still acting on behalf of the public, which is now defined as the small group itself. In this pattern of oscillating but differential social circles (*chaxugeju*), public and private are relative concepts. Standing in any circle, one can say that all those in that circle are part of the public. (p. 69)

To traditional China, the village is a public or collective space, while in the literature of Western gated communities, the enclave is treated as the 'private'. But in new urban China to what extent do Chinese residents pursue or perform collectivism as a community of homeowners? Does the gated community represent a continuation of collectivism? Rather than seeing gated communities as a reproduction of work-unit collectivism, Li Zhang (2010) argues that it is 'asserting individuality' and the creation of a new housing class:

> I would not go so far as to suggest that consumption choice in contemporary Chinese society is a mere refashioning of a deeper, unconscious commitment to the notion of collectivism. Rather, I see the emphasis on consumption practice as a pathway to a new class membership based on distinction and exclusivity. The way *jieceng* is spatialized and performed in Chinese cities echoes a global trend toward the privatisation of space, security, and lifestyle. (p. 136)

Similarly, Fulong Wu (2005) argues that while the form of gating is still used, the meaning of enclave becomes quite different. The residential decision is individually made, and in this sense it could be seen as 'private'. However, when residents come to gated communities, they form a relation as homeowners. They may socialise and hence go beyond their private sphere. But their relation is based on proprietary interests without intense social interaction. These common interests may become a force of social mobilisation, for example showing property activism. But this community is more an imagined one than an everyday life space.

The power of the homeowners' association varies but is generally limited in scope. In China, while all new estates show some form of gating, the rate of homeowners' associations varies quite significantly. For example, in Shanghai over 90 per cent of commodity housing neighbourhoods have set up their homeowners' associations, while the figure in other cities barely reaches one-third. Therefore, not all gated-form communities are governed by a homeowners' association and become a 'homeowners' association neighbourhood'.[64] But even with a homeowners' association, the neighbourhood may not have sufficient power to regulate itself. Collective action is only triggered by certain disputes over property rights because the developer has not fulfilled a promise or has violated their rights. But the disputes and conflicts are presented in a similar way to defending consumer rights. Except for these occasions, the Chinese gated community does not evolve into the public sphere of everyday life. In order to understand neighbourhood politics, we need to understand new actors.

The development of gated communities has introduced a new set of actors – the property management company and homeowners' association – besides the residents' committee and has thus complicated neighbourhood governance. The actual configuration of the governance form is variegated, depending upon the history of development, local government policies, the quality and price of properties, and the position of the estate in the property market. Chinese gated communities hence should not be regarded as a uniform governance form which is often characterised as neighbourhoods that are self-governed, market-provided, and resident participated, with limited state intervention. While the developer and property management company, the residents' committee, and homeowners' association are often regarded respectively as representations of the market, state and society,[65] their roles in neighbourhood governance are less clearly defined.

Because all new gated communities are developed from scratch, often in suburban areas, the developer plays a significant role in the creation of the residential estate. Later, when the development project has been completed, the developer may transfer property management to its subsidiary property management company to maintain the company brand or appoint an external property management company to continue the relation with the estate. The property management company provides services and charges a fee to residents. As homeowners, the residents cannot exert much influence on property management or control over neighbourhood maintenance because of this history. Unlike the gated community in the United States, the developer does not set up a homeowners' association at the beginning. If there is no severe conflict or dispute, there is not much incentive to set up a homeowners' association. In many cases homeowners' associations are dysfunctional anyway, due to the costs in both money and time. However, when conflict between homeowners and the developer or property management companies arises, residents need to ask the residents' committee to intervene; at this stage, the government encourages the establishment of a homeowners' association to sort out the property issues by the homeowners themselves. In fact, conflicts and disputes over properties are widespread in China.[66] In the following sections, main actors in gated communities are examined.

Residents' committee. Gated communities emerged mostly as commodity housing development, especially in suburban areas. In contrast to traditional neighbourhoods where the residents' committee is well established owing to the long history of residence, the suburban gated community is newly built and thus sees a governance vacuum. The residents' committee in gated communities deals with different sorts of tasks from the traditional neighbourhoods as the poverty rate is lower and most housing issues are sorted out by residents themselves. Often, the role of the residents' committee is peripheral, although the committee still has the right to intervene in the homeowners' association election even in a more market-oriented development housing estate.

In the case of resettlement housing and affordable housing estates, the state may directly organise service provision or set the standards and prices of property services for the company. Again, often these property management companies are state-owned enterprises or subsidiaries which help the local state to manage the estates.[67] In short, although the residents' committee originates from mass organisation through neighbourhood election, professionalisation has changed it into a quasi-government agency with staffed positions. The residents' committee does not have the full capacity to deal with all the 'internal' matters of gated communities. Its role has been supplemented by another type of social organisation – the homeowners' association.

Property management company. The property management company often gains control over public areas and occasionally builds some annex projects to generate a profit to subsidise estate maintenance. Because homeowners form a relation with the property management company as a consequence of property purchase, they do not choose the property management company themselves and often have disputes about the charges or the standard and quality of services. They may have a contract with the property management company to pay maintenance charges. But even if there is a contract, it is not part of the property deeds. The power of the property management company comes from the developer. The property management company, as the service provider, plays a *de facto* role of neighbourhood manager. It is difficult for individual homeowners to break out of the initial contract, as the relation is inherited from the history of development. It requires a collective decision to make a change.

In traditional neighbourhoods or work-unit compounds after housing privatisation, the street office may appoint a property management company to maintain the neighbourhood. Then, the property management company has to respond to the street office. But in commodity housing gated communities, because these estates are new and the residents are better off, the street office does not intervene too much in 'neighbourhood affairs', thinking that estate maintenance is essentially the job of the developer or the property management company representing the developer – it is their duty to ensure the quality of the product (of the properties and related environment as part of the deal). Because homeowners and the developer have a consumer relationship, the local government does not resort to the administrative approach to intervene.

Homeowners' association. According to the property law, the homeowners' association has the right to appoint the property management company. The association is set up by homeowners through an election process. However, the residents of upper-market gated communities are busy middle-class people who are reluctant to participate in the homeowners' association. A few activists may have different motivations, as it is reported that due to the lack of accountability, some activists have used the opportunity to generate financial income or receive benefits from the property management company. On the other hand, the residents' committee is supposed to supervise the homeowners' association and often regards property management as the internal affairs of the neighbourhood. Sometimes the residents' committee mediates conflicts between homeowners and the developer or the property management company. But in most cases, the residents' committee intervenes only in lower-income gated communities where residents are not able to set up their own homeowners' association. In that situation, the residents' committee or the street office may take on the responsibility to appoint the property management company to look after the public space, especially the area between individual estates in a larger residential area.

The homeowners' association is different from other territorially based or originated relations such as the association of *laoxiang* (the same origin of hometown). The former is more similar to what Park called the 'vacation association' which is based on secondary interests rather than primary social interactions.[68] Homeowners who bought properties in the same estate form a homeowners' assembly to elect the homeowners' association, which is literally the board of directors. This is a voluntary organisation for property interests. The procedure of the homeowners' association election is easily influenced by external factors, because there is not enough sociability to allow residents to know each other well and build up solidarity.

The lack of sociability is especially apparent for newly built estates in the upper housing market. It is difficult to set up a homeowners' association, and many are not fully functional. Most residents are passive and lack the energy to participate in social activities. They are mobilised only when their property rights are violated, often by the developer failing to fulfil a promise. Because of low sociability and the usual laxity or irregularity of elections, the accountability of the homeowners' association is questionable and difficult to monitor. There are often disputes among residents. The homeowners' association creates additional costs and lacks the resources and legal status to act. The legal system has not been well established to cope with the potential vast demand from neighbourhoods. Neighbourhood affairs are often deemed not to be subject to law-based governance. That is, the neighbourhood is not governed by 'private (market) contracts'.

In contrast to the shareholding cooperative in urban villages, which has a clearly defined company status, the homeowners' association's status is rather ambiguous. It does not have a legal personality, and its operation thus does not follow the rules of incorporation. Although the homeowners' association is entrusted with the responsibility to represent homeowners to manage the 'collective' property rights outside the private sphere of housing ownership of individual households, in reality it is difficult for the homeowners' association to execute these rights. Compared with the village shareholding cooperative, the homeowners' association does not really have any independent collective assets to manage. The common space is associated with the developer that initially used the property management company. The rights are executed by the developer or the property management company.

Although the public space of gated communities is collectively 'owned' by homeowners, in practice the property rights are in the hands of those who manage it. Only when the homeowners can collectively act and dismiss the management company are the property rights of homeowners executed. This is not impossible, but collective action requires the institutional building of the homeowners' association. Institution building, however, encounters an ambivalent attitude of the state towards rebuilding neighbourhood governance, because the state does not promote the 'self-governance' of homeowners. Although the government wishes to let homeowners manage their own properties in the neighbourhood through the property management company, in reality the association as a social organisation or society cannot effectively deal with the market operation of the latter. The intention has not been self-governance by residents. Self-governance by residents themselves or 'collectivism' is not a selling point in the marketing of gated communities. Rather, the selling points are often about distinctive architectural style and high-quality property and services.

In a suburban setting where the gated community of commodity housing is most widely adopted, the institution of local government has been underdeveloped. The developer and later the property management company in practice lead the development and management. To supplement the governance capacity, homeowners are encouraged to form an association, very much like the residents' committee which is officially defined as a mass organisation. In an almost fully owner-occupied housing estate, a homeowners' association (quite similar to the residents' committee) would be rather redundant. However, in reality, through 'community building' in the 2000s, the residents' committee has become a *de facto* government agency, staffed by professional staff and funded by the government. But for gated communities, residents are better off and are deemed by the government to have the capacity to manage their own neighbourhood affairs. The homeowners' association thus is the 'third sector' to help neighbourhood governance. However, the power of the homeowners' association should be constrained from the government point of view – it would be less problematic to the state if the association were a company rather than a social organisation that could evolve into a process of social mobilisation. Therefore, consequential regulations have defined the role of the homeowners' association in the sphere of property management, supervising the property management company. But for the property management role alone, the operation of a company at the neighbourhood level is too costly. In fact, many property management companies levy a charge directly on residents instead of going through the intermediary of a neighbourhood company (association).

The government initially promoted the establishment of homeowners' associations, hoping that capable and well-resourced homeowners would take care of their property-related matters. Indeed, in gated communities the demand for civic affairs is much simpler – there are no low-income welfare recipients (or so-called minimum livelihood guarantee, *dibao*) or services for unemployment. The major task is property management, and these property management issues, according to the viewpoint of the government, should be dealt with by the residents themselves as they are the property owners. If they need, they can purchase services from the market, namely through property management companies, which are not provided by the government agency, that is, the residents' committee, which simply lacks the capacity to provide property management. The state has to balance assigning the homeowners' association to take care of neighbourhood property-related affairs against preventing its evolution into an organisation that could take political action.[69] So some degree of social mobilisation is not a concern for the government. Rather, some degree of self-management is not regarded as undesirable. But because of the lack of transparency, higher costs and insufficient social capital developed in the neighbourhood, the homeowners' association does not function well. It is difficult to organise collective action until property rights interests are under threat, for example disputes over the use of green space.[70]

Understanding gated communities as a built-form product rather than a governance form helps to reveal why the property management company is so powerful in these estates. Residents do not choose gated communities as a self-governed neighbourhood – as a new form of collectivism or a totalised society in which they can maintain control through their own organisation such as the homeowners' association. Gated communities are presented to property buyers as a consumer product – a dream home of privacy and an associated high-quality environment that is professionally managed (Figure 4.11). The property rights of individual houses are defined through market transactions; but the developer often holds some assets in common areas and auxiliary structures, for example, shops at the ground floor level or clubhouses that charge a user fee and uses the property management company to continue to manage the estate. First, for the developer, there is a reputational liability to maintain the brand of the estate. Second, real estate development takes a long time; these gated communities are often developed in several phases. As such, the developer does not immediately withdraw from the estate. Some are able to use additional space to develop rental businesses to generate a profit to subsidise operation and maintenance. However, it is often difficult to collect property management fees, especially in poorer neighbourhoods.

On the other hand, it is difficult for homeowners to act collectively. The homeowners' association is less accountable and transparent – its

Figure 4.11 A professionally managed upper-market housing estate in Beijing. The estate has spacious garden and villa-style housing. Taken in 2003.

development requires substantial effort and government support. Due to the non-staffed position of the homeowners' association, unlike the board of directors of homeowners' associations in the United States, the homeowners' association does not have sufficient power, legal means, resources or trust in its members to act. Homeowners are willing to pay for a higher quality of home and the associated residential environment but are unwilling to pay a fee to a homeowners' association to fund the staffed posts that are necessary in order to act 'collectively'. There is no property tax which could be treated as a local source such as the council tax in the UK. Residents pay a quite nominal fee for property maintenance rather than substantial tax. There is a lack of economic foundation for the operation of self- or private governance in Chinese cities.

Property disputes are widespread. Residents do not exactly know what they have bought in the neighbourhood. The developer may resell public space or green space for profits or charge for car parking space. The problem often originates from property marketing to lure customers into projects. The developer boasts a wide range of services, regardless of the price tag which will be paid by residents themselves. But not all gated communities are in the upper market. In fact, many are quite ordinary, standard, mainstream housing estates. The maintenance is not cost effective. Residents cannot afford or are unwilling to pay for these services. Some lobbies of apartment buildings are decorated with marble floors, oil paintings and sofas.[71] In Liulin Court in Shanghai, mentioned at the beginning of this chapter, initially two tower buildings had security guards and coded entrance devices linking to each apartment. Now they are abandoned without guards, and the doors are left open. Only at the entrance of the estate is there a security guard, but entrance is rather lax without much checking. This is in contrast with other estates nearby which are larger in scale and still maintain a higher level of security.

The establishment of homeowners' associations and gated communities is not about the prevention of the 'free-riding' of estate facilities which often describes how residents wish to pay for their services and enjoy these facilities exclusively from outsiders. The formation of a homeowners' association is rather a reaction to a property dispute between gated community residents and developers. In gated communities in the United States, residents choose them as a governance choice. Setha Low (2003) illustrates this as a choice between municipal property tax and homeowners' fees:

> Gated communities in many cases precede annexation as a result of extreme urban sprawl — that is, urban/suburban expansion without municipal infrastructure. The gated community serves as a government-like service provider. (p. 188)

But annexation means residents now have to 'pay fees to the homeowners' association and pay high real estate taxes'. Two of her interviewees moved to another gated community 'in an attempt to escape some of these taxes, and to purchase private services at a reasonable cost'.[72] To her cases, it is a governance choice, and consequently the choice of tax versus retaining the property tax and self-funding some community service activities.

In terms of service provision, the scope of residents' self-provided and funded services is still limited in China. Homeowners' association neighbourhoods maintain amenities such as health clubs, swimming pools, tennis courts and security through the membership club. Residents pay for them as the property prices include the construction cost of tennis courts, gardens and green space. In order to maintain their operation, residents have to pay a higher estate maintenance fee. For example, business tenants in Canary Wharf in London pay a premium property management fee, which covers privately maintained gardens of a better quality than the parks maintained by local councils. However, in China, although property management fees vary according to the standard of estates, gated communities are a mainstream form of development. Although these estates boast a nice built environment, the property management fees are not sufficiently high to replace government funding for essential services. The services self-funded by the neighbourhood typically include leisure facilities such as tennis courts, some security, and garden maintenance of the gardens inside the estates. Initially, some super large estates such as Southern China Estates were built by Countryside Garden, which is known for mass housing production by a single developer. Some schools and clinics were initially built by the developer but soon these were 'incorporated' by the municipal government as public provision.

But wider social services such as schools, hospitals and police are still maintained by the local government. In China, there is no 'property tax'.[73] Services such as schools and healthcare are still covered by general taxes rather than property income. The state still provides services across central and suburban districts, even though the residential landscape in the suburbs is dominated by gated communities. The services are not much differentiated by the different standards and qualities of gated communities. While inner urban areas usually have better services, the government often supports the development of healthcare and schooling in the suburbs by setting up branches of well-known schools and hospitals in the central areas. Social services are actually provided quite uniformly across the metropolitan region. As such there is not really 'voting by foot' – residents relocating in order to choose municipal taxation or quality of facilities, i.e., to find the best match between services and their preferences.[74]

In sum, from the governance perspective, this chapter attempts to solve a puzzle: along with individualisation and rising residential privacy and property rights awareness, why have we not seen the emergence of a 'public sphere'? Here, through the investigation of the actual development and governance process, the book highlights that the Chinese gated community is not a 'private city', but neither is it a space of collectivism as shown in Fei's rural China – the social order is not built upon differential mode of association as within a totalised society. New actors such as the homeowners' association are created but cannot exert effective control. There is no contractual relation to be enforced upon its fellow residents. In other words, a homeowners' association cannot manage its social life in the neighbourhood.

Neighbourhood life and place attachment

While gated communities are characterised by some new organisational features, especially market-provided property services and rising homeowners' associations, they are not a pre-configured product of governance, engineered by the state or developer. They are presented, rather, as a choice of building style and related private life. Advertisements for gated communities barely mention a vibrant community, intense social interaction, or plenty of social activities. When the clubhouse is mentioned, it is as an illustration of high-quality facilities rather than socialisation in communal spaces. In a way, Chinese gated communities do present a vision of 'dystopia' where residents have a desire to be separated from society.[75] The Chinese gated community does not present a lifestyle for social life. If lifestyle is mentioned, it is greater residential privacy, more about the exclusive built environment and aesthetic building styles.

The development of gated communities in China is not driven by globalisation or an imported governance form of 'privately governed communities'. The gated community in China is not a neighbourhood of private governance or a 'homeowners' association neighbourhood' as it is known in the United States. Rather, regarding gated communities in China as a neighbourhood of particular governance, they are a 'product' innovation: a built form which existed in the imperial period (for example, exclusivity for the aristocrat). It is now impossible to build an estate for single family houses and apartments. So the townhouse (terraced house) or semi-detached house style (*shuangping*) is used to meet the demand for greater residential privacy. Similarly, gated condominium estates are developed in more central areas, which are built at a higher density but maintain elusive and exclusive privacy. It is in this sense that they are 'private' communities. The housing is privately owned, creating a space centred on one's private life around the nuclear family rather than on communal engagement. Residents of gated communities may encounter each other in semi-public space in a rather superficial way but they rarely pay a casual home visit (*chuanmeng*) as in the traditional alleyway neighbourhood. The gated community is not a world of acquaintances. Various residential surveys indicate that gated communities lack social and neighbourly interactions.[76]

The desire for residential privacy reflects an overall process of 'individualisation' – disillusion about collectivism and overly politicised social life. Residents wish to return to their own space of life. Such a preference for a 'normal' life is seen in the post-reform era across different social groups, not just the new rich or a privileged middle class but also ordinary people (*laobaixing*). Residential choice is a matter of choosing lifestyle or the 'spatialisation of class',[77] but at the same time residents hope to develop a *guanxi* of their choice and sharing of their 'circles', breaking away from the territorially bounded social relations that are prescribed for them. Social relations in a totalised society, such as a village or workplace (*danwei*), are unavoidable and inescapable. Instead, residents hope to find their 'association' with others outside the place of residence. Choosing gated communities is a personal retreat from the totalised society.[78] Hence, albeit with product variations, the Chinese gated community is a mainstream product. It is a community based on common interest – property value and the quality of the living environment, rather than a place where residents seek to encounter others.

Social activities are very much limited to leisure and entertainment. Because the gated community is a mainstream residential form, unlike in the United States, the form of living represents an overall decrease in sociability in neighbourhoods. Residents' committees sometimes organise social activities, hoping to promote social cohesion (collectivism) through more personal social interaction. These activities are not well received, or are only selectively participated in. In the neighbourhood garden or square, nannies or housewives with children sometimes encounter each other in a casual way. Residents use the open swimming pool or indoor gyms or participate in more 'civilised' leisure and exercise, such as strolling after dinner. It is rare to see the elderly playing *mahjong* or cards along the roadside or people playing music in a communal space. Parents centre their activities around children. Residents exchange greetings but keep a comfortable social distance without intruding into the personal territory of others. The neighbourhood is their 'home', breaking away from society. It is not a temporary place to stay but a paradise to claim their ordinary life.[79] Hence, homeowners make great efforts to choose the house style, landscaping, decoration and furniture. The construction of gated communities and their neighbourhood life aims to invent a meaning – often in a rather ordinary countryside, the 'exotic' landscape has been invented for gated communities to signify the place, presenting the glorious and prestigious status of the neighbourhood.[80] The social mentality of indifference also reflects a more superficial relation in these places.

In contrast to the lack of social interaction, residents in commodity housing estates demonstrate a strong place attachment.[81] They identify themselves strongly with the neighbourhood as residents of the place. Their place attachment is not built upon everyday encountering but rather on their common interests in the community as homeowners.[82] Their place attachment is 'interests driven' rather than 'socially mobilised'.[83]

However, their common interests have driven residents to participate in neighbourhood life in a more passive way. But because of low social capital, it is difficult for residents to exert influences over neighbourhood affairs. As Yushu Zhu (2020) observed:

> Neighbourhood attachment (i.e., place sentiment toward a neighbourhood) serves as a prerequisite for any form of participation. While neighbourhood attachment is sufficient for latent involvement, such as staying informed about neighbourhood issues through social exchanges and other spontaneous activities, social capital produces mobilising forces that motivate residents to move beyond the latent stage to influence community outcomes through manifest engagement. (p. 1)

The greater residential privacy and low social interaction in gated communities reflect the overall trend of Chinese society leaving its rurality – leaving the soil. But strong place attachment, sentiment and territorial identity mean that the 'community' does not disappear, but is based on a different foundation.

Robert Park (1915), the founder of the Chicago School of Sociology, pointed out that the social order would be built more on specialised vocational groups or guilds and that relations would be defined by interests and utilitarianism, and no longer territorially based. Although it was found that 'urban villagers' still presented more territorially based relations in ethnic and working-class neighbourhoods in the United States,[84] Chinese gated communities partially confirm Park's prediction about the transformation of neighbourhood life but at the same time disprove the claim about territory. Due to the specific setting, the neighbourhoods of Chinese cities are preserved, transformed or created. In the gated community, property interests make residents more like a vocational organisation or interest group but still largely territorially based, just like urban villages where the rental economy transformed the village into a shareholding entity. Residents of gated communities also interact through virtual social media such as neighbourhood discussion forums and form alliances in defending their property rights.

Conclusion

The Chinese gated community is not a micro-district built in the socialist era. Here, micro-district represents a master planned style of residence and the characteristics of an estate-based built form.[85] The term *fengbi* in the Chinese gated community further clarifies that these estates have security features with a high degree of residential privacy. Stressing the security highlights the nature of Chinese gated communities and helps avoid the connotation of private governance assumed in the notion of gated communities in the United States. How did the gated community appear in China? First and foremost, post-reform urban China has seen the desire for a higher quality of housing and the built environment, and secondly commodity housing buyers want a 'good life' associated with the environment.

Prior to the development of a housing market, housing development was always organised on a scale smaller than the municipality. A universal public sector did not exist on a large scale of municipal welfare. The municipality only maintained the public rental housing that had been converted from pre-socialist private housing. It did not have the capacity, and was indeed unwilling, to invest in large-scale public housing development, because housing was allocated as occupational welfare to working staff and public housing rental was low. It was a 'collective' (larger than individuals) provision. Although work-unit compounds built gates, the form of security was rather modest because society was generally safe and the crime rate was low. The neighbourhood watch was strong, and everyone was poor and did not have much personal wealth to store at home. Indeed, only when residents had household appliances such as a TV were windows with anti-theft iron bars installed. Even though they had security and gated features, these residences would not be called gated communities. The term refers to a particular mode of development – 'commodity' housing estates with some security features.

Gated communities became a practical way to organise diverse residential demand for the higher quality of the built environment. It creates a new residential landscape and social geography of greater diversity. It adds a generic type of residential neighbourhood, in contrast to largely open traditional neighbourhoods and rural villages. But within this generic type, it has seen variegated qualities (*dangci*) with different degrees of gated-ness. These gated communities with different qualities and price tags are organised on an estate-by-estate basis. Similar to the notion of 'plotting urbanism' in the peripheral urban areas of the global South,[86] we can probably call the landscape of gated communities 'estate urbanism', with greater residential differentiation built upon residences, in addition to social stratification created by urban and rural *hukou*, institutional affiliation and educational attainment (Figure 4.12 and Figure 4.13). But exactly because of this great internal variation within gated communities, it is perhaps difficult to expect that

Figure 4.12 A gated housing estate, Southern Lake Garden, in Shantou. The estate has a reasonable density compared with another high-density estate in the same city. Taken in 2013.

Figure 4.13 A high-density housing estate, Star Lake City, in Shantou. The plot ratio is much higher than Southern Lake Garden. These two photos show that gated commodity housing is now a mainstream product with varying densities and qualities. Taken in 2013.

a class of gated communities residents with a clear identity will eventually be created, while just like other forms of lifestyle consumption, living in gated communities as a residential preference shapes the social status of the middle class.[87] In the new world of gated communities, the all-inclusive relation of differential mode of association is not replicated. The gated form of residence may build walls like the Forbidden City or a French castle, or a melange of neoclassical motifs and low-density suburban subdivisions.

In newer urban areas, many services related to the property within the neighbourhood are provided by the developer rather than the government during housing construction. Homeowners did not previously know one another but become an interest group based on their properties. As a result, residents have relatively strong attachment to their community, despite low neighbourhood social interactions. But the neighbourhood has been transformed. Consumers, that is, individual homeowners, are not able to organise themselves effectively into an organisational form, because of the constraint of resources, lack of willingness to participate in public affairs and desire for residential privacy, together with a lack of demand for self-governance. Gated communities lack social capital because of low neighbourhood interaction and are not evolving into a 'civil society' that can exert political demands for governance. The extent of self-governance is limited. These residential neighbourhoods are gated on the basis of the estates built by their developers. To some extent, property services are provided by the developer, their subsidiary or recruited property management company.

The residential form originates from the market provision of housing by developers, which indeed reflects a residential change in urban China. The change brings in more residential autonomy at the neighbourhood level, which is built upon and manifests as individualisation rather than collectivism.[88] It is in this sense that the Chinese gated community is a 'private' neighbourhood, because all the properties are privately owned and the residential environment maintains a high degree of privacy with limited social interaction. But these neighbourhoods are not privately governed – or in the perspective of differential mode of association, a form of governance originating from the social relations of residents. The 'incompetence' of the homeowners' association requires state agency – the residents' committee – to be an arbitrator between developer and homeowners in residential disputes. In low- and middle-income neighbourhoods, the state has to replace the non-functional homeowners' association to deliver basic services.

If the definition of 'gated community' includes self-governance using legal forms such as CC&Rs, then *fengbi xiaoqu* is not a gated community, although they have gated forms with some security features. They are secured residential places but not places under private control, privately governed, or privatism. On the other hand, residential privacy is respected and desired, leading to weakened social relations and neighbourhood social lives. However, Chinese gated communities do not present such an extreme form of private governance as gated communities in Western market economies. The construction of these neighbourhoods started with the market provision of housing and consequent property management services. The state still plays an important role in neighbourhood governance; at the lower end of gated communities, such as resettlement housing estates, the state plays an even more direct role.[89] The configuration of governance mode becomes even more complicated when there are different combinations of actors such as the property management company, the homeowners' association, the residents' committee and street offices in diverse neighbourhood types.[90] But even within the same category of neighbourhood such as gated communities, their strength can be different, depending upon the history of development.

As for the urban life of gated communities, the developer strives to discover the meaning of the good life, understanding the desire for a modern (Western) social life. After long-term political turmoil, such an imagined Western social order became particularly appealing during China's (liberal) 'cultural renaissance' in the 1980s. But the imagination of the West originated during the collapse of imperial China. Fei Xiaotong in his book, *From the Soil*, described such a contrast:

> Western societies are somewhat like the way we collect rice straw to use to cook our food. After harvest, the rice straw is bound into small bundles; several bundles are bound into larger bundles; and these are then stacked together so that they can be carried on shoulder poles. Each piece of straw belongs in a small bundle, which in turn belongs in a larger bundle, which in turn makes up a stack. The separate stacks all fit together to make up the whole haystack. In this way, the separately bound bundles can be stacked in an orderly way. In Western society, these separate units are organisations. By making an analogy between organisations in Western societies and the composition of haystacks, I want to indicate that in Western society individuals form organisations. (Fei 1947/92, 61)

Fei then compared social organisations and asked why even basic social units such as families were so ambiguous in China:

> In my opinion, the ambiguity indicates the difference between our social structure and that of the West. Our pattern is not like distinct bundles of straws. Rather, it is like the circles that appear on the surface of a lake when a rock is thrown into it. Everyone stands at the centre of the circles produced by his or her own social influence. Everyone's circles are interrelated. One touches different circles at different times and places. (Fei 1947/92, 62–3)

Fei characterises the mode of organisation in Western society as the 'organisational mode of association' (*tuantigeju*), in contrast to differential mode of association (*chaxugeju*). For the latter, although Fei's intention was to explain the source of 'selfishness', as the boundary of the public is ambiguous and only self-interest is identifiable, *chaxugeju* represents all-inclusive and all-intrusive social relations. As Fei explained:

> In the West, the state is an organisation that creates distinct boundaries between the public and the private spheres. Like straws in a haystack, citizens all belong to the state. They have to make the state a public organisation beneficial to each individual... . But in traditional China, the concept of public was the ambiguous *tianxia* (all under heaven), whereas the state was seen as the emperor's family. Hence, the boundary between public and private has never been clear. The state and the public are but additional circles that spread out like the waves from the splash of each person's social influence. (Fei 1947/92, 70)

This feature of engagement has been increasingly regarded as undesirable, consciously or unconsciously, in the post-reform era. It is not the state but rather ordinary Chinese people who have begun to seek their private life, and as a residential choice – residential privacy. They do not have the appetite for collective action to achieve self-governance. In essence, the motivation is to find better services and a better 'material' life. But the development of a more family-oriented built environment has a profound implication for urban life – the end of collectivism or differential mode of association in traditional China.

The development of gated communities, as the residential form of commodity housing, has materialised the process of individualisation that started even before the economic reform.[91] With the massive scale of development, this form has now become the mainstream type of residence in urban China. It is in this sense that the claim made by Chinese real estate developers in the 2000s – 'residential construction transforms China' (*juzhu gaibian zhongguo*) – has come true.

As can be seen from the above, gated communities cannot be explained through simply supply- or demand-side factors. The Chinese gated community is not a pure supply-side innovation. It would be an exaggeration to suggest that the Chinese gated community was created by developers to invent a residential market. Neither is it created as the residential form of collectivism by the state to continue its control. Gated communities reflect demand for a residential environment that has more residential privacy and personal space. The construction of gated communities has led to the provision of property management at the residential neighbourhood level. The governance of neighbourhood through private provision is called private governance or 'club governance'.[92] But property management, paid for by homeowners, is often controlled by the developer. The club is not equivalent to 'collectivism', namely a social order built upon differential but closely related social relation – *chaxugeju*. The extent of self-governance is quite limited. Gated communities represent a new type of 'community' of property owners. Different from the rural village based on differential mode of association, it is an imagined community that has little actual social interaction but common interests in property rights.

In the United States, despite their increasing prevalence, gated communities still present a privileged residential form and a segment of the upper housing market. The 'white picket fence' suburb created by mass suburbanisation associated with 'white flight' was originally an open access community.[93] In contrast, the mass relocation of Chinese urbanites to the peripheral gated communities is a more mainstream choice of variegated residential qualities ranging from practically affordable housing to luxury villa compounds. Indeed, such a choice is less about governance or municipal tax issues. Choosing gated communities is basically a choice of consumer products, with different degrees of security, services and prices – the Chinese gated community is a micro consumer society.

In other words, it is not a *public* choice for different governments or governance modes. Rather, it is about housing as a consumer product, as municipal services such as hospitals, schools, nurseries and libraries are widely and universally available except in rural areas. In fact, these services are less conveniently available in suburban estates, and often the municipal government has to set up special branches in order to enhance the attractiveness of suburban residential areas. The degree of the strength of the homeowners' association is not part of the equation. Even though the children of the middle class may attend private schools, their parents cannot move into a place where they do not need to pay the tax for funding schools. In other words, school funding and choice are not linked to exclusive club goods of gated communities. Because the housing qualities of suburban gated communities and traditional neighbourhoods are so different, they are not seen as comparable choices. In the early 2000s, Shanghai residents living in alleyway housing even used 'night urine bottles' because of the lack of indoor toilets. The quality of alleyway housing was so poor and deteriorated that it would not seem a bad idea to move to a new place, even though this meant a farewell to their acquaintances. Thus, the choice is firstly seen as a selection of different living environments, rather than work-unit collectivism versus gated community privatism. But when the majority of residents 'walked outside their work-unit compounds' to suburban gated communities,[94] the strongly related and organic communities came to an end. This is literally *leaving* the soil, besides declining neo-traditionalism in workplace neighbourhoods.

Notes

1. Wu, 2005.
2. The concept of *xiaoqu*, or micro-district, has a long tradition from socialist planning; see Wu, 2015.
3. The closest translation of gated communities for occasional everyday use is *mengjin shequ*, meaning the residential community with gates. While the two words 'gated' and 'communities' are faithfully translated, *mengjin shequ* refers to a built form without its governance connotation. In this book, I use gated community and *fengbi xiaoqu* interchangeably without the connotations of its North American definition.
4. These estates include a variety of hybrid forms, for example, so-called 'affordable housing' (*jinji shiyong fang*), 'price-limited housing' (*xianjia fang*) or government-sponsored resettlement housing estates which provide homeownership to relocated residents. Thus we exclude other gated forms such as work-unit compounds, which are discussed in Chapter 2.
5. For suburban residential landscapes, see Keil, 2018, and also Keil and Wu, 2022.
6. Lu et al., 2020.
7. Tang, 2018.
8. Zhang, 2010: 136.
9. Yan, 2010.
10. Yan, 2010.
11. Wu, 2005; Huang, 2006; Huang and Low, 2008.
12. See Chapter 3; and also Kan and Wong, 2019.
13. Low, 2003.
14. Low, 2003: 181.
15. Low, 2003: 181.
16. Some homeowners' associations do manage to have a maintenance fund account that is supervised by the local housing bureau. It is generally difficult to set up an enterprise account because the association is not an enterprise.
17. Cai and He, 2021: 1.
18. Webster, 2001; Webster and Lai, 2003.

19. This is the exact treatment of a variety of gated communities in the broadest sense; Webster et al., 2006.
20. Wu, 2005.
21. In Webster's deliberation, the club form is closer to the private sphere (the 'private' city) than collectivism, in contrast to Huang and Low, 2008.
22. Lu et al., 2019.
23. To avoid the compounded meaning of the 'private' as self-governance, it is perhaps more precise to use the word 'market' in the provision of property services.
24. This is similar to 'planning gain' in a permission-based planning system such as that in the UK.
25. Karaman et al., 2020.
26. McKenzie, 2005.
27. Pow, 2009.
28. The term 'incorporation' is not used in the Chinese context. It is often used in the US context about municipal annexation which requires households in incorporated residential areas to pay a local tax. See Low, 2003.
29. Interview with the former CEO, 09/2018.
30. But in fact it handed over 800 million Yuan in total, interview.
31. Lu et al., 2020.
32. Because the land premium is calculated based on the plot ratio.
33. Interview with the former CEO, 09/2018.
34. This means that the developer actually became a primary developer, a role which was normally played by a government development corporation. The land obtained by the developer was 'raw', without much infrastructure. Also, the contribution from developers to infrastructure is limited, compared with planning gain in the UK. Mostly, the contribution is the price paid by developers to land bidding.
35. Lu et al., 2020.
36. Lu et al., 2020.
37. Lu et al., 2020.
38. Lu et al., 2020.
39. The demolition and redevelopment is described in Shao, 2013.
40. Wu, 2004b.
41. Wu, 2004b: 230.
42. Pow, 2009; Wu, 2004b; 2005; 2009a.
43. Wu and Webber, 2004.
44. Giroir, 2007.
45. Pow, 2009.
46. Interview, August 2005, Beijing.
47. See Wu, 2010a for elaboration.
48. Wu, 2009a.
49. Zhang, 2010; Wu, 2009a.
50. Webster et al., 2002.
51. Interview, November 2018.
52. Wissink, 2019a: 172.
53. Huang and Low, 2008.
54. Zhu et al., 2012.
55. But we need to understand the exact meaning of 'place attachment' in this Chinese context, which is quite different from traditional Chinese society on the foundation of *chaxugeju*, as argued in this book.
56. Zhou, 2014.
57. Zhang and Ong, 2008.
58. Wu, 2018a.
59. Huang, 2006; Huang and Low, 2008.
60. Webster et al., 2006.
61. It organised a 'mass banquet' (*baijiayan*) just days before the outbreak of COVID-19.
62. Webster et al., 2006.
63. Hendrikx and Wissink, 2017.
64. In the United States, the neighbourhood governed by the homeowners' association is noted as 'private neighbourhoods' (Low, 2003) or 'homeowners association neighbourhood' (Fraser et al., 2016).

65. He, 2015.
66. See Tomba, 2005; Yip and Jiang, 2011; Shin, 2013; Yip, 2014.
67. Lu et al., 2020.
68. Park, 1915.
69. Zhou, 2014.
70. Boland and Zhu, 2012; Fu and Lin, 2014.
71. Wu, 2010a.
72. Low, 2003: 188.
73. Except for some experiments in Shanghai and Chongqing, which provide a modest income for the local government.
74. However, moving into the catchment area of public funded school is quite common, regardless of gated communities. See Wu et al., 2018.
75. See Pow, 2015. This dystopia is compounded by 'fear for other'; Low, 2003.
76. Zhu et al., 2012; Zhu, 2020.
77. Zhang, 2010.
78. Wu, 2011.
79. Zhang, 2010.
80. Wu, 2010a.
81. Zhu et al., 2012; Zhu, 2020.
82. In the literature of gated communities, this is also known as 'common interest development' (CID).
83. Zhu, 2020.
84. Gans, 1962.
85. The term 'master-planned estate' is used in the literature in Australia to refer to gated communities; see McGuirk and Dowling, 2011. While the gated community stresses a private governance form, the master-planned estate emphasises the design and security features.
86. Karaman et al., 2020.
87. Zhang, 2010.
88. Davis, 1990.
89. Lu et al., 2020.
90. Wang and Clarke, 2021.
91. Yan, 2010.
92. Webster, 2001.
93. Keil, 2018.
94. Wu, 2002a.

5
Rethinking urban China in an urban debate

Introduction

This book has explained how China is becoming urban through examining generic yet concrete residential spaces or neighbourhoods where people conglomerate. Rather than focusing on the force of economic agglomeration and the creation of the city, my attention has been paid to the social process occurring in the microscopic spaces of everyday life. Arguably, this process is exactly an *urbanisation* process rather than general political and social change outside the 'nature of cities'.[1] This book does not depict macroeconomic political changes and the attendant changes to urban development approaches, although urban changes are placed within this broad political and social context. In other words, my perspective does not start from seeing a strong state as a defining parameter for China's urbanisation. Rather, I attempt to understand how a visible state is emerging from the urbanisation process.

The focus here is placed on urban changes, in particular at the neighbourhood level. From these generic spaces we observe changing neighbourhood life and social order. In other words, the book is about 'urbanisation' in its broader sense beyond economic changes and population concentration – increasing non-agricultural economies and rural-to-urban migration. Instead of seeing political economic changes and their impacts on the city, the perspective here is to understand urban transformation from the making of the urban and how this transformation generates implications for governance. In this sense, the political change is not deterministic but rather responsive to urbanisation on the ground.

The trend towards a greater sphere of consumption in Chinese cities was detected in the early stages of market reform.[2] In a later stage of rising consumerism, Deborah Davis (2000) scrutinised the implication

Figure 5.1 The area near Xintiandi, Shanghai, showing an upgrading process in central Shanghai. Taken in 2019.

of market development for potentially greater 'community and personal autonomy'. According to Davis, the overall transformation could be understood as a 'consumer revolution' which was profoundly changing the political and social order. However, the main limitation to the thesis of consumer revolution is the challenge to describe what existed before such a transition. A common narrative presents the society before consumer revolution as a fully bureaucratised one controlled by the state, but this ignores the interstices and close communal relations in these places.

From the understanding of neo-traditionalism,[3] the transition therefore was not from a tightly regulated society to a 'neoliberal' market society with greater social autonomy. Rather, it was a change from an organic and 'totalised' society to a more clearly defined division between individuals, class and a professionalised state, while the society itself remained underdeveloped. This does not deny diverse social life and remaining reciprocal relationships, especially among those who are not able to enter the formal urban sphere. But the overall trend is the departure from rurality to embrace greater diversity and differentiation (Figure 5.1 and Figure 5.2). We have seen declining territorial relations and more network-based interactions. The form of residential communities has been strengthened, but this 'community construction'

Figure 5.2 The dilapidated central area near the 'Little Park' in Shantou, showing a different trajectory from Xintiandi. Inner-city decline is rather rare in China. Taken in 2014.

is based more on property rights and governmental techniques. This book has examined residential changes and precisely understands this transition, which is referred to here as 'urbanisation'. Thus, changing governance goes beyond the single dimension of state control, state retreat or state regulation.

Besides housing consumption, this book has paid more attention to urban space and residential changes. In other words, the concern here is an 'urban revolution', considering the territory within which social relations are forged and transformed. Although production activities in the cities (hence the labour market) and welfare provision at the urban scale (hence urban policy or the 'urban question') are relevant to urbanisation, attention has been focused on urban neighbourhoods and changing residential relations. The overall thread of this book goes through entrepreneurial governance and changing urban life.

Although the book mainly focuses on urban neighbourhoods, including semi-urbanised villages in peri-urban areas, the trend described in these places occurs beyond the boundaries of the city. It is in this sense that this is a 'planetary' and extended urbanisation process, which has a profound impact on rural areas. Rural places are incorporated into Chinese urbanisation through massive rural-to-urban migration. In 2020, the total number of rural migrants in Chinese cities was 285.6 million.[4] Although some migrants join their families in the cities, many adopt a tactic of 'split households', staying separately in the city and countryside as a result of social exclusion as well as the high expense of living in the city.[5] Land near the cities is converted into urban uses and occupied by non-local users. Even in a faraway rural place, land is affected by urban development through the policy of so-called 'land rights transfer'.[6] Because the policy imposes a fixed annual quota of land development in each county, new development in one place has to be accompanied by demolition in another. A village site is demolished, and villages are merged to create more agricultural land – conversion from built-up area to agricultural uses generates a new 'land development quota' to be used in places near the city. Both demolition and building are processes of urbanisation, demolishing existing rurality to merge rural villages into new settlements and creating spaces that differ from rurality. The profound change in the countryside, while it is beyond the scope of this book, occurs simultaneously with what is described here as 'leaving the soil'.

This book thinks of the urban as a material base for capital accumulation and changing social relations made in the everyday lives of residents. The boundaries and categories between the urban and the rural are becoming increasingly indistinguishable. China has a long agrarian history. The book has examined Chinese cities in the context of the longevity of rural China after its socialist transformation until the recent 'urban revolution'. In countries like India or other places in the global South, colonial administration structures, that is, how subjects were governed and how the rural and the urban were designated, still affect what is 'the urban' today.[7]

Although the book is concerned only with urban China and contrasts it with rural China, this difference should not be regarded as a generic difference between spatial categories but rather as temporal change. That is, the cities and rural villages in imperial China and the earlier socialist planned economy bear similar rurality, while new urban China, including extensive direct or indirect links to rural areas, is subject to the same process of urbanisation. Rural China itself does not escape the process of urbanisation today, although the book has mainly described changes in the territory of cities. Through massive rural–urban migration, land development transfer and 'rural consolidation',[8] the urban is being made at a scale that extends across the whole territory of China.

Neighbourhood development and changes

Four generic neighbourhoods have been described here. The traditional alleyway neighbourhood largely remained untouched until the urban renewal programme initiatives in the 1990s. In the following years, especially after 'housing commodification' in 1998, the suburbs of Chinese cities have seen large-scale development, most saliently through 'gated communities'. The redevelopment of inner cities was slow until suburban development became controlled by 'land development quotas' and the policy of compact cities. Around the urban built-up area, the original rural villages were converted into informal rental housing for rural migrants, particularly near industrial areas. At the same time, better-off residents left the traditional alleyway neighbourhoods and low-income households, while mostly rural migrants working for retail, catering and other social services moved into them, leading to further deterioration of the living environment. Urban demolition reduced the areas of traditional alleyway neighbourhoods, turning some into gated condominium estates.

Perhaps the most stable neighbourhood is the workplace neighbourhood because housing was usually built as five- to six-storey buildings, which are difficult to demolish. Through housing privatisation, most sitting tenants became homeowners. Many sold their properties and moved to suburban commodity housing, while some even held on to their ownership and rent their properties out to new migrants. As the homeownership rate of original urban households in Chinese cities is as high as over 80 per cent, renters are mostly rural migrants and new graduates who have not stepped onto the property ladder.

This development history explains why the suburban gated community is the most desirable form. The quality of the living environment can be ranked in the order of commodity housing, workplace areas, traditional alleyway neighbourhoods, and finally urban villages. There are different forms of governance. The traditional alleyway neighbourhood was a marginal neighbourhood compared with workplace compounds and is still governed by the residents' committee. Its governance has become more formalised through merging small neighbourhoods into larger administrative communities, but the changing composition of residents has made it more difficult to mobilise them to maintain the features of traditionalism. It has been difficult to introduce a more market-oriented form of governance because of low affordability for the services of property management companies.

As for workplace neighbourhoods, the residents' committee was not a major mechanism for governance until the transfer of neighbourhood management to newly developed residential neighbourhoods. Its governance was achieved through the neo-traditionalism of the work-unit community. Thus, while the workplace neighbourhood seems to be the most stable in terms of residential change, its change in governance is quite significant. In contrast to newly developed suburban gated communities or upgraded condominium estates in the premium locations of the city, the workplace neighbourhood lacks both affordability for property management and demand for 'private governance', because the remaining residents in the original place are poorer than those who were able to purchase newer housing, although some may wish to stay in central and school catchment areas.

No matter what the reasons, housing refurbishing and decoration are widespread among Chinese residents. The dismantling of collective consumption organised by the state has led to a more self-fulfilled form of homemaking under the 'consumer revolution', but workplace neighbourhoods have not advanced to the extent that residents resort to private services and governance. Indeed, it is difficult to maintain costly property services. The built environment is deteriorating, and often the new administrative community has to undertake some duties and play a leading role in neighbourhood governance. In short, the transition is from sectoral to territorial governance, rather than from the state to the market. It has been difficult to establish homeowners' associations. Despite the neo-traditionalist history, these places encounter difficulties maintaining their collectivism.

In contrast, urban villages had no history of formal urban governance during the socialist period. The villagers' committee would not have been able to cope with the sudden increase in private rentals which were mostly self-built. But the collective land of the former 'production brigade' was converted into the assets of villagers' shareholding cooperatives. Services for villagers largely rely on rental income from collective assets. The traditional organisations of clan and lineage continue to exert influence but only for a minority of residents. The majority – over 90 per cent – are rural migrant renters who are excluded from governance. The formal social order is increasingly maintained by the extension of state administrative agency. If urban villages are demolished, they are converted into urban administration under the governance of a residents' committee. For new rental housing created from extra units of resettlement housing, governance is achieved through the landlord and tenant symbiotic relation, bearing some features of 'private governance' of rental economy. However, the whole resettlement housing neighbourhood created from urban village redevelopment is still subject to formal administrative management – reflecting the formalisation process of redevelopment.

Finally, for gated communities, homeownership is the dominant form of housing tenure, although the actual occupancy rate may be low. The gated community neighbourhood has the most complex governance structure. With the introduction of property management companies to take over property services performed by the state or workplaces, together with homeowners' associations to represent residents for property-related affairs and the residents' committee to play a more formal administrative role, the structure of governance is not fixed and is contextually dependent on the individual development histories of these estates. But the overall trend is that these gated estates are not solely governed by homeowners' associations, as the role of the homeowners' association is confined within the remit of property rights.

The lack of transparency and governance legitimacy makes it difficult for the homeowners' association to play a greater role in neighbourhood governance. But residents' strong vested interests in property rights occasionally lead to 'rightful resistance' or collective actions when homeowners feel their rights are being violated. Residents do have a stronger identity and 'place' attachment to the estate based on their property rights, and participate in neighbourhood leisure and entertainment activities, although these remain at a superficial level, different from the intimate neighbouring seen in traditional alleyway neighbourhoods. In other words, neighbourhood identity is maintained through common property rights interests more than everyday life experience.

In short, these four types of neighbourhoods demonstrate a common trend in that traditional features have been dismantled and distinctive new traits have been created. As mentioned earlier, another commonality is that the transition is triggered by the introduction of the market as a coordination mechanism into places where such a mechanism was suppressed or had not become dominant. But the market mechanism does not rise to the extent that it can determine the course of governance. The change does not give rise to a self-governed or stronger society. Informality is transformed and remains; relations transcend territorial boundaries; greater urbanity is created. Everyday lives are no longer confined through the order of differential mode of association, constituting new urban China. Other than pointing out the departure of new urban China from its traditionalism or rurality, these new traits have quite variegated manifestations in different places. Hence, these neighbourhoods remain as generic categories – due to their different histories and political economic positions in China's overall societal transformation.

Placing urban China in the 'urban' debates

The Chinese city has a long history. The word 'city' in Chinese is actually composed of two characters, *cheng* (city) and *shi* (market). The book *Spring and Autumn Annals of Wu and Yue* written in 25–220 AD describes the origin of the city as: 'building the city for the emperor; developing the market for people. This is the origin of the city'. The Chinese definition points out two forces in city building: economic activities and governance.[9] Therefore, it is helpful to think about the city beyond being a pure space container for economic activities. Understanding governance and behind it, social relations and mentality, is necessary.

It is imperative to understand the city as the outcome of both economic agglomeration and the politics of development. It is intriguing to ask what the driving forces for the concentration of population and economic activities into the city are and for the more variegated and concrete spatial forms of neighbourhoods. Recently, in the field of urban studies, there has been a debate over the 'nature' of the city,[10] and a rethinking of the distinction between the city and the urban.[11] Such a distinction is meaningful for understanding what the exact changes in Chinese urban neighbourhoods are, because, although the Chinese city as a built form has existed for a long time, only now has Chinese society been drastically urbanised, leaving its roots of rurality. A new form of social relation, governance and order, and social mentality has been formed. Now we place the understanding of urban China in three major debates over the city.

The 'nature' of cities

There is a debate on the understanding of the city. The 'nature' of cities, according to Allen Scott and Michael Storper (2015), is an outcome of economic agglomeration. Its concrete spatial form is further moulded by the 'land nexus' consisting of competition over location and regulatory intervention. They argue that 'agglomeration is the basic glue that holds the city together as a complex congeries of human activities, and that underlies – via the endemic common pool resources and social conflicts of urban area – a highly distinctive form of politics' (pp. 6–7). The nature of cities thus involves 'combining two main processes, namely, the dynamics of agglomeration and polarization, and the unfolding of an associated nexus of locations, land uses and human interactions' (p. 1). They suggest that the formation of the city is driven by the force of agglomeration, extending through dispersion. They further formally state that:

> The city represents a very specific scale of economic and social interaction generated by agglomeration processes and focused on the imperative of proximity, and almost always endowed with governance arrangements that attempt to deal with the problematical effects of density and propinquity. (Storper and Scott 2016, 1119)

By emphasising this force of agglomeration, out of competition for the central location, which is essential and unique to the city, they hope to identify the process that is the inherently urban rather than more general social phenomena and processes. These general social processes may be related to urban life but cannot be essentially defined as the city. They suggest that the definition of the city should separate general social processes from the process of creating the city.

Implicitly, underlying this notion of the essential agglomeration process that creates the city is an attention to the economic sphere, apart from social and political dynamics. It is this exclusive focus on the economic sphere that incurs various criticisms. Others argue that there is a need to understand everyday life and urban experience in order to define the city, such as blacks' different experience of cities[12] and the experience of women during urbanisation.[13] The urban experience is heterogeneous, as shown in the association of blacks with urban lives.[14] While other scholars argue for the need to understand the city in relation to policy,[15] political economy suggests that the urban process is a spatial concentration of economic surplus by ruling classes and the state,[16] or the politics of governance in a form of assemblage crossing the defined boundaries of the city.[17] Thinking from a postcolonial standpoint, Ananya Roy (2016) argues that the understanding of the urban must be placed in governmentality in the case of a postcolonial society, or how the colonial history affects the classification of the city today. She explains how

> [T]he urban does not have a priori meaning in India as a governmental category. Instead, it comes into being through programs of government, through the populations classified and named by such programs, as well as by the tussles and claims generated through such mediations. (Roy 2018, p. 41)

From thinking about assemblage, cities are connected sites and are constructed by those who live in them.[18] The agencies of actors, learning from other places and acting across a defined space, are important forces in the formation of the city.[19] This later relates to the understanding of the city as a defined space or an extended form of urbanisation, which will be discussed later.

Now, placing urban China in this debate, this book has revealed the social and governance dynamics of Chinese urbanisation. In China, during the feudal period, the city was more or less an administrative centre, occupied by the rich aristocratic class and built with a government compound (*yamen*) and a Confucian temple. The city could hardly exert its influence over the vast rural area which was under self-governance by its 'natural' order. The position of the city was defined by the imperial order rather than the division of labour, which made the city superior to the rural and able to exploit it.

The Chinese city, as suggested by its name *shi* and as argued by Scott and Storper (2015), was also the hub of market exchange; but the city itself was not 'urbanised' in a way that presents a striking social difference from other rural communities. It was a marketplace with a concentration of population and a labour force of craftsmen in small workshops and traders who both were by no means ostentatious and were in fact looked down upon. Despite an ephemeral republican era and then the socialist revolution, the Chinese city remained a city without urbanisation. In fact, through socialist transformation, suppression of consumption and economising urbanisation, the socialist city reversed the trend towards growing urbanity in the republican period – an era now narrated as 'Shanghai nostalgia'.[20] The socialist city is a settlement without urbanism. In the socialist period, the city was an instrument or site for industrial production – 'industrialisation without urbanisation' – as consumption and the urban life were constrained and regarded as 'non-productive'.

In the post-reform era, the city and various associated spatial forms have been rediscovered and transformed into a new instrument for economic growth. The application of the market form of development means the city is used in a different way, as Scott and Storper (2015) suggest, as a hub of market exchange. But the rising of market exchange is only one aspect of change. Considering political economic thinking, the city is also a place for handling surplus capital accumulation, and even the base to launch financial operations – the creation of capital for growth.[21] The role of the city as a spatial fix[22] and assetisation[23] – an essential but specific economic role – has been elaborated elsewhere.

Here, this book depicts a broader process that is now making the Chinese city an urban world, as shown in the residential changes in four generic neighbourhoods, namely, how these neighbourhoods, as fragments, finally constitute the urban – 'urban China' as we know it now. This book, while examining these 'spatial' components, is about social life; understanding the urban through the social relations forged in these places, which are different from the Chinese rurality of differential mode of association. Consequently, there are great challenges in dealing with a marketised society – it is no longer a society with traditionalism and neo-traditionalism – which drives the changing mode of governance. In this sense, the process is not a general social process but rather the 'urban process'.[24]

Such a society seriously lacks self-governance capacities. The market has captured the territory usually performed by society (in, for example, the 'commodification of neighbourhood services'). Greater social inequality means that the poor lack economic resources to support their activities, and the scope of reciprocal relations has been significantly reduced. 'Natural' rights to community based on the differential mode of association and territorial embedding have been excluded by newly emerged market relations (for example, the village shareholding cooperative excluding rural migrants who are renters). This raises the imperative for the state to reshape its function and extend its governmental techniques. While agglomeration is intrinsic to urbanisation, as the Chinese city has become the site of the world's workshop, the formation of urban China is beyond the economically driven dynamics described by a term such as 'agglomeration'.

The city as concentrated form versus the urban as assemblages

There is a debate over the conceptualisation of the city as a concentrated form versus an extended assemblage. Precisely, the debate is about the distinction between the urban and the city – being wider and planetary, the urban is not a bounded geographical concept, and urbanisation is a process.[25] While the city is thought of as a defined object, the urban represents a process, a trend or an assemblage of social relations.

As mentioned earlier in discussing the first debate, Scott and Storper (2015) conceptualise the city as an outcome of agglomeration towards a defined location; then its shape is differentiated by different capacities for securing the central location.[26] According to this understanding, the city is a defined object with a 'land nexus'. However, starting from a critique of the 'urban age' as a statistical artefact, Neil Brenner and Christian Schmid (2014) argue that the statistical distinction between the city and the rural is not helpful. Their criticism is not about the statistical definition of the city *per se*. Rather, they criticise the conceptualisation of the city as a bounded entity. They envisage an extended form of urbanisation rather than a defined boundary between the urban versus the non-urban world under modern capitalism:

> The resultant, unevenly woven urban fabric (Lefebvre, 2003[1970]) is today assuming extremely complex, polycentric forms that no longer remotely approximate the concentric rings and linear density gradients associated with the relatively bounded industrial city of the nineteenth century, the metropolitan forms of urban development that were consolidated during the opening decades of the twentieth century or, for that matter, the tendentially decentralising, nationalised urban system that crystallised across the global North under Fordist-Keynesian capitalism. (Brenner and Schmid 2014, 743)

Instead of thinking of the city as a defined category, they focus on urbanisation as a major social process in the contemporary world, arguing that 'the urban and urbanisation are theoretical categories'. 'The urban is not a pregiven, self-evident reality, condition or form – its specificity can only be delineated in theoretical terms, through an interpretation of these core properties, expressions or dynamics' (p. 749). They conceive 'urbanization as a process of continual sociospatial transformation' (p. 750). Further, they elaborated this new epistemology of the urban:

> New forms of urbanization are unfolding around the world that challenge inherited conceptions of the urban as a fixed, bounded and universally generalisable settlement type. (p. 151)

While Storper and Scott (2016) insist on the existence of the land nexus and the defined spatial unit of the city, the debate between the city and the urban is not about statistical or morphological difference. The city and its neighbourhoods exist as a concentrated form where a large number of people live.

However, the process related to the making of the city is not bounded within a defined territory and is more permeable. It is in this sense that Brenner and Schmid (2014) argue for the concept of 'planetary urbanization' which extends to the rest of the world. The substantial difference is that Scott and Storper (2015) think the latter social process is not necessarily the urban: they argue that thinking of the nature of cities as agglomeration helps 'to distinguish intrinsically urban phenomena from the rest of social reality' (p. 1). The distinction between the two sides is the different understanding of what is an urban process: advocacy for a defined urban land nexus and thus a spatial unit of the city perceives an exclusively city-shaping agglomeration effect, while the thesis of planetary urbanisation regards these broader social processes as exactly constituting the 'urban process', that the urban is an oeuvre of the everyday life of their dwellers, according to the insights of Lefebvre (1991). This exclusive attention to a concentrated form as the city is criticised as 'methodological cityism'[27] from an understanding of the metabolic process of the city. But thinking of the political process inherent in city-building, the urban presents a form of assemblage across defined boundaries.[28] The city-region is such an example.

This book does not look at the regional scale of urbanisation or city-region formation in China, which has been discussed elsewhere.[29] Neither is the Chinese city examined as a single and generic entity. This book has investigated the diverse forms of urbanisation, a process of difference with attention to neighbourhoods, and looked into the strikingly different residential landscapes that constitute the Chinese city. These neighbourhoods are not only the material forms but also the social fabric of the city. They are components of the urban. The residential changes in these neighbourhoods have been examined with reference to the social life of residents. Thus the 'level' of urbanisation is measured not as a quantity of urban population, a critique made by Brenner and Schmid (2014) about the bounded city.

In China, more than 50 per cent of the population now reside in places 'classified' as the city – a historical milestone passed since 2014. But there is a need to understand urbanisation as a process beyond rural-to-urban migration. In China urban studies, 'internal' neighbourhood change is rarely regarded as a process of urbanisation. But according to the understanding of the 'urban' as everyday life and the urban revolution as a radical turn towards the growing city as an oeuvre or assemblage of everyday life,[30] the transformation of traditional neighbourhoods and the making of new urban villages and gated communities are part of urbanisation processes. Rurality, once typical in Fei Xiaotong's Kaixiangong village but to a variegated extent in workplace communities of the socialist industrial city or in alleyway neighbourhoods (as shown in the genre of Shanghai nostalgia), is fading and diminishing. This 'fading' of rurality is urbanisation (Figure 5.3).

Figure 5.3 A rural village left vacant near the convention centre in Wuxi new town. This area was originally planned for Wuxi eco-town. The place is not far from Kaixiangong village in Wujiang, also near the Taihu Lake, which is the setting for Fei Xiaotong's book *From the Soil*. The photo shows the disappearance of *Rural China*. Taken in 2017.

These four neighbourhoods, as a constellation of the urban, are differentiated and dispersed, in terms not only of their locations but also of their different positions in governmentality. The book not only pays attention to the central area (fully urbanised) but also to the quite dispersed and in fact scattered semi-urbanised and informal areas of urban villages and suburban estates. Looking from a distance, the development of the Chinese city presents a concentrated form, not only regionally in the east but increasingly in the middle and western mega-cities too, but also as a built-up area with CBDs and industrial zones. The impact of the agglomeration effect is visible in uneven development. But beyond this obvious uneven development, the city is not just a land-use pattern of residential differentiation but also a differentiated world of life.

Albeit focusing here on internal urban space, the city itself is a world of cities (neighbourhoods), made out of their specific history, in relation to Chinese society and various actions (for example, applying the market mechanism to the production of space). They are constituted by the everyday life of residents in these places in response to political economic changes. For example, residents seek residential privacy and thus are susceptible to real estate lures to a 'paradise of the good life', engineered by the developer, which are packaged with exotic landscape design.[31] This understanding points to suburban development in relation to the state strategy of promoting urban growth,[32] residents' desire for a different relation with the state, and perhaps also to their employers' and the developers' tactics of profit making. The creation of 'exotic' suburban landscapes is an imaginary learnt from the West. The most 'exotic' landscape is in fact a banal suburban single-house division, using names such as 'Orange County', which is actually the name of an upper market estate.[33] Though expensive, these large single houses called 'villas' in China are not exotic at all. Many are simply suburban divisions as in North America.

The commodification of public housing in both traditional and workplace neighbourhoods has reduced reciprocal relations and neighbourhood help. They are affected by urban land economics (land finance) for example, as these neighbourhoods are produced and reproduced in a more market-oriented way. But the change is not solely created as a process of agglomeration, competing for a central location known as the city.

Metaphorically, this book has described how the process is 'leaving the soil' – becoming different from the rural China of differential mode of association (*chaxugeju*). Certainly, these neighbourhoods have higher densities than more scattered villages and a tranquil rural life with a close-knit social fabric, often built upon clan, lineage or the 'natural' membership of a workplace. Such association or entitlement is 'non-deprivable'. But the rights to these new neighbourhoods are increasingly tied up with differentiated and class-based consumption status; hence they are changeable and are to be made. In essence, thinking of the urban as (changing) social relations allows us to review the commonality of these diverse places.

As these generic neighbourhoods in Chinese cities reveal, the urban is characterised by a more commodified relation outside a world of acquaintance. This does not mean that the urban is an isolated world, with few linkages between people. The urban is actually seeing intense, more frequent interaction and dynamism. Residents do not necessarily feel that they are entirely rootless – the commodity housing estate shows a stronger 'place attachment' because residents share the same interests in property rights and can be mobilised into social action to defend them, often as 'rightful resistance' (defending by law). However, they can no longer claim their rights simply by staying in the place longer (as their everyday life) or by being entitled to a political community.

Urban dwellers understand this change, thus embracing the new social mentality of the urban.

This new form of society is different from its precedents – rural villages, alleyway neighbourhoods and workplace living quarters. Urban villages and gated communities are apparently new fragments, but this is not a contrast between the built forms of Chinese terraced housing with portal stone gates (*shikumen*) and five to six walk-ups in workplace (*danwei*) and newer residential areas. All evolve and co-exist. Hence, their existence and transformation represent a process rather than a defined spatial entity. Here, residential location 'choice' is not seen just as a competition for locations, not even as a choice of a particular form of governance.[34] They are parallel urban worlds constructed out of their development history and the regime of spatial production. For gated communities, the Chinese middle class, driven by market forces, pursue greater residential privacy, and do not organise themselves into 'private governance'. Organic traditionalism is not replicated in newer gated communities. There are consumer activities in these neighbourhoods, literally in the 'club houses' of gated communities. Although residents belong to the same neighbourhood, they are not very different from other consumer clubs, and hence do not form or represent the 'third realm'.[35]

Particularism versus generalisation

The field of urban studies has recently seen a debate over particularism versus generalisation. The postcolonial critique argues that theories developed in the West should not be seen as universal and applicable to the global South without considering their particularities. Even more importantly, the global South should be the site where theories are generated. This argument is forcefully put by Ananya Roy (2009a) as the 'geographies of theory'. Instead of focusing on the 'global city' in the North, urban studies should examine 'ordinary cities': as every city has the potential to be theoretically relevant, the focus should be on these cities as 'sites of difference'.[36] In other words, instead of seeing a universal replication of Western theories, as Jennifer Robinson (2011) argues, we need to think across differences and see 'a world of cities'. Urban theory needs to be constructed through a 'comparative gesture' to emphasise distinctive features.[37] Thinking in relational terms, that is, in 'inter-reference' between different policy practices, the notion of 'worlding' is put forward to describe cosmopolitan and postcolonial urbanism.[38]

According to this advocacy of particularism, specific colonial history, social practices and governance practices can help us understand current urbanism in the global South. On the other hand, urban theory should be provincialised, recognising the 'parochial character of universal knowledge claims'.[39] Instead of focusing on the effect of globalisation on cities in the global South, attention should be paid to 'subaltern urbanism' and everyday life beyond the categories of the state, capital and civil societies,[40] for example the essential feature of 'informality'.[41] Criticising the 'nature' of cities', Helga Leitner and Eric Sheppard (2016) argue that:

> [No] single theory suffices to account for the variegated nature of urbanization and cities across the world. Such provincialisation requires a serious engagement with both mainstream and critical Anglophone urban theory, challenging the seeming naturalness of knowledge claims through rigorous theoretical and empirical scrutiny from the standpoint of peripheral perspectives located outside the core. (p. 228)

In response to the criticism, Storper and Scott (2016) insist on the need to 'ask for a clear and direct demonstration of the fundamental incommensurability of urban phenomena in different parts of the world' and 'theoretically generalisable features of urbanisation as a whole' (p. 1122). They criticise the 'exceptionalism of the Global South' as leading to exclusive attention to 'favoured themes such as poverty, slums, informal labour markets, vulnerable property rights, inadequate infrastructure and lack of sanitation' (p. 1123).

Regarding particularism and generalisation, Jamie Peck (2015) advocates that a 'conjunctural' approach might be more appropriate, which considers particular social practices but also some meta processes and trends that prevail across different worlds. Together with agencies and particular histories and social processes in different places, a major theme such as governance financialisation is identified. In the case of Chinese market reform and its relation to neoliberalism, according to this conjunctural approach, China has seen a variegated version of overall trends,[42] which is not just worlding or policy mobility but is also driven by fundamental political economic conditions in China and the world.

This book is not about general urban theory but rather focuses on the Chinese city. Naturally, the concerns are inherently particular. Special attention has been paid to the historically and geographically concrete conditions of Chinese urbanisation. While set in the overall context of political economic changes, the book is particularly interested in changing social life and how the urban is constructed in diverse neighbourhoods. Economic forces and development approaches, such as land-financed development, are mentioned but are not the core concern of this book.[43] The intention is to contrast Chinese rurality, socialist collectivism and post-reform urbanism. Attention to the specific histories would reveal a process beyond Chinese specificity – that urbanisation is becoming a generalised process across the whole society, despite variegated and specific built forms.

The process has not been entirely engineered by the dominant actor (here the state) and its institution (for example, *hukou*, which is used to explain everything about the poverty of rural migrants in China-related literature). Besides seeing a series of practical actions in the specific historical contexts which lead to subsequent changes, the book has aimed to think about the more general conditions that we face in the contemporary urban world, arguably a process of 'planetary urbanisation'. In fact, besides particular history and culture, the concern here shares a remarkable similarity to anomie, a concept raised by Emile Durkheim in connection with earlier urbanisation in the West and the implications of 'metropolitan mental life',[44] and the concern in *Bowling Alone: The Collapse and Revival of American Community* by Robert Putnam (2000)[45] – declining social capital. But Putnam paid particular attention to television as a major leisure form in the United States since the 1960s. Considering the Chinese city, more attention here is paid to residential changes under the application of marketisation to a previously totalised society.

As suggested earlier, China has a long history of city building.[46] Its pace of urbanisation, however, has speeded up over the last four decades since the market reform. Owing to its specific development history and the large scale of city building, the Chinese experience of urbanisation may bring a new perspective to the understanding of 'emerging cities', here a trend from the absence of urbanism to greater urban life.

For example, the development of 'edge cities' and 'post-suburbia' has been understood through post-industrial restructuring and flexible accumulation. But the Chinese case indicates the need to understand the role of political leaders, and more generally the state in the process of urban development, as described by the thesis of 'the state acting through the market'.[47] Similarly, gated communities are widely understood in terms of lifestyle choice, a rising concern for security and a preference for 'private governance'. But the making of Chinese gated communities indicates a more supply-side reason. Associated with real estate projects, developers try to create an imaginary Western suburbia to brand suburban and rural areas. Gated communities are part of an overall development strategy supported by the entrepreneurial local state, which is incentivised by land-based development from land sales and constrained by its means of mobilising financial resources, because of the restriction on the local government raising money directly from the capital market.[48]

However, as discussed in Chapter 4, the development of gated communities is also indigenously driven by residents' desire for greater residential privacy, a better quality of living environment, a controlled personal sphere and family life, often as an imagined good life after the political turmoil.[49] These specificities mean that the overall trend might be generalised but would not be an exclusive agglomeration effect with differentiated capacities to bid on the land by different social groups.

This book has adopted a historical view of neighbourhood changes. Rather than seeing the state leading the whole process or engineering reform as a well-designed, coherent and intended project, there has been in fact no clear road map. The tactic was fairly pragmatic – 'across the river by groping stones'. It is also a 'worlding' practice.[50] Learning from successful East Asian newly industrialising economies and their developmental states, China initiated the market reform and switched to export-oriented industrialisation. This is an understanding of particularism about the particular Chinese state with its history of leading socialist revolution but maintaining neo-traditionalism throughout industrialisation. Industrialisation without urbanism sounds very particular, but there are both resemblances of the former socialist city under controlled urbanisation and persistence of 'street corner society' and 'urban villages', or 'ethnic enclaves' in the industrialised West.

Also, similar to the postcolonial global South where the understanding of the urban needs to relate to the classification of governance subjects (hence 'political society' rather than 'civil society') and re-mapping of the urban as governmental techniques,[51] the understanding of the implications of particular histories of rurality and state socialism for urban China reflects the 'geography of theories'.[52] But this particularism is not without a more general concern for urbanisation and social order, which was raised in earlier sociological studies of the urban.[53] Similarly, since the application of marketisation, Chinese society has embarked on a journey towards greater complexity, diversity and heterogeneity – a process observed at a close neighbourhood scale in this book.

This process is part of planetary urbanisation, which permeates every corner of the city and every fragment beyond the city. Social totality began to break down and, despite the techniques of governance, the city is no longer under a fundamental, singular control, reminiscent of anomie during rapid urbanisation, a universal proposition suggested by Emile Durkheim in nineteenth-century Europe. As we see in China, the market does not rise to a status that can dictate the whole of society, or the so-called 'market society' by Karl Polanyi (1944). Neither can the state leave the social order to a self-governed society. There was a *de facto* tendency of increasing autonomous spaces, as predicted by the consumer revolution thesis. But this has not led to urban China as a new civil society beyond 'rightful resistance'.[54] Rather, it is a process of urbanisation which has driven Chinese society away from its stable, static and predictable rurality, which raises the practical need for and possible approaches to the restoration of a social mentality which requires a social order emerging neither from the state nor from self-governed citizens. This is what we have observed in diverse neighbourhoods. These neighbourhoods are the building blocks of urban China, which may eventually return to an indigenously generated social order if they are not broken into chaos and might eventually provide the foundation of future Chinese society.

New urban China: informality, network and urbanity

Considering the classic notion of urbanism as anonymity, high density and diversity, we can identify some features of the Chinese city which have not been uniformly transformed into a 'market society'. New urban China is not a sterile place without social interaction. But sociality does not generate power – the right to the city. The society is underdeveloped. In the following pages we speculate about some features of new urban China.

First, informality still exists in Chinese neighbourhoods and their urban life. As Ananya Roy (2005) argues that informality represents a 'mode of urbanisation' in the global South, informal rental housing and the under-regulated built environment and accompanying social relations persist in China. Chinese urban villages are created by the 'everyday life' of rural migrants and the informal rental practices of farmers in peri-urban areas. These places naturally contain some features of the traditional society such as more frequent neighbouring and social interactions among renters.[55] Especially, in inner urban neighbourhoods, migrants encounter and interact more frequently with urban locales and develop social trust to some extent.[56] These neighbourhoods contain some sociability. In terms of governance, the form is also less hierarchical but involves multiple actors participating in an assemblage, crossing administrative boundaries.⁵⁷ The villagers' committee is largely a type of rural governance institution, underdeveloped in the socialist period compared with the more formal governance of state-owned enterprises. New shareholding cooperatives are horizontally linked with investors and developers. This is compounded by the legacies of clans and lineages.

The newly developed neighbourhoods are not sterile places. Even though urban villages occupy a marginal status, a vibrant everyday life still exists there, not only because of reciprocal support but also due to sharing informal communal spaces as well as the hawkers and street markets in these places. Because the state allows greater autonomy in both urban villages and gated communities, wishing that residents should look after themselves and sort out their daily lives and their own property maintenance, the dwellers in these places maintain informal social relations and interaction. For example, Yongshen Liu and Yung Yau (2020) observed in urban villages near Guangzhou University Town (a project of state entrepreneurialism):

> Vendors occupy the streets and roads selling barbecued food or snacks to cater to students' preference for a 'midnight-snack culture'. (p. 279)
>
> Empowered by the market rule, villagers, student-oriented commercial developers and self-employed migrant entrepreneurs extorted their power by developing a market society directed at the actual students and consumers of the area: university students and low-income tenants. (p. 285)

Similar to the 'urban villagers' described by Herbert Gans (1962) in the Italian neighbourhood of Boston, Chinese urban dwellers also engage in close interaction in their neighbourhoods where some features of the traditional society still persist.

This does not contradict the overall trend of transformation of social relations and urban life, because the traditional neighbourhoods and new rural villages in the city demonstrate a more organic everyday life of traditionalism than middle-class gated communities. The latter represent a more formal development in social life. This book suggests that even with intense interaction, a new social relation is largely forged on the basis of individuals rather than collectivism. The existence of informality thus does not mean that these new neighbourhoods remain like a static traditional society. Further informality is an outcome of the process of individualisation and will continue.

Second, new urban China becomes a translocal networked society, not only with greater linkage between Chinese cities and the outside world as well as the influx of migrants from rural to urban areas, but also with more intense interactions through networks across residential boundaries. Besides 'enclave urbanism',[58] there exists 'borderland urbanism'[59] where residents between different residential enclaves interact and associate in everyday life. When looking at the actual everyday lives of residents, they are seen as not bounded and isolated by these enclaves. Bart Wissink (2019a) suggests that 'an alternative relational comparative view', which 'understands enclaves as assemblages of heterogeneous elements that are themselves part of multiple assemblages operating on various "scales"' (p. 172) is more appropriate. A close examination of migrants' social networks reveals some diverse patterns which are not bounded by the neighbourhood.[60] In part, social interaction crossing boundaries is due to increasing residential mobility, as many no longer reside within the same neighbourhood but maintain contacts.[61] Intergroup interactions exist within and across neighbourhoods and social trust has been developed, though in an asymmetric form.[62]

The transformation of social contact and networks in China cannot be simply summarised as the dystopia that is typically characterised in the literature of the prototypical gated community.[63] The change of social contact and mentality cannot be measured just in terms of the distance of spatial reach. Or, if indeed spatial reach is considered, urban China has seen a pattern of 'planetary urbanisation', linking the urban with the vast rural area through migrant inflow and their translocal contacts, and crossing urban boundaries between spatially confined collectivism in rural villages or traditional alleyway neighbourhoods.

Both urban residents and rural migrants are more mobile. Despite spatially extended contacts and perhaps precisely due to this greater encountering, similar to what George Simmel described in the 'metropolis', residents become more atomised, centred upon self and family. The role of the residential community in urban life is declining (Figure 5.4), although the strength of neighbourhoods associated with a more 'economic man' and formal administratively oriented governance has been strengthened.

In the case of urban and rural villages, this intermediate space of sociability, which was once based on clans and lineages as 'collective' social structures, is replaced by shareholding companies of 'investors'. While the clan or territorially derived relation (people with the same origin of hometown, *laoxiang*) has not totally disappeared and continues to

Figure 5.4 A private club near Xintiandi, Shanghai. The club, on the upper floor of a jewellery store with the same owner, has become a venue for fashion and business. Taken in 2019.

exert an effect, its influence is mediated through social relations in the new urbanised context.

In the case of gated communities, social mobilisation is based on shared interests in properties, rather than a moral order established by and derived from a closer 'community'. Gated communities may also be spaces of social entertainment and leisure; but none of the members have sufficient information or comprehensive knowledge about the others. As such, following the description of the 'blasé metropolitan attitude',[64] they present an indifference towards others, a respect for residential privacy and a clearer distinction between the public and private spheres. Hence, these residential neighbourhoods are socially under-mobilised, except in the extreme form of 'neighbourhood activism' to defend their property rights.[65]

Third, new urban China also sees greater urbanity. The sphere of consumption demonstrates great diversity and discretionary styles (Figure 5.5). Everyday leisure, entertainment and spontaneous cultural activities are organised by grassroots residents,[66] potentially forming a new 'public space'.[67] While dancing in public squares and parks has been read politically as contestation to regulated everyday life by the

Figure 5.5 Taking a photo and strolling in Daning Park, Shanghai. Near the park are new commodity housing estates. The area is being upgraded with large shopping malls and green amenities. The scene shows everyday life in urban China. Taken in 2018.

authoritarian state,[68] public dancing as morning or evening exercise in fact reflects the desire for a more private reason of pleasure and health rather than a political and social purpose, in contrast to the political rallies seen in the socialist past in public squares (Figure 5.6).[69] Because of the shortage of leisure space, especially for low-income neighbourhoods in inner-urban areas, residents tend to occupy any possible communal space, streets and pavements by offices and commercial buildings during the evening. These are informal, spontaneous activities.

The leisure activities are apolitical. Awareness of the public sphere does not necessarily emerge from consumerism. Although dancing in public is a new phenomenon since economic reform, the informality and sociality is not a surprise as even during the peak of the socialist period, traditional neighbourhoods and to a lesser extent workplace neighbourhoods still demonstrated quite organic features. Instead of thinking of public dancing as a political statement, it exists mostly for leisure and health reasons. Noise and interference with other residents often cause tension and quarrels, demanding more stringent regulation. In traditional neighbourhoods, and even in more modern public housing estates, residents still

Figure 5.6 Dancing in a public park, Shanghai. Dancing in public spaces is an ordinary event. Owing to the high-density living environment, residents tend to use spare space for exercise, less for socialising and club formation. The elderly prefer free public space rather than commercially run gyms and clubs. Taken in 2019.

play *mahjong* along the roadside or in public spaces; public dancing is a natural extension as an increasing concern for health. There are commercially operated 'leisure centres' or 'card and chess playrooms' (*qipaishi*), but the elderly are unwilling or cannot afford to use these premises.

In upper-market housing estates, public dancing in the garden or square is rare. These gated communities have tennis courts, swimming pools or gyms for exercise. While informal leisure activities in traditional and inner urban areas continue to exist, the development of gated communities indicates the transformation of urban life along with residential changes. In all the types of neighbourhoods depicted in this book, neighbourhood social and entertainment activities are promoted by the state to enhance neighbourhood cohesion. As discussed in the implications for governance, emergent greater urbanism does not mean the development of a public realm. Along with individualisation and diminishing differential mode of association, the space of collectivism has been reduced. Instead of seeing the logic of rising consumerism and the creation of public space, in the context of 'urban revolution' a new social relation

Figure 5.7 A club, as the shop sign reads, for gymnastics, yoga and coffee. The commercially run club is becoming very popular with the Chinese middle class who are increasingly aware of health and a healthy lifestyle while facing high work pressure and busy urban life. This photo can be seen in comparison with the earlier photo of dancing in parks. Taken in 2019.

has been forged, less based on parochialism. Everyday life, neighbouring and social networks, and informal leisure activities continue to exist. But as we observe in urban neighbourhoods, there is a tendency that residents should now dance in community-organised leisure activities in a state-supplied community centre or in commercially operated gyms (Figure 5.7). Therefore, this communal space, used by a wide range of people for diverse activities, has not formed the Western meaning of public space from which a civil society emerges.

In short, the notion of anonymous urban life might be an exaggeration of the new urban China, as the legacy of the traditional society exists in the everyday life of urban dwellers, even though the level of intimacy has declined. The urban way of living characterised by anonymity, detachment from the neighbourhood and secondary relationships does not apply to all Chinese neighbourhoods.[70] In the world of rural migrants, such a state without full assimilation can exist for a prolonged time. For example, in the most developed city of Shenzhen, rural migrant workers in Foxconn may get stuck as manual workers living in a factory dormitory, subject to strict social management.[71] Similarly, many living in urban villages in the peri-urban area may never find a way to become an urban citizen, hence spatially and socially 'getting stuck' in industrial parks.[72] Their lives may never be fully 'anonymised' as a consumer since they are involved in social interaction in a network form with great informality and urbanity.

Notes

1. For the 'nature of cities', see Scott and Storper, 2015; see the debate later in this chapter.
2. Davis et al., 1995; Davis, 2000.
3. Walder, 1986.
4. The figure was released by the National Statistical Bureau on 30 April 2021.
5. Fan et al., 2011.
6. See Shi and Tang, 2020; Shao et al., 2020. See also, Smith, 2021, for an in-depth study of Chongqing.
7. See Roy, 2016, who argues that the urban question in India is an agrarian question. See also Gururani, 2020.
8. Zhu, 2019.
9. See Wu, 2020a.
10. Scott and Storper (2015) argue that it is important to distinguish the essence of the city from other social phenomena existing inside the city. The essence is an agglomerated form of activities.
11. For example, Brenner and Schmid (2014) argue that we should not treat the urban as a bounded entity like the city. The urban is a process, representing a special social relation.
12. Simone, 2016.
13. Peake, 2016.
14. Simone, 2016.
15. Parnell and Pieterse, 2016.
16. Walker, 2016.
17. Cochrane, 2018.
18. Robinson, 2011.
19. Robinson, 2011; McFarlane, 2011; Dovey et al., 2018; Cochrane, 2018.
20. Zhang, 2008.
21. Wu et al., 2020.
22. See Wu, 2020a; for the case of new town and the assemblage of governance, see Shen et al. (2020).
23. See Wu et al., 2020.
24. Indeed, Harvey (1978) explains the 'urban process' under capitalism.
25. Brenner and Schmid, 2015.
26. Scott and Storper, 2015.
27. Angelo and Wachsmuth, 2015.
28. Cochrane, 2018.
29. Wu, 2016a.
30. Lefebvre, 1991.
31. Wu, 2010a.
32. Wu, 2015.
33. Wu, 2004b.
34. In the sense of 'public choice' theory, for gated communities.
35. Huang, 1993 and 2019.
36. Robinson, 2006.
37. Robinson, 2006. See also, Wissink (2019b) on the comparison of gated communities.
38. Roy and Ong, 2011.

39. Sheppard et al., 2013: 895.
40. Sheppard et al., 2013.
41. Roy, 2009a.
42. Peck and Zhang, 2013.
43. See Wu et al. (2007) for urban development, Wu (2015) for city planning, and more recently Wu et al. (2020) and Wu (2022) for the condition of financialisation.
44. See Parker, 2015: 44.
45. Please note, the community does not exclusively refer to residential neighbourhoods.
46. From Wu, 2020a.
47. Wu, 2020c.
48. Wu, 2022.
49. See also Wu, 2004b.
50. Roy and Ong, 2011.
51. Roy, 2016.
52. Roy, 2009a.
53. Parker, 2015.
54. O'Brien and Li, 2006.
55. Wu and Logan, 2016.
56. Wang et al., 2017b.
57. See Allen and Cochrane (2007) for the idea of assemblage in governance.
58. Wu, 2005; He, 2013; Hendrikx and Wissink, 2017.
59. Iossifova, 2015.
60. Wissink et al., 2014.
61. Hazelzet and Wissink, 2012.
62. Wang et al., 2016; Wang et al., 2017b.
63. Pow, 2015.
64. The expression was developed by George Simmel.
65. Shin, 2013; Cai and Sheng, 2013; Yip and Jiang, 2011.
66. Qian, 2014; Qian, 2019.
67. Orum et al., 2009.
68. Kraus, 2000.
69. Gaubatz, 2019.
70. Wu and Wang, 2019: 50. Perhaps this classic generalisation of urbanism does not apply to anywhere, and it has been subject to wide critique, especially from the perspective of the production of space and the urban as assemblage of everyday life.
71. Li et al., 2019.
72. Shen, 2017.

Conclusion: a visible state emerging from urban revolution

This book has documented the impact of marketisation on Chinese society. Observing grassroots society, I have depicted the landscape of urbanisation – an urban revolution – and explained the urban roots of a visible state. In this way, I do not start from authoritarianism as a defining feature, as an ideal type of Chinese model or Chinese characteristics, in the sense of 'neoliberalism with Chinese characteristics'.[1] Rather, I have taken a reverse direction of enquiry, seeking to understand the new features of governance from a grounded understanding of the process of urbanisation. Therefore, the book is more about China's urbanism than its governance and politics.[2] The current book does not engage much with the rich literature of political studies on China,[3] though this would be a fruitful future endeavour.

Studies on Chinese politics often take a macroscopic view, though they may be developed through specific cases. They are not in the field of urban studies. On the other hand, urban geographical studies often regard the general social process as a defining parameter for the city and tend to discover urban changes as variegated manifestations of the general social process.[4] However, this study aims to understand how the urban process generates urban governance features.

The initial de-collectivisation and fiscal decentralisation in rural areas generated great incentives for village cadres to become local entrepreneurs, turning the local state into what Jean Oi (1992) termed 'local state corporatism'. The initial rural reform created township and village enterprises (TVEs) and introduced quasi-corporate governance.[5] However, rural village administration was still underdeveloped, remaining as self-governing collectives and influenced by traditional structures such as lineages.[6] Therefore, Chinese rural society has been partially urbanised into a hybrid of village shareholding economy and traditional societies. However, near the central cities, rural villages have become 'urban villages'. Village-initiated real estate projects and related corporate governance, in the form of villagers' 'self-expropriation' and reaction towards state-led urban expansion, turned the rural village into the 'village-as-the-city'.[7] This has meant a profound change in Chinese society, as Nick Smith described in *The End of the Village* (2021):

> For a nation long defined by its rural institutions and culture (Fei [1947]1992), the loss of its villages would represent a fundamental change. (p. 242)

This book has provided a nuanced understanding of this *major* aspect of urban change, which is complementary to existing studies on social and governance changes in China. In the 1990s, there was a debate on 'market transition' and its implications for social stratification. Market transition predicts declining state redistribution and rising market actors who participate directly in production and market exchange.[8] However, the thesis of power persistence suggests the continuation of state officials in the new market economy and the persisting influence of socialist redistribution institutions such as the workplace system on housing differentiation and residential segregation and benefits.[9] Regarding the 'transition' debate, this book has pinpointed the exact change. Concurring with the transition argument, observed in inner-urban neighbourhoods and rural villages before this 'market transition', we witnessed the disappearance of traditionalism built upon its differential mode of association and the appearance of a seemingly pervasive market society. However, Chinese urbanity differs from an imagined self-organising market society which might not work in any circumstance.[10] In this regard, the book is in agreement with the power persistence thesis and highlights the development of a more visible state managing society in the process of urbanisation. However, different from seeing the *continuation* of socialist institutions in history, the book reveals changes in governance. As mentioned, this book tends to complement existing China and urban studies on transition and continuation rather than offer a complete shift of paradigm. This is largely dependent upon the emphasis on a 'half-empty bottle'.

First, political studies on China continue to focus on Chinese state authoritarianism, which is regarded as a continuation of its governance feature despite new market mechanisms in economic development.[11] While the original intention of Andrew Walder seemed to explore the features of authoritarianism (though it had a traditional root), this book stresses the 'traditionalism' feature in workplace neighbourhoods. From political studies on China, state adaptability and resilience have been noted,[12] and so have other political and economic changes, such as the 'informalisation' of Chinese workforces[13] and land-driven economic development entailing land grabs, village demolition and relocation of villagers into high-rise apartments in urbanised areas.[14] However, the state maintains control over the pace of urbanisation, the size and distribution of cities,[15] strengthening the management of grassroots society,[16] and bureaucratisation. Very few studies link micro and macro studies together. This is the value of urban studies for understanding politics. Mark Frazier (2019) scales down his unit of analysis to the level of the city and compares contentious politics in Shanghai and Bombay. He suggests that place-based politics have a generative implication, which he terms 'the power of place', for a national political landscape. This book takes a similar stance. In short, as summarised elsewhere,[17] across different scales of neighbourhoods, metropolitan areas and city-regions, the role of the state in urban governance is visible. On the other hand, China's urbanisation is incomplete and some 'traditional' features may still remain even in today's China, as many researchers have found when they paid visits to Chinese neighbourhoods.[18]

Second, looking at social studies on China, the remaining features of traditional societies are stressed in a vast literature of Chinese studies.[19] For example, social network analysis (about *guanxi*) has been developed, derived from the differential mode of association.[20] However, the concept of *guanxi* is now often used in a modern corporate context. In this regard, the spread of *guanxi* might be also seen as an indication of the collapse of traditionalism rather than a revival of traditionalism. Further, an extensive literature on urban villages emphasises the degree of informality, with reference to traditional features of lineage and clan, and continuing collective economies.[21] This book, on the other hand, argues that the source of informality derives from marketisation (if not neoliberalisation) which becomes a *new* mode of governance, similar to other places in the global South.[22] Social relations in changing traditional alleyway and workplace neighbourhoods, urban villages and gated communities become more about exchange than reciprocity. Social control built upon the traditional relations of the 'society of acquaintance' no longer works. Fast urbanisation imposes profound challenges to the social and moral order, as witnessed by more advanced Western market societies in their respective stages of urbanisation. However, the attention paid to Chinese traditionalism as social and cultural particularism is useful in that it helps to go beyond an understanding of urbanism as the contrast between the *generic* urban and rural ecologies. Thus, by depicting a landscape of urban revolution, now becoming 'planetary', this book highlights how urbanism unfolds in a geographically distinct context – Chinese social topography. One salient feature is the lack of self-organising society resulting from the end of the differential mode of association, which creates an imperative for a visible state. Despite observation of social actors, residual collectivism and prolonged traditionalism, the replacement of the differential mode of association by urbanism does not have a sufficiently strong foundation (the 'soil' in Fei Xiaotong's words) to meet the challenge of pervasive marketisation witnessed in Chinese society.

Urban governance seen from neighbourhoods

This book has observed residential changes from diverse urban neighbourhoods to think through political and governance implications. In particular, society is brought into scope to understand changing state and market relations, usually framed as 'neoliberalism'.[23] Is there a consumer revolution leading to the development of neighbourhoods as 'consumer clubs' under 'private governance'? The postcolonial perspective attempts to answer such a question in a similar context by looking into the colonial history. The structure of colonial governance continues to affect current governance and the construction of social order, not leading to a civil society but rather to a 'political society' in terms of a politically associated relation of residents with the state.[24] This is manifested as the detachment of certain groups (the 'subaltern') from the governance structure, though they continue to exert their influence through their contestation, actions and agencies. This form of governance is noted as 'subaltern urbanism'.[25] Similarly, this book has attempted to look into China's urban history – the making of the urban – to understand its governance features.

Over the last four decades, the overarching political economic change for the Chinese city has been market reform. There are debates about whether we should characterise the urban change as 'neoliberal urbanism' in China.[26] Earlier studies have described a fully-fledged process of marketisation and commodification. Later studies have seen modifications and revisions of the original thesis into a variegated form. Jamie Peck and Jun Zhang (2013) regard Chinese capitalism as a variegated type between the ideal types of liberal market economies modelled on the US and coordinated market economies modelled on Germany. The strength of their analysis is to understand the dynamics through a Polanyian perspective.

Aggressive market development in the 1990s, after Deng Xiaoping's southern tour in 1992, most decisively in the commodification of labour and land, has created a tendency to move towards a 'market society'. 'Land finance' as a major source of government income further led to what You-tien Hsing (2010) called 'urban transformation' – a far-reaching 'urbanisation' of the Chinese state. For the state, 'urban modernity, more than industrial modernity, now captures the political imagination of local state leaders' (pp. 4–5). The social and urban changes are seen as the outcomes of this political economic change. Further, to cope with a series of social crises, society's self-protection mechanism started to work. More precisely, after the initial radical reform in the 1990s, the 2000s saw a 'double movement' during which the state played a more visible role. The campaign of 'community construction' was initiated in this context at that time. From the more visible roles of the state since the 2010s, it has been speculated that China has departed from neoliberalism to move closer to the 'state developmentalism' of East Asia.[27]

It is evident that the Chinese state has strengthened its roles in neighbourhood governance through the campaign of 'community construction' – systematic grassroots governance,[28] and later a specific technology of 'grid governance'.[29] It is not about the degree of state intervention,[30] which is not disputable in research as shown in the need to denote 'neoliberalism with Chinese characteristics'.[31] It is a question of the *origin* of strong and visible state roles while an opposite market mechanism is prevailing. A further modification of the thesis might be using the 'growth machine' or growth coalition between the state and capital, suggesting that capital is becoming dominant and so the state is serving the interest of capitalists. But through neighbourhood governance, we have revealed the foundation of strengthened state roles in urban life.

To restore social order in urban space, a new mode of governance has been experimented with, similar to the account of the 'double movement', which moves beyond neoliberalism and comes closer to state developmentalism in East Asia. Here the attention to East Asian culture is useful – pointing to the origins of a collectivism that has existed in these societies for a long time. These societies may not have been very neoliberal, despite drastic market development. In the case of China, market reform is neither for the interest of a new bourgeois class nor leading to the dominance of market coordination.[32]

The use of the market is instrumental but the market remains an instrument while the centrality of planning power persists.[33] The transition to the market and the retention of state intervention might be intentional (as a national developmental strategy) but is perhaps imperative (as a 'double movement'). It was hard for the state to remain, or to hide, inside the society as it used to be. In that context, it used to operate as a small administrative class of 'cadres' (though their status is ambiguous as they were also, according to the ideology, 'serving the people', or were part of the proletarian class) together with a largely 'totalised', 'self-governed' and organic society before China was 'completely urbanised'[34] through an 'urban revolution'. In that kind of society, ideological positioning was important as society had to accept the principle of self-regulation and mutual monitoring. Now, it is necessary to resort to a more technical governance, as China is becoming urban. For example, in the case of the Fifth Village, a woman migrant was required to show her marriage certificate. But in her rural village, this would not have been necessary as everyone would know her marriage status. Similarly, even in the early stage of economic reform, work-units still issued letters to prove the marriage status of their employees because the workplace knew their employees well. These characterised the traditional society from the soil – and in consequence a totalised governance form.

Market reform has created greater inequalities and has led to the dismantling of traditional society and greater alienation. After the state's initial retreat, state capacity building, seen as a Polanyian turn, was initiated in the 2000s and continued in the 2010s. The year 2020 perhaps marks a watershed. The global pandemic, the shrinkage of the global market and rising populism demand more than ever a stronger and more active state. This might not reverse the 'urban revolution' started after market reform, but the making of the urban is also more important and imperative than before as a new form of economy and society.

There has been serious doubt about 'whether neoliberalism can capture the central stories or trajectories of Chinese urban transformation', according to Yu Zhou, George Lin and Jun Zhang (2019):

> By citing examples of recent urban China research, we show that the neoliberalism framework, even in its 'variegated' or 'assemblage' version, tends to trap China's analysis within a frame of reference comfortable to Western researchers, and ultimately hinders the development of diversified, potentially more fruitful inquiries of the urban world. (p. 33)

They argue that previous more political economic–oriented studies did not pay sufficient attention to the urban sphere. The political economic perspective, according to them, focuses more on the omnipotent state or its specific forms of state governance, for example, fragmented authoritarianism – sectoral and territorial fragmentation,[35] central and local government relations, and the entrepreneurial state. They appeal for an understanding of a 'spontaneous recombination and reconfiguration of the urbanising society at the grassroots level' (p. 39).

It is true to some extent that urban development under state socialism presented an 'organised' feature. But this does not mean that the Chinese city at that time was an entirely modernised industrial entity operated by the state apparatus. Traditional features did continue in Chinese state-organised consumption. It is also true that urban development in the post-reform era demonstrated the role of the entrepreneurial state and its greater willingness to deploy market instruments.[36] But again the application of the market mechanism does not mean that the Chinese city has become a more self-organised society where the market rules through private governance. The difference here, as stressed in this book, is the extent of urbanisation.

The key point stressed in this book on urban neighbourhoods is that society before market transformation had many of the features of a traditional society with close and territorial social relations. The transition is not from a state-controlled society to a society of public/civic life based on social interaction and 'communities'. Instead, as described by 'bargained authoritarianism',[37] the state is more responsive to the practical needs of stability, crisis management and problems through policy initiatives and actions. There is indeed great agency within society. The urbanisation process transforms traditional features, and is also accompanied by 'individualisation' and consumerism as already described in anthropological[38] and sociological studies,[39] leading to the creation of a new urban space which is simultaneously a new state space.

The direction of the transition seems to be opposite to what has been described so far[40] – from a bureaucratic and authoritarian state-controlled society to an organic and communitarian society. Partly this is because earlier studies understated the 'organic' features of the socialist city. Residential communities have been transformed. In the post-reform Chinese city, there is now a more networked society, and the scope of communities has expanded to consumer clubs which may not be territorially based. But the course of urbanisation is not singularly designed or led by the state. The state hoped to get rid of 'administrative burdens' and pragmatically applied the market mechanism and instruments to the Chinese economy.[41] But in reality, the state is being led by the ever-changing process of urbanisation – an urban revolution – and further, the state is being remade, at least in its urban governance function. A whole set of changes has been created, including urbanisation, which have subsequently transformed the relations between the state and society, so that the state has become disembedded from its previous position, creating the imperative for 'urban governance', often through complex interactions with society and the market.

While recent political and sociological studies are able to present a more nuanced and complex picture of the Chinese state through concepts such as 'fragmented authoritarianism'[42] or 'bargained authoritarianism',[43] the notion of authoritarianism is convenient but problematic. It is not an authoritarianism that became fragmented or has had to bargain with the rising power of the society. A more dynamic view is required to treat the state beyond its static feature – as if an omnipotent position of authoritarian state remains.

From the field of urban studies, this book has documented the emergence of a 'modern' state in these neighbourhoods during market reform. This perspective shows that the state was embedded in a totalised society in the past and marketisation began to generate a new governance functionality of the state. That is, the state does not retreat from neighbourhood governance or follow the course of neoliberalism. It is an application of the market rule but also a consequential professionalisation of the state. The state is no longer embedded within a totalised society which now demonstrates features that are different from those of a traditional society. China is becoming an 'urbanised' society, leaving the foundation of the differential mode of association.

Urban revolution in China

The thesis of the 'private city' emerges from the context of the nation state of Keynesianism in the West.[44] Now, a small group of actors, or the 'club realm', controls fragmented urban spaces, assets and their management through corporate organisations. In this club realm theory, the state is absent, transaction costs are reduced, and the efficiency of service provision is increased. Hence, it is appropriately noted as 'neoliberal urbanism'.

In contrast, China did not have universal citizenship. In the collectivist tradition, a small group, either village or work-unit, is known as the 'public'. There was no modernist state or metropolitan 'urban'.[45] Similar to the socialist city where urbanism and the spontaneity of the urban landscape was absent,[46] the Chinese city and countryside comprised an assemblage of public collectives before the urban revolution. In a sense, they were 'villages'. In the tradition of East Asia, this feature might be attributed to its collectivist culture.

Now, urban revolution in China should be seen as the end of traditional collectivism and the creation of a new way of urban life. This is not the replacement of a universal welfare state by private (collective) governance. The previous socialist approach of 'industrialisation without urbanisation', which refers not only to the low level of the urban population due to *hukou* constraints but also to the lack of urbanity, has been abandoned with the adoption of globalisation and making Chinese society 'urban' as the 'workshop of the world'. It is true that initial urbanisation might have occurred in the villages of the Pearl River Delta where overseas Chinese investors set up small workshops. But this is exactly the urbanisation of the countryside. Since then, the Chinese city has no longer seen the compact, built-up world of the state realm. The urban is becoming a pervasive process outside the boundary of the city, similar to what is described by 'planetary urbanisation'.[47] Most importantly, the urbanisation process is also embodied in concrete residential changes in these neighbourhoods which are transforming and emerging, as described in this book. This urban world is diverse and consists of people who are in practice living an everyday urban life but may not officially be classified as urban and do not enjoy entitlements – rural migrants living in urban villages may be similar to the subaltern in the global South.[48] In other words, this urban world is characterised by 'local capitalisms, local citizenships'.[49]

The urban revolution is characterised by diminishing traditionalism as the traditional society of collectivism experiences transformation from close neighbourhood engagement to a more diverse, individualised and networked life. Collective space is pressured from two fronts: the market and the state. The increasing, pervasive operation of the market in urban development has introduced a new governance of development. In rural villages and then in urban villages, the corporatisation of villagers' collective assets through shareholding cooperatives has transformed the residential neighbourhood of collective space into an asset-holding community. As for informal urban villages, the state strives to regularise them through demolition and the development of a more formal rental housing market. Demolition and resettlement signify an entire transformation of rural collective society. In many remaining urban villages, the state takes a rather lax approach before demolition, which is often read as 'neoliberal' as the state does not deliver public services and infrastructure, as in fact the rural farmers had never been inside the welfare system of the socialist state.

The problems created by informal developments such as the village of Tangjialing in Beijing from time to time require the state to take action, demonstrating some features of the developmental state creating and regulating the formal economy. The poor informal environment is not up to the aspirations of the rising middle class, and the development of gated and enclosed estates is the norm rather than the exception. For example, in 2017, a fire in the village in the Daxing district of Beijing triggered large-scale demolition and redevelopment. The policy of redevelopment is known as 'dispersing, regulating and upgrading'.[50] The upgrading of informal space aims to 'optimise' the function of Beijing as a world-class capital. The emergence of urban villages and gated estates indicates the creation of new urban spaces that are not under traditional collectivism.

Reading the Chinese urban revolution requires us to develop new narratives and vocabularies. In the post-industrial West, the concepts of gentrification and suburbanisation have been commonly invoked as the key aspects of urban transformation. However, they may not capture *all* the aspects of urbanisation in China.[51] Despite a now substantially expanded connotation to include upgrading, displacement, dispossession and demolition,[52] gentrification may still be quite specific, and perhaps it would be better for the concept to retain some specificity as its meaning is much clearer when this is so.[53]

Certainly, many aspects of gentrification occur in Chinese neighbourhoods. For example, some alleyway neighbourhoods are being gentrified, and gated estates in the peri-urban areas could also be seen as the displacement of the original rural farmers, hence rural gentrification. However, the emergence and transformation of all the neighbourhoods described in this book cannot be summarised as gentrification. As the title of Ruth Glass's book – *London: Aspects of Change* (1964) – suggests, gentrification is seen as an overarching description to capture the 'aspects of change' in cities like London. Similarly, in this spirit, by visiting diverse neighbourhoods in China, this book has attempted to discover the *major* aspect of change in urban China. I believe that it is *urbanisation* in its broad sense of 'leaving the soil' – an urban revolution or departure from 'the society from the soil' as seminally captured by renowned Chinese sociologist Fei Xiaotong in the early 20th century.

This book has demonstrated the dismantling of the differential mode of association (*chaxugeju*) and 'neo-traditionalism' in new urban China. From investigating urban neighbourhoods, I have identified two mechanisms. First, the state uses the market as an instrument to promote economic growth and deliver services in Chinese cities. This is known as 'state entrepreneurialism'. Thus, the state has become an actor in urban development. Market development has driven greater consumer choice and consumerism, creating a new space outside traditionalism. Second, the intensification of 'urban' problems and governance challenges pulled the state out of its neo-traditionalist position embedded within society. Compared with an underdeveloped society threatened by marketisation, the state has taken a role as arbitrator between the market and society, leading to the final separation of the state and society. The reform of neighbourhood governance demonstrates not only the intention to 'control' society but also a necessary and practical way, seen by the state, to develop social protection mechanisms and to maintain a social order.[54]

Conclusion

This book depicts the landscape of 'urban revolution' in China, which started in 1979 – the turning point when the state decided to introduce the market mechanism into economic production and social reproduction, initially as a pragmatic solution to the problem of lagging development. Later, the application of market instruments was broadened and included coordination and governance. Manifested as large-scale rural-to-urban migration, urban sprawl and extension, urban demolition and residential relocation, this urban revolution has propelled residential changes and led to greater residential diversity. New neighbourhoods such as urban villages and gated communities have been created, while traditional neighbourhoods have been demolished and transformed. An extensive literature has documented urban construction or city-building.[55] To a lesser extent, the emergence of urbanism and urban China as social transformation has been understood in its entirety.[56] While specific social changes such as residential segregation, displacement and rural-to-urban migration have been extensively studied, a holistic view is much needed to rethink the nature of the urban in post-reform China.

China's market transition is essentially a response to the growth constraints inherent in the earlier extensive and military-oriented industrialisation period.[57] In other words, market reform was adopted as a fix to an economy suffocated by the lack of growth space. Market-oriented urban changes thus opened up a new space for accumulation. However, by applying the market instrument to urban development, a distinct form of urbanism has been produced, in sharp contrast to socialism which emphasises uniformity and collectiveness.[58]

In the context of advanced Western capitalism, David Harvey (2008) convincingly argues for such a thorough process of commodification, suggesting that:

> the most recent radical expansion of the urban process has brought with it incredible transformations of lifestyle… . The quality of urban life has become a commodity, as has the city itself, in a world where consumerism, tourism, cultural and knowledge-based industries have become major aspects of the urban political economy. The postmodernist penchant for encouraging the formation of market niches – in both consumer habits and cultural forms – surrounds the contemporary urban experience with an aura of freedom of choice. (p. 31)

Along with market development, a new urban way of life, called 'new urbanism' by Neil Smith (2002), is prevailing,[59] which emphasises choice, diversity and the private governance of development, for example in the form of gated communities. In the United States, the wide spread of gated communities and private control of urban space have led to concern over the 'demise of the public space'.[60] In short, this new form of urbanism has been produced as an outcome of neoliberalisation.

In China, we are witnessing the development of a distinct form of urbanism characterised by great diversity and emphasis on the private residential realm.[61] In the past, uniformity and collectiveness were the basic features of Chinese urbanism under state socialism.[62] The construction of workplace compounds or workers' quarters[63] reinforced what Andrew Walder (1986) called 'communist neo-traditionalism', which lacked the diversity normally associated with an urban realm. The private sphere was constrained or intruded on by the state through state-organised collective consumption. Housing developed in the pre-1949 era was converted into public rentals and became a living space of multiple occupancies. Residents even had to share a kitchen and toilet and communal space. The workplace affiliation reinforced close relations in residential neighbourhoods.

Market development brings in a new consumerism to rebalance the private and public spheres. The new middle class experiences unprecedented choice and mobility. Coincident with disillusion over the socialist utopia, they begin to search for a new lifestyle in gated communities. As they retreat to a more private residential realm, we witness a similar trend of changing residential preference, under China's market-oriented urban changes, from utopia to 'myopia' or 'dystopic' urban space.[64] Similar to American suburbia, which is characterised by single-family housing, great social homogeneity and a particularly gendered way of life,[65] Chinese suburbia meets the demand of the upwardly mobile middle class for a new fantasy of the good life. Many gated communities in China have fancy Western names, such as Orange County, Riviera, Fontainebleau or Thames Town.

As a result, the Chinese city shows increasing diversity and inequality. These development projects emphasise individual preference and choice and the private form of consumption. Just as the planned residential district known as 'mikroraion' in the former Soviet Union, which was to cultivate the spirit of the 'socialist man',[66] these newly built residences in the suburbs of Chinese cities attempt to produce a pool of consumers who can appreciate the aesthetics of built forms. As a result, design features are constantly boasted about by developers, to suggest that their development represents a new form of urbanism.[67] Novelty is not measured through a sense of time alone: older imperial or colonial forms can be re-invented under the name of 'heritage preservation', for example the Xintiandi project as part of Shanghai nostalgia.[68]

Market-oriented urban changes and the new form of urbanism have a dialectical relationship. Under market-oriented urban development, the city is used as a 'spatial fix' to absorb surplus capital and defer an over-accumulation crisis. Through market-oriented urban changes, for example commodity housing development, new forms of the built environment and lifestyles have been produced. On the other hand, the new form of urbanism is advocated to attract consumers so as to make development viable.[69] The new form of urbanism is not a passive result of market transition. Rather, it has been consciously developed and branded as a more modern, more civilised and more desirable living environment.[70]

Therefore, since the 1990s we have seen the wide spread of practices to transplant Western residential landscapes, construct iconic buildings, and conduct city beautification in Chinese cities.[71] Similar to the role of Haussmannisation in Paris in early capitalist development, these practices, through a set of new cultural forms and symbols, play a crucial function in sustaining market-oriented urban changes. As such, broadly defined 'neoliberalisation' should include, in addition to the changing state–market relation, wider social-cultural changes associated with market development, which transform everyday practices under the principle of market exchange, namely a process of so-called 'bourgeois societalisation', according to Bob Jessop (2002). This book has explored similar social processes and consequences of market development in

China, but without presuming that this would be a neoliberal urban trajectory towards a civil society.

Focusing on diverse neighbourhoods, this book has contrasted today's changing neighbourhoods with a more rural China – Kaixiangong village as depicted by Fei Xiaotong in 1947 – and with workers' villages and more marginal alleyway neighbourhoods in socialist industrialising China, before China embarked on the journey to 'urban revolution'. The overall trend of social life is that these neighbourhoods are 'leaving the soil' – metaphorically the foundation of rural China – and witnessing a new form of urbanism. This has been forerun by individualisation away from clans and lineages in rural areas and subsequently in the Chinese city.[72]

Now, the new urban has seen the breaking out of individuals from the previous bonded collectivism established by the differential mode of association (*chaxugeju*). The dismantling of collectivism and the social class behind 'traditionalism' means that 'private governance' might be an option to maintain a social order and for residents to make sense of urban life. But in reality, private governance does not work for most neighbourhoods, except in the urban village where the shareholding cooperative seems to impose some authority over the renters of collective village assets. But even so, the rental of housing is largely managed by individual households themselves. In other words, we have not seen an emergent civil society based on their participation in the market.

Instead of seeing the creation of private governance and an associated civil society in China, the imperative of developing an administrative order has been forged. Fast urbanisation presents great challenges and is seen as problematic because it cannot easily be comprehended by the administrative system, which indeed imposes serious governance demands. In solving various practical problems generated by applying the market mechanism to an organic society which had not been fully transformed by the socialist revolution in 1949, the state has intentionally or unintentionally but in practice become 'professionalised'. This process of professionalisation, the establishment of a more bureaucratic social order, is often read as the evidence for a visible authoritarian state. But this book has revealed its urban roots.

While the initiative of 'community construction' starting in the 2000s tried to restore an organic society of collectivism and create a buffer or a new interface between the state and individualised citizens, the space of traditionalism is increasingly becoming narrower. Although great efforts have been made to mobilise 'society', the tide of individualisation is difficult to reverse. The promotion of residential communities – whether physically through the development of new village resettlement estates in places such as Tangjialing new town in Beijing where the 'ant tribe' lived, suburban gated housing estates, or socially by creating homeowners' associations or neighbourhood sociability through leisure activities – does not overcome the desire for greater residential privacy. It is impossible to replicate a new collectivism in these places. As a result, these spaces have embarked on the journey towards greater urbanism. We are now seeing a new urban China and a more visible state no longer in an embedded relation with society. Thinking about the differential (*chaxu*) mode (*geju*) of association which characterised Chinese society before its urban revolution, differential relations (*guanxi*) persist but the mode, rationality, or order (*geju*) has perished.

Notes

1. See Harvey, 2005.
2. This might be a different book in the future, about Chinese state entrepreneurialism.
3. This is the core of China studies; see Saich, 2015; Heilmann and Perry, 2011; Thornton, 2013.
4. One useful perspective is to examine property rights so as to understand how different property rights regimes define consequential urban forms. See Qian, 2022.
5. See also Oi, 1999; Smith, 2021.
6. See also Tsai, 2007; Oi, 1999; Smith, 2021.
7. Smith, 2021: 180.
8. Nee, 1989.
9. Bian and Logan, 1996.
10. Here, this is a Polanyian argument.
11. For example, the authoritarian state encounters great difficulties in collecting economic performance data; Wallace, 2016.
12. Heilmann and Perry, 2011.
13. Frazier, 2011; Giles et al., 2006; Park and Cai, 2011.
14. See Ong, 2014; Rithmire, 2015; Yep and Forrest, 2016; Yep and Wu, 2020.
15. Wallace, 2014; Jaros, 2019.
16. Perry and Goldman, 2007; Read, 2012; Thornton, 2013.
17. Wu and Zhang, 2022
18. For example, Audin, 2020; Tynen, 2019.
19. For example, village shareholding cooperatives; see Wong, 2016; Sargeson, 2018; Kan, 2019b.
20. Bian, 2019. See Dillon and Oi (2008) for the application of networks and actors in state-building in republican Shanghai.
21. For example, Sa, 2021.
22. Here I refer to Ananya Roy (2005).
23. See Keith et al. (2014) and Buckingham (2017) for the critique of applying the concept of neoliberalism to China.
24. Chatterjee, 2004.
25. Roy, 2016.
26. There is a large body of literature on this topic: Walker and Buck, 2007; He and Wu, 2009; Wu, 2008; 2010b; 2018b; Chu and So, 2012; Peck and Zhang, 2013; Zhou et al., 2019.
27. Chu and So, 2012.
28. Tomba, 2014.
29. Tang, 2020.
30. Wu and Zhang, 2022.
31. Harvey, 2005.
32. This is elaborated in Wu, 2010b.

33. Wu, 2018b.
34. Brenner and Schmid, 2011.
35. For fragmented authoritarianism, see Mertha, 2009.
36. Wu et al., 2007; Wu, 2015; Wu, 2018b.
37. The concept is developed by Lee and Zhang, 2013.
38. Yan, 2010.
39. Davis, 2000.
40. As represented in Davis et al. (1995) and Davis (2000).
41. As presented in discarding ideological argument and focusing on 'economic efficiency'.
42. Mertha, 2009.
43. Lee and Zhang, 2013.
44. Glasze et al., 2006.
45. Municipal institutions were experimented with in republican China; see Stapleton, 2000.
46. Andrusz et al., 1996; Hirt, 2012.
47. Brenner and Schmid, 2015.
48. Simone and Pieterse, 2018; Roy, 2011, 2016.
49. Smart and Lin, 2007.
50. Cecilia Wong et al., 2018.
51. Perhaps other places too; see Wu, 2020c.
52. Lees, 2012; Lees et al., 2016.
53. For an introduction to the concept, see Hamnett, 2021; for the debate on the usage, see Schmid et al., 2018.
54. This is to some extent captured by the thesis of bargained authoritarianism; Lee and Zhang, 2013.
55. Wu et al., 2007; Campanella, 2008; Lin, 2009.
56. With the exception of Friedmann, 2005, and more recently Forrest et al., 2019.
57. Wu, 2010b.
58. Szelenyi, 1996.
59. Smith, 2002. Others have called this 'neoliberal urbanism'; Walks, 2006.
60. Low, 2003.
61. Wu, 2005; Pow, 2009; Wu, 2010a.
62. Lin, 2007; Wu, 2009a.
63. Bray, 2005; Lu, 2006; Wu, 2015.
64. See MacLeod and Ward, 2002, and Pow, 2015.
65. Beauregard, 2006.
66. French and Hamilton, 1979.
67. Wu, 2009b; 2010b.
68. He and Wu, 2005; Ren, 2008.
69. See Wu et al., 2020, for housing financialisation and its contribution to the overall Chinese regime of accumulation.
70. Vis-à-vis moral geography, see Pow, 2009; 2015.
71. Wu, 2007b; 2016b; 2020a.
72. Rising consumerism contributes to this process.

References

Aalbers, Manuel B., Loon, Jannes Van, & Fernandez, Rodrigo. (2017). The financialization of a social housing provider. *International Journal of Urban and Regional Research, 41*(4), 572–87.
Abramson, Daniel Benjamin. (2007). The aesthetics of city-scale preservation policy in Beijing. *Planning Perspectives, 22*(2), 129–66.
Allen, John, & Cochrane, Allan. (2007). Beyond the territorial fix: Regional assemblages, politics and power. *Regional Studies, 41*(9), 1161–75.
Andrusz, G. M., Harloe, M., & Szelenyi, I. (Eds). (1996). *Cities after Socialism: Urban and Regional Change and Conflict in Post-Socialist Societies*. Oxford: Blackwell.
Angelo, Hillary, & Wachsmuth, David. (2015). Urbanizing urban political ecology: A critique of methodological cityism. *International Journal of Urban and Regional Research, 39*(1), 16–27.
Argenbright, Robert. (1999). Remaking Moscow: New places, new selves. *The Geographical Review, 89*, 1–22.
Arkaraprasertkul, Non. (2018). Gentrification and its contentment: An anthropological perspective on housing, heritage and urban social change in Shanghai. *Urban Studies, 55*(7), 1561–78.
Audin, Judith. (2020). Street-corner society and everyday politics in the Beijing hutong. In M. Gibert-Flutre & H. Imai (Eds), *Asian Alleyways: An Urban Vernacular in Times of Globalization* (pp. 57–82). Amsterdam: Amsterdam University Press.
Barbalet, Jack. (2021a). The analysis of Chinese rural society: Fei Xiaotong revisited. *Modern China, 47*(4), 355–82.
Barbalet, Jack. (2021b). *The Theory of Guanxi and Chinese Society*. Oxford: Oxford University Press.
Beauregard, Robert A. (2006). *When America Became Suburban*. Minneapolis: University of Minnesota Press.
Belsky, Richard. (2000). The urban ecology of late imperial Beijing reconsidered: The transformation of social space in China's late imperial capital city. *Journal of Urban History, 27*(1), 54–74.
Belsky, Richard David. (2005). *Localities at the Center: Native Place, Space, and Power in Late Imperial Beijing* (Vol. 258). Cambridge, MA: Harvard University Asia Center.
Bestor, Theodore C. (1989). *Neighborhood Tokyo*: Stanford: Stanford University Press.
Bian, Yanjie. (2019). *Guanxi: How China Works*. Cambridge: Polity Press.
Bian, Yanjie, & Logan, John R. (1996). Market transition and the persistence of power: The changing stratification system in urban China. *American Sociological Review, 61*, 739–58.
Blokland, Talja, & Nast, Julia. (2014). From public familiarity to comfort zone: The relevance of absent ties for belonging in Berlin's mixed neighbourhoods. *International Journal of Urban and Regional Research, 38*(4), 1142–59.
Boland, Alana, & Zhu, Jiangang. (2012). Public participation in China's green communities: Mobilizing memories and structuring incentives. *Geoforum, 43*(1), 147–57.
Bracken, Gregory Byrne. (2013). *The Shanghai Alleyway House: A Vanishing Urban Vernacular*. London: Routledge.
Bray, David. (2005). *Social Space and Governance in Urban China: The Danwei System from Origins to Reform*. Stanford, CA: Stanford University Press.
Brenner, Neil, & Schmid, Christian. (2011). Planetary urbanization. In M. Gandy (Ed.), *Urban Constellations* (pp. 10–13). Berlin: Jovis.
Brenner, Neil, & Schmid, Christian. (2014). The 'urban age' in question. *International Journal of Urban and Regional Research, 38*(3), 731–55.
Brenner, Neil, & Schmid, Christian. (2015). Towards a new epistemology of the urban? *City, 19*(2–3), 151–82.

Buckingham, Will. (2017). Uncorking the neoliberal bottle: Neoliberal critique and urban change in China. *Eurasian Geography and Economics*, 58(3), 297–315.

Cai, Rong, & He, Shenjing. (2021). Governing homeowner associations in China's gated communities: The extension of state infrastructural power and its uneven reach. *Urban Geography*, 1–23. Last accessed 14 June 2020. https://doi.org/10.1080/02723638.2021.1878429.

Cai, Yongshun, & Sheng, Zhiming. (2013). Homeowners' activism in Beijing: Leaders with mixed motivations. *The China Quarterly*, 215, 513–32.

Campanella, Thomas J. (2008). *The Concrete Dragon: China's Urban Revolution and What It Means for the World*. New York: Princeton Architectural Press.

Castells, Manuel. (1977). *The Urban Question*. London: Edward Arnold.

Chatterjee, Partha. (2004). *The Politics of the Governed: Popular Politics in Most of the World*. New York: Columbia University Press.

Chu, Yin-Wah, & So, Alvin Y. (2012). The transition from neoliberalism to state neoliberalism in China in the turn of the twenty-first century. In C. Kyung-Sup, B. Fine, & L. Weiss (Eds), *Developmental Politics in Transition: The Neoliberal Era and Beyond* (pp. 166–87). Basingstoke: Palgrave Macmillan.

Cochrane, Allan. (2018). Rethinking the urban of urban politics. In K. Ward, A. E. Jonas, B. Miller, & D. Wilson (Eds), *The Routledge Handbook on Spaces of Urban Politics* (pp. 14–25). London: Routledge.

Davis, Deborah S., Kraus, Richard, Naughton, Barry, & Perry, Elizabeth J. (Eds). (1995). *Urban Space in Contemporary China: The Potential for Autonomy and Community in Post-Mao China*. Cambridge: Cambridge University Press.

Davis, Deborah S. (Ed.). (2000). *The Consumer Revolution in Urban China*. Berkeley: University of California Press.

Davis, Mike. (1990). *City of Quartz: Excavating the Future in Los Angeles*. London: Verso.

De Soto, Hernando (2000). *The Mystery of Capital*. New York: Basic Books.

Dillon, Nara, & Oi, Jean Chun (Eds). (2008). *At the Crossroads of Empires: Middlemen, Social Networks, and State-Building in Republican Shanghai*. Stanford: Stanford University Press.

Dovey, Kim, Rao, Fujie, & Pafka, Elek. (2018). Agglomeration and assemblage: Deterritorialising urban theory. *Urban Studies*, 55(2), 263–73.

Esherick, Joseph W. (Ed.). (2000). *Remaking the Chinese City: Modernity and National Identity, 1900–1950*. Honolulu: University of Hawaii Press.

Evans, Harriet. (2014). Neglect of a neighbourhood: Oral accounts of life in 'old Beijing' since the eve of the People's Republic. *Urban History*, 41(4), 686–704.

Fan, C. Cindy, Sun, Mingjie, & Zheng, Siqi. (2011). Migration and split households: A comparison of sole, couple, and family migrants in Beijing, China. *Environment and Planning A*, 43, 2164–85.

Fang, Ke, & Zhang, Yan. (2003). Plan and market mismatch: Urban redevelopment in Beijing during a period of transition. *Asia Pacific Viewpoint*, 44(2), 149–62.

Fei, Xiaotong. (1947/1992). *From the Soil: The Foundations of Chinese Society* (a translation of Fei Xiaotong's *Xiangtu Zhongguo*, by Gary G. Hamilton and Wang Zhen). Berkeley: University of California Press.

Feng, Jian, Zhou, Yixing, Logan, John, & Wu, Fulong. (2007). Restructuring of Beijing's social space. *Eurasian Geography and Economics*, 48(5), 509–42.

Feng, Jian, Zhou, Yixing, & Wu, Fulong. (2008). New trends of suburbanization in Beijing since 1990: From government-led to market-oriented. *Regional Studies*, 42(1), 83–99.

Fields, Desiree, & Uffer, Sabina. (2016). The financialisation of rental housing: A comparative analysis of New York City and Berlin. *Urban Studies*, 53(7), 1486–1502.

Forrest, Ray, Ren, Julie, & Wissink, Bart. (2019). *The City in China: New Perspectives on Contemporary Urbanism*. Bristol: Bristol University Press.

Forrest, Ray, & Yip, Ngai Ming (2007). Neighbourhood and neighbouring in contemporary Guangzhou. *Journal of Contemporary China*, 16(50), 47–64.

Fraser, James, Bazuin, Joshua Theodore, & Hornberger, George. (2016). The privatization of neighborhood governance and the production of urban space. *Environment and Planning A*, 48(5), 844–70.

Frazier, Mark W. (2002). *The Making of the Chinese Industrial Workplace: State, Revolution, and Labor Management*. Cambridge: Cambridge University Press.

Frazier, Mark W. (2011). *Socialist Insecurity: Pensions and the Politics of Uneven Development in China*. Ithaca, NY: Cornell University Press.

Frazier, Mark W. (2019). *The Power of Place: Contentious Politics in Twentieth-Century Shanghai and Bombay*. Cambridge: Cambridge University Press.

Frazier, Mark W. (2022). Housing the socialist worker: The 'workers' new village' in Shanghai. In I. Francechini & C. Sorace (Eds), *Proletarian China*. London: Verso.

French, Richard Anthony, & Hamilton, F. E. Ian (Eds). (1979). *The Socialist City: Spacial Structure and Urban Policy*. Chichester: John Wiley and Sons.

Friedmann, John. (1987). *Planning in the Public Domain: From Knowledge to Action*. Princeton, NJ: Princeton University Press.

Friedmann, John. (2005). *China's Urban Transition*. Minneapolis: University of Minnesota Press.

Friedmann, John. (2007). Reflection on place and place-making in the cities of China. *International Journal of Urban and Regional Research*, *31*(2), 257–79.

Friedmann, John. (2010). Place and place-making in cities: A global perspective. *Planning Theory and Practice*, *11*(2), 149–65.

Fu, Qiang, & Lin, Nan. (2014). The weaknesses of civic territorial organizations: Civic engagement and homeowners associations in urban China. *International Journal of Urban and Regional Research*, *38*(6), 2309–27.

Gans, Herbert. (1962). *The Urban Villagers*. New York: Free Press.

Gaubatz, Piper Rae. (1996). *Beyond the Great Wall: Urban Form and Transformation on the Chinese Frontiers*. Stanford, CA: Stanford University Press.

Gaubatz, Piper. (2019). New China Square: Chinese public space in developmental, environmental and social contexts. *Journal of Urban Affairs*, *43*(9), 1235–62.

Gelder, Jean-Louis van. (2009). Legal tenure security, perceived tenure security and housing improvement in Buenos Aires: An attempt towards integration. *International Journal of Urban and Regional Research*, *33*(1), 126–46.

Ghertner, D. Asher. (2015). *Rule by Aesthetics: World-Class City Making in Delhi*. Oxford: Oxford University Press.

Gibert-Flutre, Marie, & Imai, Heide (Eds). (2020). *Asian Alleyways: An Urban Vernacular in Times of Globalization*. Amsterdam: Amsterdam University Press.

Giles, John, Park, Albert, & Cai, Fang. (2006). How has economic restructuring affected China's urban workers? *The China Quarterly*, *185*, 61–95.

Giroir, Guillaume. (2005). A globalized golden ghetto in a Chinese garden: The Fontainebleau Villas in Shanghai. In F. Wu (Ed.), *Globalization and the Chinese City* (pp. 208–26). London: Routledge.

Giroir, Guillaume. (2007). Spaces of leisure: Gated golf communities in China. In F. Wu (Ed.), *China's Emerging Cities: The Making of New Urbanism* (pp. 234–55). Abingdon, Oxon: Routledge.

Glass, Ruth. (1964). *London: Aspects of Change*. London: Centre for Urban Studies, University College London.

Glasze, Georg, Webster, Chris, & Frantz, Klaus (Eds). (2006). *Private Cities: Global and Local Perspectives*. London: Routledge.

Gu, Honghuan, Logan, John R., & Wu, Ruijun. (2021). Remaking Shanghai: New divisions in an expanding metropolis. *International Journal of Urban and Regional Research*, *45*(1), 80–98.

Guo, Youliang, Zhang, Chengguo, Wang, Ya Ping, & Li, Xun. (2018). (De-) Activating the growth machine for redevelopment: The case of Liede urban village in Guangzhou. *Urban Studies*, *55*(7), 1420–38.

Gururani, Shubhra. (2020). Cities in a world of villages: Agrarian urbanism and the making of India's urbanizing frontiers. *Urban Geography*, *41*(7), 971–89.

Hamnett, Chris. (2021). *Advanced Introduction to Gentrification*. Cheltenham: Edward Elgar.

Harvey, David. (1978). The urban process under capitalism. *International Journal of Urban and Regional Research*, *2*(1–3), 101–31.

Harvey, David. (2005). *A Brief History of Neoliberalism*. Oxford: Oxford University Press.

Harvey, David. (2008). The right to the city. *New Left Review*, *53*, 23–39.

Haussermann, Hartmut, & Haila, Anne. (2005). The European city: a conceptual framework and normative project. In Y. Kazepov (Ed.), *Cities of Europe* (pp. 43–64). Oxford: Blackwell.

Hazelzet, Arjan, & Wissink, Bart. (2012). Neighborhoods, social networks, and trust in post-reform China: The case of Guangzhou. *Urban Geography*, *33*(2), 204–20.

He, Qiong, Musterd, Sako, & Boterman, Willem. (2021). Understanding different levels of segregation in urban China: A comparative study among 21 cities in Guangdong province. *Urban Geography*, 1–26. Last accessed 25 August 2022. https://doi.org/10.1080/02723638.2021.1893049.

He, Shenjing. (2007). State-sponsored gentrification under market transition: The case of Shanghai. *Urban Affairs Review, 43*(2), 171–98.

He, Shenjing. (2010). New-build gentrification in central Shanghai: Demographic changes and socioeconomic implications. *Population, Space and Place, 16*(5), 345–61.

He, Shenjing. (2012). Two waves of gentrification and emerging rights issues in Guangzhou, China. *Environment and Planning A, 44*(12), 2817–33.

He, Shenjing. (2013). Evolving enclave urbanism in China and its socio-spatial implications: The case of Guangzhou. *Social & Cultural Geography, 14*(3), 243–75.

He, Shenjing. (2015). Homeowner associations and neighborhood governance in Guangzhou, China. *Eurasian Geography and Economics, 56*(3), 260–84.

He, Shenjing, Li, Lingyue, Zhang, Yong, & Wang, Jun. (2018). A small entrepreneurial city in action: Policy mobility, urban entrepreneurialism, and politics of scale in Jiyuan, China. *International Journal of Urban and Regional Research, 42*(4), 684–702.

He, Shenjing, Liu, Yuting, Webster, Chris, & Wu, Fulong. (2009). Property rights redistribution, entitlement failure and the impoverishment of landless farmers in China. *Urban Studies, 46*(9), 1925–49.

He, Shenjing, Wang, Dong, Webster, Chris, & Chau, Kwong Wing. (2019). Property rights with price tags? Pricing uncertainties in the production, transaction and consumption of China's small property right housing. *Land Use Policy, 81*, 424–33.

He, Shenjing, & Wu, Fulong. (2005). Property-led redevelopment in post-reform China: A case study of Xintiandi redevelopment project in Shanghai. *Journal of Urban Affairs, 27*(1), 1–23.

He, Shenjing, & Wu, Fulong. (2007). Socio-spatial impacts of property-led redevelopment on China's urban neighbourhoods. *Cities, 24*(3), 194–208.

He, Shenjing, & Wu, Fulong. (2009). China's emerging neoliberal urbanism: Perspectives from urban redevelopment. *Antipode, 41*(2), 282–304.

He, Shenjing, Zhang, Mengzhu, & Wei, Zongcai. (2020). The state project of crisis management: China's Shantytown Redevelopment Schemes under state-led financialization. *Environment and Planning A: Economy and Space, 52*(3), 632–53.

Heilmann, Sebastian, & Perry, Elizabeth J. (Eds). (2011). *Mao's Invisible Hand: The Political Foundations of Adaptive Governance in China*. Cambridge, MA: Harvard University Press.

Hendrikx, Martijn, & Wissink, Bart. (2017). Welcome to the club! An exploratory study of service accessibility in commodity housing estates in Guangzhou, China. *Social & Cultural Geography, 18*(3), 371–94.

Hirt, Sonia A. (2012). *Iron Curtains: Gates, Suburbs and Privatization of Space in the Post-Socialist City*. Oxford: Wiley-Blackwell.

Honig, Emily. (1992). *Creating Chinese Ethnicity: Subei People in Shanghai, 1850–1980*. New Haven, CT: Yale University Press.

Hsing, You-tien. (2010). *The Great Urban Transformation: Politics of Land and Property in China*. Oxford: Oxford University Press.

Huang, Philip C. C, (1993). 'Public Sphere'/'Civil Society' in China? The third realm between state and society. *Modern China, 19*(2), 216–40.

Huang, Philip C. C. (2019). Rethinking 'the Third Sphere': The dualistic unity of state and society in China, past and present. *Modern China, 45*(4), 355–91.

Huang, Youqin. (2006). Collectivism, political control, and gating in Chinese cities. *Urban Geography, 27*(6), 507–25.

Huang, Youqin, & Low, Setha M. (2008). Is gating always exclusionary? A comparative analysis of gated communities in American and Chinese cities. In J. R. Logan (Ed.), *Urban China in Transition* (pp. 182–202). Oxford: Blackwell.

Hubbard, Phil. (2018). Retail gentrification. In *Handbook of Gentrification Studies* (pp. 294–309). Cheltenham: Edward Elgar.

Iossifova, Deljana. (2015). Borderland urbanism: Seeing between enclaves. *Urban Geography, 36*(1), 90–108.

Jacobs, Jane. (1961). *The Death and Life of Great American Cities*. New York: Vintage.

Jacoby, Sam, & Cheng, Jingru. (2021). *The Socio-Spatial Design of Community and Governance: Interdisciplinary Urban Design in China*. Singapore: Springer Nature.

Jaros, Kyle A. (2019). *China's Urban Champions*. Princeton, NJ: Princeton University Press.

Jessop, Bob. (2002). *The Future of the Capitalist State*. Cambridge: Polity Press.

Kan, Karita. (2019a). Accumulation without dispossession? Land commodification and rent extraction in peri-urban China. *International Journal of Urban and Regional Research, 43*(4), 633–48.

Kan, Karita. (2019b). A weapon of the weak? Shareholding, property rights and villager empowerment in China. *The China Quarterly*, *237*, 131–52.
Kan, Karita, & Wong, Rebecca W. Y. (2019). Gated villages: Community governance and social control in peri-urban China. In R. Yep, J. Wang, & T. Johnson (Eds), *Handbook on Urban Development in China* (pp. 248–61). Cheltenham: Edward Elgar.
Karaman, Ozan, Sawyer, Lindsay, Schmid, Christian, & Wong, Kit Ping. (2020). Plot by plot: Plotting urbanism as an ordinary process of urbanisation. *Antipode*, *52*(4), 1122–51.
Keil, Roger. (2018). *Suburban Planet: Making the World Urban from the Outside in*. Cambridge: Polity Press.
Keil, Roger, & Wu, Fulong (Eds). (2022). *After Suburbia: Urbanization on the Planet's Periphery*. Toronto: University of Toronto Press.
Keith, Michael, Lash, Scott, Arnoldi, Jakob, & Rooker, Tyler. (2014). *China Constructing Capitalism: Economic Life and Urban Change*. London: Routledge.
Kipnis, Andrew B. (2016). *From Village to City: Social Transformation in a Chinese County Seat*. Berkeley: University of California Press.
Knox, Paul L. (1991). The restless urban landscape: Economic and sociocultural change and the transformation of Metropolitan Washington, DC. *Annals of the Association of American Geographers*, *87*(2), 181–209.
Kraus, Richard. (2000). Public monuments and private pleasures in the parks of Nanjing: A tango in the ruins of the Ming emperor's palace. In D. S. Davis (Ed.), *The Consumer Revolution in Urban China* (pp. 287–311). Berkeley: University of California Press.
Lee, Ching Kwan, & Zhang, Yonghong. (2013). The power of instability: Unraveling the microfoundations of bargained authoritarianism in China. *American Journal of Sociology*, *118*(6), 1475–1508.
Lee, Leo Ou-fan. (1999). *Shanghai Modern: The Flowering of a New Urban Culture in China, 1930–1945*. Cambridge, MA: Harvard University Press.
Lees, Loretta. (2012). The geography of gentrification: Thinking through comparative urbanism. *Progress in Human Geography*, *36*, 155–71.
Lees, Loretta, Shin, Hyun Bang, & López-Morales, Ernesto. (2016). *Planetary Gentrification*. Cambridge: Polity.
Lefebvre, Henri. (1970/2003). *The Urban Revolution*. Minneapolis: University of Minnesota Press.
Lefebvre, Henri. (1991). *The Production of Space*. London: Blackwell.
Leitner, Helga, & Sheppard, Eric. (2016). Provincializing critical urban theory: Extending the ecosystem of possibilities. *International Journal of Urban and Regional Research*, *40*(1), 228–35.
Li, Jie. (2015). *Shanghai Homes: Palimpsests of Private Life*. New York: Columbia University Press.
Li, Wei. (2009). *Ethnoburbs: The New Ethnic Community in Urban America*. Honolulu: University of Hawaii Press.
Li, Zhigang, & Gou, Feicui. (2020). Residential segregation of rural migrants in post-reform urban China. In S. Musterd (Ed.), *Handbook of Urban Segregation* (pp. 55–75). Cheltenham: Edward Elgar.
Li, Zhigang, Ou, Shunixan, & Wu, Rong. (2019). A study of socio-spatial segregation of rural migrants in Shenzhen: A case of Foxconn. In R. Forrest, J. Ren, & B. Wissink (Eds), *The City in China: New Perspectives on Contemporary Urbanism* (pp. 185–206). Bristol: Bristol University Press.
Li, Zhigang, & Wu, Fulong. (2006). Socio-spatial differentiation and residential inequalities in Shanghai: A case study of three neighbourhoods. *Housing Studies*, *21*(5), 695–717.
Li, Zhigang, & Wu, Fulong. (2008). Tenure-based residential segregation in post-reform Chinese cities: A case study of Shanghai. *Transactions of the Institute of British Geographers*, *33*(3), 404–19.
Li, Zhigang, & Wu, Fulong. (2013). Residential satisfaction in China's informal settlements: A case study of Beijing, Shanghai, and Guangzhou. *Urban Geography*, *34*(7), 923–49.
Liang, Samuel Y. (2014). *Remaking China's Great Cities: Space and Culture in Urban Housing, Renewal, and Expansion*. Abingdon, Oxon: Routledge.
Liao, Banggu, & Wong, David W. (2015). Changing urban residential patterns of Chinese migrants: Shanghai, 2000–2010. *Urban Geography*, *36*(1), 109–26.
Lin, George C. S. (2006). Peri-urbanism in globalizing China: A study of new urbanism in Dongguan. *Eurasian Geography and Economics*, *47*(1), 28–53.
Lin, George C. S. (2009). *Developing China: Land, Politics and Social Conditions*. London: Routledge.

Lin, George C. S. (2007). Chinese urbanism in question: State, society, and the reproduction of urban spaces. *Urban Geography, 28*(1), 7–29.

Lin, Sainan, Wu, Fulong, & Li, Zhigang. (2020). Social integration of migrants across Chinese neighbourhoods. *Geoforum, 112*, 118–28.

Lin, Sainan, Wu, Fulong, & Li, Zhigang. (2021). Beyond neighbouring: Migrants' place attachment to their host cities in China. *Population, Space and Place, 27*(1), e2374.

Lincoln, Toby. (2021). *An Urban History of China*. Cambridge: Cambridge University Press.

Lindner, Christoph. (2011). The postmetropolis and mental life: Wong Kar-Wai's cinematic Hong Kong. In G. Bridge & S. Watson (Eds), *The New Blackwell Companion to the City* (pp. 327–36). Oxford: Blackwell.

Liu, Ran, Wong, Tai-Chee & Liu, Shenghe (2012). Peasants' counterplots against the state monopoly of the rural urbanization process: Urban villages and 'small property housing' in Beijing, China. *Environment and Planning A, 44*(5), 1219–40.

Liu, Siyao, Zhang, Fangzhu, & Wu, Fulong. (2022). Contrasting migrants' sense of belonging to the city in selected peri-urban neighbourhoods in Beijing. *Cities, 120*, 103499.

Liu, Ye, Li, Zhigang, Liu, Yuqi, & Chen, Hongsheng. (2015). Growth of rural migrant enclaves in Guangzhou, China: Agency, everyday practice and social mobility. *Urban Studies, 52*(16), 3086–3105.

Liu, Yongshen, & Yau, Yung. (2020). Urban entrepreneurialism vs market society: The geography of China's neoliberal urbanism. *International Journal of Urban and Regional Research, 44*(2), 266–88.

Liu, Yuqi, Wu, Fulong, Liu, Ye, & Li, Zhigang. (2017). Changing neighbourhood cohesion under the impact of urban redevelopment: A case study of Guangzhou, China. *Urban Geography, 38*(2), 266–90.

Liu, Yuting, & Wu, Fulong. (2006). Urban poverty neighbourhoods: Typology and spatial concentration under China's market transition, a case study of Nanjing. *Geoforum, 37*(4), 610–26.

Logan, John R., & Molotch, Harvey Luskin (1987). *Urban Fortunes: The Political Economy of Place*. Berkeley: University of California Press.

Low, Setha. (2003). *Behind the Gates: Life, Security, and the Pursuit of Happiness in Fortress America*. London: Routledge.

Low, Setha. (2006). Towards a theory of urban fragmentation: A cross-cultural analysis of fear, privatization, and the state. *Cybergeo: European Journal of Geography*. Last accessed 14 June 2022. https://doi.org/10.4000/cybergeo.3207.

Lu, Duanfang. (2006). *Remaking Chinese Urban Form: Modernity, Scarcity and Space, 1949–2005*. London: Routledge.

Lu, Hanchao. (1995). Creating urban outcasts: Shantytowns in Shanghai, 1920–1950. *Journal of Urban History, 21*(5), 563–96.

Lu, Hanchao. (1999). *Beyond the Neon Lights: Everyday Shanghai in the Early Twentieth Century*. Berkeley: University of California Press.

Lu, Hanchao. (2020). More than half the sky: Women and urban neighbourhood workshops in China, 1958–1978. *The China Quarterly, 243*, 757–79.

Lu, Tingting, Zhang, Fangzhu, & Wu, Fulong. (2018). Place attachment in gated neighbourhoods in China: Evidence from Wenzhou. *Geoforum, 92*, 144–51.

Lu, Tingting, Zhang, Fangzhu, & Wu, Fulong. (2019). The meaning of 'private governance' in urban China: Researching residents' preferences and satisfaction. *Urban Policy and Research, 37*(3), 378–92.

Lu, Tingting, Zhang, Fangzhu, & Wu, Fulong. (2020). The variegated role of the state in different gated neighbourhoods in China. *Urban Studies, 57*(8), 1642–59.

Lu, Tingting, Zhang, Fangzhu, & Wu, Fulong. (2022). The sense of community in homeowner association neighborhoods in urban China: A study of Wenzhou. *Housing Policy Debate, 32*(4–5), 642–60.

Lü, Xiaobo, & Perry, Elizabeth J. (1997). *Danwei: The Changing Chinese Workplace in Historical and Comparative Perspective*. Armonk, NY: M.E. Sharpe.

Ma, Laurence J. C., & Xiang, Biao (1998). Native place, migration and the emergence of peasant enclaves in Beijing. *The China Quarterly, 155*, 546–81.

Ma, Laurence J. C. (2009). Chinese urbanism. In R. Kitchin & N. Thrift (Eds), *International Encyclopedia of Human Geography* (pp. 65–71). Oxford: Elsevier.

MacLeod, Gordon, & Ward, Kevin. (2002). Spaces of utopia and dystopia: Landscaping the contemporary city. *Geografiska Annaler, 84B*(3–4), 153–70.

Marcuse, Peter. (1996). Privatization and its discontents: Property rights in land and housing in the transition in Eastern Europe. In G. M. Andrusz, M. Harloe, & I. Szelenyi (Eds), *Cities after Socialism: Urban and Regional Change and Conflict in Post-Socialist Societies* (pp. 119–91). Oxford: Blackwell.

McFarlane, Colin. (2011). Assemblage and critical urbanism. *City*, *15*(2), 204–24.

McGuirk, Pauline, & Dowling, Robyn. (2011). Governing social reproduction in masterplanned estates: Urban politics and everyday life in Sydney. *Urban Studies*, *48*(12), 2611–28.

McKenzie, Evan (2005). Constructing the pomerium in Las Vegas: A case study of emerging trends in American gated communities. *Housing Studies*, *20*(2), 187–203.

McMillian, David W., & Chavis, David M. (1986). Sense of community: A definition and theory. *Journal of Community Psychology*, *14*(1), 6–23.

Mertha, Andrew. (2009). 'Fragmented authoritarianism 2.0': Political pluralization in the Chinese policy process. *The China Quarterly*, *200*, 995–1012.

Meyer, Michael. (2009). *The Last Days of Old Beijing: Life in the Vanishing Backstreets of a City Transformed*. New York: Walker.

Monkkonen, Paavo, Comandon, Andre, & Zhu, Jiren. (2017). Economic segregation in transition China: Evidence from the 20 largest cities. *Urban Geography*, *38*(7), 1039–61.

Myers, Garth. (2020). *Rethinking Urbanism: Lessons from Postcolonialism and the Global South*. Bristol: Bristol University Press.

Nee, Victor. (1989). A theory of market transition: From redistribution to markets in state socialism. *American Sociological Review*, *54*(5), 663–81.

O'Brien, Kevin J., & Li, Lianjiang. (2006). *Rightful Resistance in Rural China*. Cambridge: Cambridge University Press.

Oi, Jean C. (1992). Fiscal reform and the economic foundations of local state corporatism. *World Politics*, *45*, 99–126.

Oi, Jean C. (1999). *Rural China Takes Off: Institutional Foundations of Economic Reform*. Berkeley: University of California Press.

Ong, Aihwa. (2006). *Neoliberalism as Exception: Mutations in Citizenship and Sovereignty*. Durham, NC: Duke University Press.

Ong, Lynette H. (2014). State-led urbanization in China: Skyscrapers, land revenue and 'concentrated villages'. *The China Quarterly*, *217*, 162–79.

Orum, Anthony M., Bata, Sidney, Shumei, Li, Jiewei, Tang, Yang, Sang, & Trung, Nguyen Thanh. (2009). Public man and public space in Shanghai today. *City & Community*, *8*(4), 369–89.

Pan, Tianshu. (2005). Historical memory, community-building and place-making in neighborhood Shanghai. In L. J. C. Ma & F. Wu (Eds), *Restructuring the Chinese City: Changing Society, Economy and Space* (pp. 122–37). London: Routledge.

Park, Albert, & Cai, Fang. (2011). The informalization of the Chinese labor market. In S. Kuruvilla, C. K. Lee, & M. Gallagher (Eds), *From Iron Rice Bowl to Informalization: Markets, Workers, and the State in a Changing China*. Ithaca, NY: Cornell University Press.

Park, Robert E. (1915). The city: Suggestions for the investigation of human behavior in the city environment. *American Journal of Sociology*, *20*(5), 577–612.

Parker, Simon. (2015). *Urban Theory and the Urban Experience: Encountering the City* (2nd ed.). London: Routledge.

Parnell, Susan, & Pieterse, Edgar. (2016). Translational global praxis: Rethinking methods and modes of African urban research. *International Journal of Urban and Regional Research*, *40*(1), 236–46.

Peake, Linda. (2016). The twenty-first-century quest for feminism and the global urban. *International Journal of Urban and Regional Research*, *40*(1), 219–27.

Peck, Jamie. (2015). Cities beyond compare? *Regional Studies*, *49*(1), 160–82.

Peck, Jamie, & Zhang, Jun. (2013). A variety of capitalism … with Chinese characteristics? *Journal of Economic Geography*, *13*(3), 357–96.

Perry, Elizabeth J., & Goldman, Merle (Eds). (2007). *Grassroots Political Reform in Contemporary China*. Cambridge, MA: Harvard University Press.

Po, Lanchih. (2008). Redefining rural collectives in China: Land conversion and the emergence of rural shareholding co-operatives. *Urban Studies*, *45*(8), 1603–23.

Po, Lanchih. (2012). Asymmetrical integration: Public finance deprivation in China's urbanized villages. *Environment and Planning A*, *44*(12), 2834–51.

Po, Lanchih. (2020). Women's land activism and gendered citizenship in the urbanising Pearl River Delta. *Urban Studies*, *57*(3), 602–17.

Polanyi, Karl. (1944). *The Great Transformation: The Political Economic Origin of Our Time*. New York: Farrar & Rinehart.

Portes, Alejandro, & Zhou, Min (1993). The new second generation: Segmented assimilation and its variants. *Annals of the American Academy of Political and Social Science, 530*, 74–96.

Pow, Choon-Piew. (2009). *Gated Communities in China: Class, Privilege and the Moral Politics of the Good Life*. Abingdon, Oxon: Routledge.

Pow, Choon-Piew. (2015). Urban dystopia and epistemologies of hope. *Progress in Human Geography, 39*(4), 464–85.

Putnam, Robert D. (2000). *Bowling Alone: The Collapse and Revival of American Community*. New York: Simon and Schuster.

Qian, Junxi. (2014). Performing the public man: Cultures and identities in China's grassroots leisure class. *City & Community, 13*(1), 26–48.

Qian, Junxi. (2019). Making urban public space amidst modern Chinese urbanism. In R. Yep, J. Wang, & T. Johnson (Eds), *Handbook on Urban Development in China* (pp. 156–70). Cheltenham: Edward Elgar.

Qian, Junxi, & Tang, Xueqiong. (2019). Theorising small city as ordinary city: Rethinking development and urbanism from China's south-west frontier. *Urban Studies, 56*(6), 1215–33.

Qian, Junxi, & Wei, Lei. (2020). Development at the edge of difference: Rethinking capital and market relations from Lugu Lake, Southwest China. *Antipode, 52*(1), 246–69.

Qian, Zhu. (2022). *Property Rights and Urban Transformation in China*. Cheltenham: Edward Elgar.

Read, Benjamin L. (2012). *Roots of the State: Neighborhood Organization and Social Networks in Beijing and Taipei*. Stanford, CA: Stanford University Press.

Ren, Julie. (2021). Exceptionalism and theorizing spatial inequality: Segregation research on cities in China. *Journal of Urban Affairs*, 1–13. https://doi.org/10.1080/07352166.2021.1921592.

Ren, Xuefei. (2008). Forward to the past: Historical preservation in globalizing Shanghai. *City and Community, 7*(1), 23–43.

Ren, Xuefei. (2014). The political economy of urban ruins: Redeveloping Shanghai. *International Journal of Urban and Regional Research, 38*(3), 1081–91.

Rithmire, Meg E. (2015). *Land Bargains and Chinese Capitalism: The Politics of Property Rights under Reform*. Cambridge: Cambridge University Press.

Robinson, Jennifer. (2006). *Ordinary Cities: Between Modernity and Development*. London: Routledge.

Robinson, Jennifer. (2011). Cities in a world of cities: The comparative gesture. *International Journal of Urban and Regional Research, 35*(1), 1–23.

Rowe, Peter G., Forsyth, Ann, & Kan, Har Ye. (2016). *China's Urban Communities: Concepts, Contexts, and Well-being*. Berlin; Boston: Birkhäuser.

Roy, Ananya. (2005). Urban informality: Towards an epistemology of planning. *Journal of the American Planning Association, 71*(2), 147–58.

Roy, Ananya. (2009a). The 21st-century metropolis: New geographies of theory. *Regional Studies, 43*(6), 819–30.

Roy, Ananya. (2009b). Why India cannot plan its cities: Informality, insurgence and the idiom of urbanization. *Planning Theory, 8*(1), 76–87.

Roy, Ananya. (2011). Slumdog cities: Rethinking subaltern urbanism. *International Journal of Urban and Regional Research, 35*(2), 223–38.

Roy, Ananya. (2016). What is urban about critical urban theory? *Urban Geography, 37*(6), 810–23.

Roy, Ananya. (2018). Urban studies and the postcolonial encounter. In S. Hall & R. Burdett (Eds), *The SAGE Handbook of the 21st Century City* (pp. 32–46). London: SAGE.

Roy, Ananya, & Ong, Aihwa (Eds). (2011). *Worlding Cities: Asian Experiments and the Art of Being Global*. Oxford: Wiley-Blackwell.

Sa, Haoxuan. (2021). Urban village shareholding: Cooperative economic organization in Northeast China. *American Journal of Economics and Sociology, 80*(2), 665–97.

Sa, Haoxuan, & Haila, Anne. (2021). Urban villagers as real estate developers: Embracing property mind through 'planting' housing in North-east China. *Housing Studies*, 1–21. https://doi.org/10.1080/02673037.2021.1888889.

Saich, Tony. (2015). *Governance and Politics of China* (4th ed.). London: Macmillan.

Sargeson, Sally. (2018). Grounds for self-government? Changes in land ownership and democratic participation in Chinese communities. *The Journal of Peasant Studies, 45*(2), 321–46.

Scheen, Lena. (2015). *Shanghai Literary Imaginings: A City in Transformation*. Amsterdam: Amsterdam University Press.

Schmid, Christian, Karaman, Ozan, Hanakata, Naomi C., Kallenberger, Pascal, Kockelkorn, Anne, Sawyer, Lindsay, ... Wong, Kit Ping. (2018). Towards a new vocabulary of urbanisation processes: A comparative approach. *Urban Studies, 55*(1), 195–2.

Scott, Allen J., & Storper, Michael. (2015). The nature of cities: The scope and limits of urban theory. *International Journal of Urban and Regional Research, 39*(1), 1–15.

Sennett, Richard. (1977). *The Fall of Public Man*. New York: Alfred A. Knopf.

Shao, Qin. (2013). *Shanghai Gone: Domicide and Defiance in a Chinese Megacity*. Lanham, MD: Rowman & Littlefield.

Shao, Zinan, Xu, Jiang, Chung, Calvin King Lam, Spit, Tejo, & Wu, Qun. (2020). The state as both regulator and player: The politics of transfer of development rights in China. *International Journal of Urban and Regional Research, 44*(1), 38–54.

Shen, Jie. (2017). Stuck in the suburbs? Socio-spatial exclusion of migrants in Shanghai. *Cities, 60*, 428–35.

Shen, Jie, Luo, Xiang, & Wu, Fulong. (2020). Assembling mega-urban projects through state-guided governance innovation: The development of Lingang in Shanghai. *Regional Studies, 54*(12), 1644–54.

Shen, Jie, & Wu, Fulong (2013). Moving to the suburbs: Demand-side driving forces of suburban growth in China. *Environment and Planning A, 45*(8), 1823–44.

Shen, Jie, & Xiao, Yang. (2020). Emerging divided cities in China: Socioeconomic segregation in Shanghai, 2000–2010. *Urban Studies, 57*(6), 1338–56.

Sheng, Mingjie, Gu, Chaolin, & Wu, Weiping. (2019). To move or to stay in a migrant enclave in Beijing: The role of neighborhood social bonds. *Journal of Urban Affairs, 41*(3), 338–53.

Sheppard, Eric, Leitner, Helga, & Maringanti, Anant. (2013). Provincializing global urbanism: A manifesto. *Urban Geography, 34*(7), 893–900.

Shi, Chen, & Tang, Bo-sin. (2020). Institutional change and diversity in the transfer of land development rights in China: The case of Chengdu. *Urban Studies, 57*(3), 473–89.

Shih, Mi. (2010). The evolving law of disputed relocation: Constructing inner-city renewal practices in Shanghai, 1990–2005. *International Journal of Urban and Regional Research, 34*(2), 350–64.

Shih, Mi. (2017). Rethinking displacement in peri-urban transformation in China. *Environment and Planning A: Economy and Space, 49*(2), 389–406.

Shin, Hyun Bang. (2009). Residential redevelopment and the entrepreneurial local state: The implications of Beijing's shifting emphasis on urban redevelopment policies. *Urban Studies, 46*(13), 2815–39.

Shin, Hyun Bang. (2010). Urban conservation and revalorisation of dilapidated historic quarters: The case of Nanluoguxiang in Beijing. *Cities, 27*, S43–S54.

Shin, Hyun Bang. (2013). The right to the city and critical reflections on China's property rights activism. *Antipode, 45*(5), 1167–89.

Shin, Hyun Bang. (2016). Economic transition and speculative urbanisation in China: Gentrification versus dispossession. *Urban Studies, 53*(3), 471–89.

Simmel, George. (1903/2002). The metropolis and mental life. In G. Bridge & S. Watson (Eds), *The Blackwell City Reader* (pp. 11–19). Oxford: Blackwell.

Simone, Abdoumaliq. (2016). It's just the city after all! *International Journal of Urban and Regional Research, 40*(1), 210–18.

Simone, AbdouMaliq, & Pieterse, Edgar. (2018). *New Urban Worlds: Inhabiting Dissonant Times*. Cambridge: Polity Press.

Skinner, George William (Ed.). (1977). *The City in Late Imperial China*. Stanford, CA: Stanford University Press.

Slater, Tom. (2006). The eviction of critical perspectives from gentrification research. *International Journal of Urban and Regional Research, 30*(4), 737–57.

Smart, Alan, & Lin, George C. S. (2007). Local capitalisms, local citizenship and translocality: Rescaling from below in the Pearl River Delta region, China. *International Journal of Urban and Regional Research, 31*(2), 280–302.

Smith, Neil. (2002). New globalism, new urbanism: Gentrification as global urban strategy. *Antipode, 34*(3), 427–50.

Smith, Nick R. (2021). *The End of the Village: Planning in Urbanization of Rural China*. Minneapolis: University of Minnesota Press.

Solinger, Dorothy J. (1999). *Contesting Citizenship in Urban China: Peasant Migrants, the State, and the Logic of the Market*. Berkeley: University of California Press.

Stapleton, Kristin. (2000). *Civilizing Chengdu: Chinese Urban Reform, 1895–1937*. Cambridge, MA: Harvard University Press.

Stenning, Alison. (2005). Post-socialism and the changing geographies of the everyday in Poland. *Transactions of the Institute of British Geographers*, *30*(1), 113–27.

Stenning, Alison, Smith, Adrian, Rochovská, Alena, & Świątek, Dariusz. (2011). *Domesticating Neo-Liberalism: Spaces of Economic Practice and Social Reproduction in Post-Socialist Cities*. Chichester: John Wiley & Sons.

Storper, Michael, & Scott, Allen J. (2016). Current debates in urban theory: A critical assessment. *Urban Studies*, *53*(6), 1114–36.

Strand, David. (2000). 'A high place is no better than a low place': The city in the making of modern China. In W.-H. Yeh (Ed.), *Becoming Chinese: Passages to Modernity and Beyond* (pp. 98–136). Berkeley: University of California Press.

Su, Xiaobo. (2015). Urban entrepreneurialism and the commodification of heritage in China. *Urban Studies*, *52*(15), 2874–89.

Su, Xing, & Qian, Zhu. (2020). Neoliberal planning, master plan adjustment and overbuilding in China: The case of Ordos City. *Cities*, *105*, 102748.

Sun, Liping. (2004). Transformation and division: Changing social structure since economic reform. Beijing: Tsinghua University Press (in Chinese).

Sun, Liping. (2008). Societal transition: New issues in the field of the sociology of development. *Modern China*, *34*(1), 88–113.

Szelenyi, Ivan (1996). Cities under socialism – and after. In G. M. Andrusz, M. Harloe, & I. Szelenyi (Eds), *Cities after Socialism: Urban and Regional Change and Conflict in Post-Socialist Societies* (pp. 286–317). Oxford: Blackwell.

Tan, Xiaohong, & Altrock, Uwe. (2016). Struggling for an adaptive strategy? Discourse analysis of urban regeneration processes–A case study of Enning Road in Guangzhou City. *Habitat International*, *56*, 245–57.

Tang, Beibei. (2015). 'Not rural but not urban': Community governance in China's urban villages. *The China Quarterly*, *223*, 724–44.

Tang, Beibei. (2018). *China's Housing Middle Class: Changing Urban Life in Gated Communities*. London: Routledge.

Tang, Beibei. (2020). Grid governance in China's urban middle-class neighbourhoods. *The China Quarterly*, *241*, 43–61.

Tang, Wenfang. (2016). *Populist Authoritarianism: Chinese Political Culture and Regime Sustainability*. Oxford: Oxford University Press.

Thornton, Patricia M. (2013). The advance of the Party: Transformation or takeover of urban grass-roots society? *The China Quarterly*, *213*, 1–18.

Tian, Li. (2008). The Chengzhongcun land market in China: Boon or bane? – a perspective on property rights. *International Journal of Urban and Regional Research*, *32*(2), 282–304.

Tomba, Luigi. (2005). Residential space and collective interest formation in Beijing's housing disputes. *The China Quarterly*, *184*, 934–51.

Tomba, Luigi. (2014). *The Government Next Door: Neighborhood Politics in Urban China*. Ithaca, NY: Cornell University Press.

Tsai, Lily L. (2007). *Accountability without Democracy: Solidary Groups and Public Goods Provision in Rural China*. Cambridge: Cambridge University Press.

Turner, John. (1976). *Housing by People: Towards Autonomy in Building Environments*. London: Boyars.

Tynen, Sarah. (2019). Lived space of urban development: The everyday politics of spatial production in Nanjing, China. *Space and Culture*, *22*(2), 172–88.

Varley, Ann. (2002). Private or public: Debating the meaning of tenure legalization. *International Journal of Urban and Regional Research*, *26*(3), 449–61.

Visser, Robin. (2010). *Cities Surround the Countryside: Urban Aesthetics in Postsocialist China*. Durham, NC: Duke University Press.

Wacquant, Loïc. (2008). *Urban Outcasts: A Comparative Sociology of Advanced Marginality*. Cambridge: Polity Press.

Walder, Andrew G. (1986). *Communist Neo-traditionalism: Work and Authority in Chinese Industry*. Berkeley: University of California Press.

Walker, Richard A. (2016). Why cities? A response. *International Journal of Urban and Regional Research*, *40*(1), 164–80.

Walker, Richard, & Buck, Daniel. (2007). The Chinese road: Cities in the transition to capitalism. *New Left Review*, *46*, 39–46.

Walks, R. Alan. (2006). Aestheticization and the cultural contradictions of neoliberal (sub)urbanism. *Cultural Geographies*, *13*(3), 466–75.
Wallace, Jeremy. (2014). *Cities and Stability: Urbanization, Redistribution, and Regime Survival in China*. Oxford: Oxford University Press.
Wallace, Jeremy L. (2016). Juking the stats? Authoritarian information problems in China. *British Journal of Political Science*, *46*(1), 11–29.
Wang, Manqi, Zhang, Fangzhu, & Wu, Fulong. (2022). Governing urban redevelopment: A case study of Yongqingfang in Guangzhou, China. *Cities*, *120*, 103420.
Wang, Ying, & Clarke, Nick. (2021). Four modes of neighbourhood governance: The view from Nanjing, China. *International Journal of Urban and Regional Research*, *45*(3), 535–54.
Wang, Zheng, Zhang, Fangzhu, & Wu, Fulong. (2016). Intergroup neighbouring in urban China: Implications for the social integration of migrants. *Urban Studies*, *53*(4), 651–68.
Wang, Zheng, Zhang, Fangzhu, & Wu, Fulong. (2017a). Affective neighbourly relations between migrant and local residents in Shanghai. *Urban Geography*, *38*(8), 1182–1202.
Wang, Zheng, Zhang, Fangzhu, & Wu, Fulong. (2017b). Social trust between rural migrants and urban locals in China–Exploring the effects of residential diversity and neighbourhood deprivation. *Population, Space and Place*, *23*(1), e2008.
Wang, Zheng, Zhang, Fangzhu, & Wu, Fulong. (2020). The contribution of intergroup neighbouring to community participation: Evidence from Shanghai. *Urban Studies*, *57*(6), 1224–42.
Webster, Chris. (2001). Gated cities of tomorrow. *Town Planning Review*, *72*(2), 149–69.
Webster, Chris. (2002). Property rights and the public realm: Gates, green belts, and Gemeinschaft. *Environment and Planning B*, *29*(3), 397–412.
Webster, Chris, Glasze, Georg, & Frantz, Klaus. (2002). The global spread of gated communities. *Environment and Planning B*, *29*(3), 315–20.
Webster, Chris J., & Lai, Lawrence W. C. (2003). *Property Rights Planning and Markets: Managing Spontaneous Cities*. Cheltenham: Edward Elgar.
Webster, Chris, Wu, Fulong, & Zhao, Yanqin. (2006). China's modern gated cities. In G. Glasze, C. Webster, & K. Frantz (Eds), *Private Neighbourhoods: Global and Local Perspectives* (pp. 153–69). London: Routledge.
Wellman, Barry, & Leighton, Barry. (1979). Networks, neighborhoods, and communities. *Urban Affairs Quarterly*, *14*, 363–90.
Whyte, Martin K., & Parish, William L. (1984). *Urban Life in Contemporary China*. Chicago: University of Chicago Press.
Wijburg, Gertjan, Aalbers, Manuel B., & Heeg, Susanne. (2018). The financialisation of rental housing 2.0: Releasing housing into the privatised mainstream of capital accumulation. *Antipode*, *50*(4), 1098–1119.
Wirth, Louis. (1938). Urbanism as a way of life. *American Journal of Sociology*, *40*, 1–24.
Wissink, Bart. (2019a). Enclave urbanism in China: A relational comparative view. In R. Yep, J. Wang, & T. Johnson (Eds), *Handbook on Urban Development in China* (pp. 171–86). Cheltenham: Edward Elgar.
Wissink, Bart. (2019b). Learning from Chicago (and LA)? The contemporary relevance of western urban theory for China. In R. Forrest, J. Ren, & B. Wissink (Eds), *The City in China: New Perspectives on Contemporary Urbanism* (pp. 61–80). Bristol: Bristol University Press.
Wissink, Bart, & Hazelzet, Arjan. (2012). Social networks in 'neighbourhood Tokyo'. *Urban Studies*, *49*(7), 1527–48.
Wissink, Bart, Hazelzet, Arjan, & Breitung, Werner. (2014). Migrant integration in China: Evidence from Guangzhou. In F. Wu, F. Zhang, & C. Webster (Eds), *Rural Migrants in Urban China: Enclaves and Transient Urbanism* (pp. 99–120). London: Routledge.
Wong, Cecilia, Qiao, Miao, & Zheng, Wei. (2018). 'Dispersing, regulating and upgrading' urban villages in suburban Beijing. *Town Planning Review*, *89*(6), 597–621.
Wong, Siu Wai. (2015). Land requisitions and state–village power restructuring in southern China. *The China Quarterly*, *224*, 888–908.
Wong, Siu Wai. (2016). Reconsolidation of state power into urbanising villages: Shareholding reforms as a strategy for governance in the Pearl River Delta region. *Urban Studies*, *53*(4), 689–704.
Wong, Siu Wai, Tang, Bo-Sin, & Liu, Jinlong. (2018). Village redevelopment and desegregation as a strategy for metropolitan development: Some lessons from Guangzhou City. *International Journal of Urban and Regional Research*, *42*(6), 1064–79.

Woodman, Sophia. (2016). Local politics, local citizenship? Socialized governance in contemporary China. *The China Quarterly, 226*, 342–62.

Woodworth, Max D., & Wallace, Jeremy L. (2017). Seeing ghosts: Parsing China's 'ghost city' controversy. *Urban Geography, 38*(8), 1270–81.

Wu, Fulong. (1996). Changes in the structure of public housing provision in urban China. *Urban Studies, 33*(9), 1601–27.

Wu, Fulong. (1997). Urban restructuring in China's emerging market economy: Towards a framework for analysis. *International Journal of Urban and Regional Research, 21*(4), 640–63.

Wu, Fulong. (2002a). China's changing urban governance in the transition towards a more market-oriented economy. *Urban Studies, 39*(7), 1071–93.

Wu, Fulong. (2002b). Real estate development and the transformation of urban space in Chinese transitional economy: With special reference to Shanghai. In J. R. Logan (Ed.), *The New Chinese City: Globalization and Market Reform* (pp. 154–66). Oxford: Blackwell.

Wu, Fulong. (2003). Transitional cities. *Environment and Planning A, 35*(8), 1331–38.

Wu, Fulong. (2004a). Urban poverty and marginalization under market transition: The case of Chinese cities. *International Journal of Urban and Regional Research, 28*(2), 401–23.

Wu, Fulong. (2004b). Transplanting cityscapes: The use of imagined globalization in housing commodification in Beijing. *Area, 36*(3), 227–34.

Wu, Fulong. (2005). Rediscovering the 'gate' under market transition: From work-unit compounds to commodity housing enclaves. *Housing Studies, 20*(2), 235–54.

Wu, Fulong. (2007a). The poverty of transition: From industrial district to poor neighbourhood in the city of Nanjing, China. *Urban Studies, 44*(13), 2673–94.

Wu, Fulong (Ed.). (2007b). *China's Emerging Cities: The Making of New Urbanism*. London: Routledge.

Wu, Fulong. (2008). China's great transformation: Neoliberalization as establishing a market society. *Geoforum, 39*(3), 1093–6.

Wu, Fulong. (2009a). Neo-urbanism in the making under China's market transition. *City, 13*(4), 418–31.

Wu, Fulong. (2009b). The state and marginality: Reflections on Urban Outcasts from China's urban transition. *International Journal of Urban and Regional Research, 33*(3), 841–47.

Wu, Fulong. (2010a). Gated and packaged suburbia: Packaging and branding Chinese suburban residential development. *Cities, 27*(5), 385–96.

Wu, Fulong. (2010b). How neoliberal is China's reform? The origins of change during transition. *Eurasian Geography and Economics, 51*(5), 619–31.

Wu, Fulong. (2010c). Property rights, citizenship and the making of the new poor in urban China. In F. Wu & C. Webster (Eds), *Marginalization in Urban China: Comparative Perspectives* (pp. 72–89). Basingstoke: Palgrave Macmillan.

Wu, Fulong. (2011). Retreat from a totalitarian society: China's urbanism in the making. In G. Bridge & S. Watson (Eds), *The New Blackwell Companion to the City* (pp. 701–12). Oxford: Blackwell.

Wu, Fulong. (2012). Neighborhood attachment, social participation, and willingness to stay in China's low-income communities. *Urban Affairs Review, 48*(4), 547–70.

Wu, Fulong. (2015). *Planning for Growth: Urban and Regional Planning in China*. London: Routledge.

Wu, Fulong. (2016a). China's emergent city-region governance: A new form of state spatial selectivity through state-orchestrated rescaling. *International Journal of Urban and Regional Research, 40*(6), 1134–51.

Wu, Fulong. (2016b). Emerging Chinese cities: Implications for global urban studies. *Professional Geographer, 68*(2), 338–48.

Wu, Fulong. (2016c). Housing in Chinese urban villages: The dwellers, conditions and tenancy informality. *Housing Studies, 31*(7), 852–70.

Wu, Fulong. (2016d). State dominance in urban redevelopment: Beyond gentrification in urban China. *Urban Affairs Review, 52*(5), 631–58.

Wu, Fulong. (2018a). Housing privatization and the return of the state: Changing governance in China. *Urban Geography, 39*(8), 1177–94.

Wu, Fulong. (2018b). Planning centrality, market instruments: Governing Chinese urban transformation under state entrepreneurialism. *Urban Studies, 55*(7), 1383–99.

Wu, Fulong. (2020a). Emerging cities and urban theories: A Chinese perspective. In D. Pumain (Ed.), *Theories and Models of Urbanization* (pp. 171–82). Switzerland: Springer.

Wu, Fulong. (2020b). Scripting Indian and Chinese urban spatial transformation: Adding new narratives to gentrification and suburbanisation research. *Environment and Planning C, 38*(6), 980–97.

Wu, Fulong. (2020c). The state acts through the market: 'State entrepreneurialism' beyond varieties of urban entrepreneurialism. *Dialogues in Human Geography*, *10*(3), 326–29.

Wu, Fulong. (2022). Land financialisation and the financing of urban development in China. *Land Use Policy*, *112*, 104412.

Wu, Fulong, Chen, Jie, Pan, Fenghua, Gallent, Nick, & Zhang, Fangzhu. (2020). Assetisation: The Chinese path to housing financialisation. *Annals of the American Association of Geographers*, *110*(5), 1483–99.

Wu, Fulong, & He, Shenjing. (2005). Changes in traditional urban areas and impacts of urban redevelopment: A case study of three neighbourhoods in Nanjing, China. *Tijdschrift voor Economische en Sociale Geografie*, *96*(1), 75–95.

Wu, Fulong, He, Shenjing, & Webster, Chris. (2010). Path dependency and the neighbourhood effect: Urban poverty in impoverished neighbourhoods in Chinese cities. *Environment and Planning A*, *42*, 134–52.

Wu, Fulong, & Logan, John. (2016). Do rural migrants 'float' in urban China? Neighbouring and neighbourhood sentiment in Beijing. *Urban Studies*, *53*(4), 2973–90.

Wu, Fulong, & Phelps, Nicholas A. (2011). (Post-)suburban development and state entrepreneurialism in Beijing's outer suburbs. *Environment and Planning A*, *43*(2), 410–30.

Wu, Fulong, & Shen, Jie. (2015). Suburban development and governance in China. In P. Hamel & R. Keil (Eds), *Suburban Governance: A Global View* (pp. 303–24). Toronto: University of Toronto Press.

Wu, Fulong, & Wang, Zheng. (2019). Moral order in the post-socialist Chinese city: Generating a dialogue with Robert E. Park's 'The City'. In R. Forrest, J. Ren, & B. Wissink (Eds), *The City in China: New Perspectives on Contemporary Urbanism* (pp. 41–60). Bristol: Bristol University Press.

Wu, Fulong, & Webber, Klaire. (2004). The rise of 'foreign gated communities' in Beijing: Between economic globalization and local institutions. *Cities*, *21*(3), 203–13.

Wu, Fulong, & Webster, Chris (Eds). (2010). *Marginalization in Urban China: Comparative Perspectives*. Basingstoke: Palgrave Macmillan.

Wu, Fulong, Webster, Chris J., He, Shenjing, & Liu, Yuting. (2010). *Urban Poverty in China*. Cheltenham: Edward Elgar.

Wu, Fulong, Xu, Jiang, & Yeh, Anthony Gar-On. (2007). *Urban Development in Post-reform China: State, Market and Space*. London: Routledge.

Wu, Fulong, & Zhang, Fangzhu. (2022). Rethinking China's urban governance: The role of the state in neighbourhoods, cities and regions. *Progress in Human Geography*, *46*(3): 775–97.

Wu, Fulong, Zhang, Fangzhu, & Liu, Yuqi. (2022). Beyond growth machine politics: Understanding state politics and national political mandates in China's urban redevelopment. *Antipode*, *54*(2), 608–28.

Wu, Fulong, Zhang, Fangzhu, & Webster, Chris. (2013). Informality and the development and demolition of urban villages in the Chinese peri-urban area. *Urban Studies*, *50*(10), 1919–34.

Wu, Fulong, & Zhou, Lan. (2013). Beautiful China: The experience of Jiangsu's rural village improvement program. In J. Colman & C. Gossop (Eds), *Frontiers of Planning: Visionary Futures for Human Settlements* (pp. 156–69). The Hague: ISOCARP.

Wu, Liangyong. (1999). *Rehabilitating the Old City of Beijing: A Project in the Ju'er Hutong Neighbourhood*. Vancouver: University of British Columbia Press.

Wu, Qiyan, Edensor, Tim, & Cheng, Jianquan. (2018). Beyond space: Spatial (Re) production and middle-class remaking driven by Jiaoyufication in Nanjing City, China. *International Journal of Urban and Regional Research*, *42*(1), 1–19.

Wu, Weiping. (2006). Migrant intra-urban residential mobility in urban China. *Housing Studies*, *21*(5), 745–65.

Xiang, Biao. (2017). The dilemma of formalisation: Beijing Zhejiang Village and the changes of Chinese society in the last twenty years. *The 21st Century* (in Chinese), *159*(2), 81–97.

Xu, Mengran, Wu, Fulong, & Li, Zhigang. (2022). Understanding the intergroup relations of migrants in China. *Population, Space and Place*, *28*(2), e2540.

Xue, Desheng, & Wu, Fulong. (2015). Failing entrepreneurial governance: From economic crisis to fiscal crisis in the city of Dongguan, China. *Cities*, *43*, 10–17.

Yan, Yunxiang. (2003). *Private Life under Socialism: Love, Intimacy, and Family Change in a Chinese Village, 1949–1999*. Stanford, CA: Stanford University Press.

Yan, Yunxiang. (2010). The Chinese path to individualization. *The British Journal of Sociology*, *61*(3), 489–512.

Yang, You-Ren, & Chang, Chih-hui. (2007). An urban regeneration regime in China: A case study of urban redevelopment in Shanghai's Taipingqiao area. *Urban Studies*, *44*(9), 1809–26.

Yeh, Anthony Gar-On, Xu, Xueqiang, & Hu, Huaying (1995). The social space of Guangzhou city, China. *Urban Geography*, *16*(7), 595–621.

Yeh, Wen-Hsin. (2008). *Shanghai Splendor: Economic Sentiments and the Making of Modern China, 1843–1949*. Berkeley: University of California Press.

Yep, Ray, & Forrest, Ray. (2016). Elevating the peasants into high-rise apartments: The land bill system in Chongqing as a solution for land conflicts in China? *Journal of Rural Studies*, *47*, 474–84.

Yep, Ray, & Wu, Ying. (2020). How 'peasant apartments' could undermine rural governance in China: Spatial realignment, moral reconfiguration and local authority. *The China Quarterly*, *242*, 376–96.

Yip, Ngai-Ming (Ed.). (2014). *Neighbourhood Governance in Urban China*. Cheltenham: Edward Elgar.

Yip, Ngai-ming, & Jiang, Yihong. (2011). Homeowners united: The attempt to create lateral networks of homeowners' associations in urban China. *Journal of Contemporary China*, *20*(72), 735–50.

Yu, Hai, Chen, Xiangming, & Zhong, Xiaohua. (2015). Commercial development from below: The resilience of local shops in Shanghai. In S. Zukin, P. Kasinitz, & X. Chen (Eds), *Global Cities, Local Streets: Everyday Diversity from New York to Shanghai* (pp. 59–89). New York: Routledge.

Zhan, Yang. (2021). Beyond neoliberal urbanism: Assembling fluid gentrification through informal housing upgrading programs in Shenzhen, China. *Cities*, *112*, 103111.

Zhang, Donia. (2013). *Courtyard Housing and Cultural Sustainability: Theory, Practice, and Product*. Farnham, UK: Ashgate.

Zhang, Li. (2001). *Strangers in the City: Reconfiguration of Space, Power, and Social Networks within China's Floating Population*. Stanford, CA: Stanford University Press.

Zhang, Li. (2010). *In Search of Paradise: Middle-Class Living in a Chinese Metropolis*. Ithaca: NY: Cornell University Press.

Zhang, Li, & Ong, Aihwa (Eds). (2008). *Privatizing China: Socialism from Afar*. Ithaca, NY: Cornell University Press.

Zhang, Li, Zhao, Simon X. B., & Tian, Jie P. (2003). Self-help in housing and Chengzhongcun in China's urbanization. *International Journal of Urban and Regional Research*, *27*(4), 912–37.

Zhang, Xudong. (2008). *Postsocialism and Cultural Politics: China in the Last Decade of the Twentieth Century*. Durham, NC: Duke University Press.

Zhang, Yunpeng. (2018). Domicide, social suffering and symbolic violence in contemporary Shanghai, China. *Urban Geography*, *39*(2), 190–213.

Zhao, Chunlan. (2004). From shikumen to new-style: A rereading of lilong housing in modern Shanghai. *The Journal of Architecture*, *9*(1), 49–76.

Zhao, Yanjing, & Webster, Chris. (2011). Land dispossession and enrichment in China's suburban villages. *Urban Studies*, *48*(3), 529–51.

Zheng, Siqi, Long, Fenjie, Fan, C. Cindy, & Gu, Yizheng. (2009). Urban villages in China: A 2008 survey of migrant settlements in Beijing. *Eurasian Geography and Economics*, *50*(4), 425–46.

Zhou, Mujun. (2014). Debating the state in private housing neighborhoods: The governance of homeowners' associations in urban Shanghai. *International Journal of Urban and Regional Research*, *38*(5), 1849–66.

Zhou, Yu, Lin, George C. S., & Zhang, Jun. (2019). Urban China through the lens of neoliberalism: Is a conceptual twist enough? *Urban Studies*, *56*(1), 33–43.

Zhu, Jieming. (2002). Urban development under ambiguous property rights: A case of China's transition economy. *International Journal of Urban and Regional Research*, *26*(1), 41–57.

Zhu, Jieming. (2019). *Urban Development in China Under the Institution of Land Rights*. London: Routledge.

Zhu, Yushu. (2020). Interests driven or socially mobilized? Place attachment, social capital, and neighborhood participation in urban China. *Journal of Urban Affairs*, 1–18. https://doi.org/10.1080/07352166.2020.1773837.

Zhu, Yushu, Breitung, Werner, & Li, Si-ming. (2012). The changing meaning of neighbourhood attachment in Chinese commodity housing estates: Evidence from Guangzhou. *Urban Studies*, *49*(11), 2439–57.

Index

acquaintance 1, 11, 20, 53, 65, 67, 107, 157, 162, 207, 216, 233, 249
activism 198, 241
aesthetics 186, 259
alienation 40, 70, 99, 111, 252,
  see also anomie
alleyways 7, 30, 66–7, 73, 103–4,
  housing 22, 59, 62–5, 68, 71, 80–1, 85, 105–7, 172, 216,
  neighbourhoods 4, 18, 40, 45–6, 51, 58, 60–1, 75, 100, 102, 114, 207, 223, 225, 231, 249, 256
  in urban village 34, 139, 120, 145, 138
Ancestor hall 153–5, 168
anomie 47, 236, 238
  see also alienation
anonymity 39, 51–2, 67, 238
Ant tribe (*yizu*) 19, 136, 138, 141, 261
arcade housing (*qilou*) 88, 90
assemblage 20, 227–9, 231, 238, 240, 254
assimilation, 165, 244
authoritarianism 8, 10, 14, 19, 55–6, 114, 169, 247–8, 253–4, 262, 267, 269, 272
autonomy 12, 38, 118, 212, 220, 239

Baiwanzhuang, Beijing 32, 69
Baojia 3, 14, 52
bargained authoritarianism 253–4, 262
  see also authoritarianism
Beautiful China 130
Beijing Sun City 177, 180, 188
Bestor, Theodore 61, 91, 108, 110
BOT (build-operate-transfer) 89
Bracken, Gregory 64
Brenner, Neil 39, 56, 230–1, 245
bureaucratisation 3, 5, 8, 10, 29, 40, 53, 99, 249

Caoyang New Village, Shanghai 70–2
Castells, Manuel 8, 39
Chaxugeju (the differential mode of association) 1–2, 16–17, 21, 52–3, 197, 214–15, 217, 233, 256, 260
Chicago School 8, 38–9, 46–7, 157
Chongqing Tiandi, Shanghai 83–4
  see also Xintiandi
citizenship, 134–5, 161, 254, 265, 269
civil society 4, 8–10, 13, 20, 103, 169, 196, 208, 212, 237, 244, 250, 238, 260, 266

clan organisation 136, 144, 151, 153
  see also lineage
club governance 176, 196, 215
  see also club realm
club realm 195, 254
  see also club governance
clubhouse 82, 178, 182, 203, 207
co-renting (*qunzu*) 107–8, 122
cohesion 163, 243
  neighbourhood 109, 243, 268
  social 208
collective
  action 128, 136, 196, 201, 214, 225
  assets 96, 142, 144, 167, 168, 201, 224, 255
  consumption 8, 9, 39, 51, 69, 109, 111–12, 191, 224, 258
  economy, 67, 85, 95–6, 108, 128, 168
collectively owned land / collective land 138, 143–4, 152, 163, 167, 224
collectivism 1, 19, 38, 40, 45–6, 125–127, 130, 164, 174, 177, 186, 194, 196–7, 206–8, 212, 214–17, 224, 239, 240, 243, 250–1, 255–6, 260–1
commodification 26, 45, 48–9, 95, 101, 165, 169, 173, 186, 223, 229, 233, 250, 251, 266
community building 12, 52, 202
  see also community construction
community centre 97, 244
community construction 18, 67, 99, 103, 113, 220, 251, 260
  see also community building
conjunctural approach, 235
conservation 76, 78–80, 82
  see also preservation
consumer revolution 14–15, 21, 77, 220, 224, 238, 250
  see also consumerism
consumerism 6, 12, 15, 29–30, 219, 242–3, 253, 257–8
  see also consumer revolution
cosmopolitan / cosmopolitanism 6–7, 11, 66, 234
courtyard 7, 18, 51, 58–9, 66, 77, 79, 81, 100, 104, 107
  housing 30, 63–4, 76, 78, 101, 172
covenants, contracts and restrictions (CC&Rs) 175–6, 179, 194, 213
creative industries 50, 54, 85, 88
cultural quarter 85

dancing 241–4
Daning Park 242
Daning Plaza, Zhaibei District 30
Dashalar, Beijing 79
Davis, Deborah 13, 14, 219, 220
decorative gate 178, 180, 188
deeds 131, 200
demolition 45, 46, 48–9, 55–6, 60, 68, 76–7, 79, 81, 86–90, 93, 103–106, 112, 115, 121, 136–8, 141, 143, 149, 155, 158, 164, 166, 177, 217, 222–3, 249, 255–7
densification 7, 58, 64, 66, 75, 107, 117, 148
development corporation 48–50, 147, 149, 157, 177–8
development zones 13, 149, 170
  see also industrial zones
dilapidated neighbourhoods (laojiu xiaoqu) 60, 73, 92
displacement 49, 50, 79, 87, 104–5, 144, 256–7
dormitory 35, 118, 133, 245
double movement 251–2
Durkheim, Emile, 47, 236, 238
dystopia 47, 207, 240

earth-bounded society 1, 2, 4, 7, 8, 17, 21, 53, 111
East Asia 61, 109, 114, 237, 251, 255
Eastern Europe / European 8, 11–12, 39
economic development land / economic reserved land 151, 168
enclave urbanism 195, 240
enclosed estates (fengbi xiaoqu) 36, 136, 256
enclosed management 130, 158
Enning Road, Guangzhou 88, 90–1
entitlement failure 165
entrepreneurial governance / state / local state 49, 79, 96, 108, 196, 237, 253
ethnic community 134
  see also ethnoburbs
ethnic enclaves, 237
  see also immigrant enclaves
Ethnoburbs 134
  see also ethnic community, ethnic enclaves,
Exceptionalism 235
Exotic landscapes 191, 233
  see also transplanted landscapes

Fei, Xiaotong 1–2, 16–17, 20–2, 46, 52, 197, 213, 232, 250, 256, 260
Fifth Village, Nanjing 15, 18, 48, 73–5, 92, 96–7, 102, 104, 107–9, 156, 252
financialisation 50, 128, 235
fire hazard 122–3, 136, 139
Fire, Daxing district, Beijing 256
  see also fire hazard
flexible labour regime 134
floating population 44, 160, 164
formalisation 44, 94, 113, 149, 171, 225, 275
Frazier, Mark, 22, 72, 249
French concession areas 6, 81, 83, 117

Gans, Herbert 239
Gaojiabang, Shanghai 19, 119, 133, 145–50, 157, 168, 170
garment workshops / business / manufacturers 131–136

gated communities 16, 19–20, 24, 28–9, 33, 37, 41, 43–60, 72–3, 113, 128, 130, 154, 158, 163–4, 172–9, 183–7, 189, 191–210, 212–8, 223, 225, 231, 234, 236–7, 239, 241, 243, 245, 249, 257, 258–9
gentrification 18, 45, 48, 50, 60, 73, 79, 104–108, 111, 115–6, 149, 256
gentry 3, 4, 69, 105
Glass, Ruth 104, 111, 256
global South 117, 120, 143, 156, 210, 222, 234–5, 237–8, 249, 255
gossip 51, 65, 67, 112
governmentality 227, 232
grade (dangci) 179, 210
grid governance / management 18, 98–9
guanxi (relation) 2, 21, 41, 129, 134–135, 170, 174, 208, 261, 263
gyms 208, 243–4

Hancunhe, Beijing 124–6, 196
Harvey, David 39, 245, 258
He, Shenjing 86
heritage preservation 78, 259
homeowners' association 29, 37, 46, 128, 175–6, 183, 196, 198–200, 204–5, 216, 224–5, 261, 276
Hongkou Football Stadium, Shanghai 184–5
housing commodification 26, 48–9, 101, 173, 186, 223
housing plots (zaijidi) 149, 160
Howard, Ebenezer 72
Hsing, You-tien 127, 251
Huajin, Wuhan 93–4, 110
Huang, Youqin 184, 194–5
hutong (alleyways) 18, 30, 58, 62–3, 76–9, 100

immigrant enclaves 165
incremental redevelopment (weigaizao) 49–50, 60, 88, 91, 93–4
India 4, 119, 222, 227
individualisation 20, 40, 111, 114, 174, 186, 195, 206–7, 212, 214, 239, 243, 253, 260
individualism 2, 216, 195
industrial zones 232
  see also development zones
industrialisation without urbanisation 17, 40, 228, 237, 255
informal rental 63, 105, 117, 120, 151, 159–60, 173, 223, 238
informal tenancy 159–60
informalisation 105, 117, 129, 130, 249
informality 11, 105, 120, 129, 143–4, 156, 158–9, 164, 167, 169, 225, 235, 238–9, 242, 249
inner urban areas 52, 28, 60, 62, 64, 65, 67, 75, 100, 206, 242–3
international settlements 5, 6, 82, 117
IT migrants 137

Jessop, Bob 259
Jiading new town, Shanghai 190
Ju'er hutong, Beijing 18, 77–8

Kaixiangong Village 4, 20, 232, 260
Kan, Karita 127
Keynesianism 254
Knox, Paul 186

278   INDEX

land appropriation 117, 127, 183
land development quota, 222–3
land rights transfer 222
Li, Jie 7, 61, 64, 67
Li, Zhigang 25, 133
Liang, Samuel 69, 82
Liede, Guangzhou 19, 144, 1146, 148, 150–7, 168
Lilong (lanes) 30, 58, 63, 80, 83–4, 100
  see also longtang
Lin, George 252
Linan Tiandi, Guangzhou 83
lineage 2, 15, 21, 114, 125, 127, 155, 163, 165, 197, 224, 233, 239–40, 247, 249, 260
  see also clan organisation
Little Hubei, Guangzhou 131–2, 133–6, 162, 164
little urbanites 66, 117–19, 165
local state corporatism 247
  see also village corporatism
Logan, John 28, 108, 161–2, 171
Longtang (lanes) 30, 66
  see also lilong.
Low, Setha 194–5, 205
Lu, Hanchao 84, 118
Lujiazui Financial and Trade Zone, Shanghai 27, 50

Ma, Laurence 5, 126, 135–6
management committee (*guanweihui*) 149
market coordination 251
market society 2, 14, 61, 238–9, 248, 251
market transition 248, 257, 259, 266, 268–9, 274
mentality (also social mentality) 18, 38–40, 42, 45–8, 114, 176, 187, 226
micro-district (*xiaoqu*) 12, 36, 37, 40, 70–3, 75, 101, 172, 209, 216
middle class 6, 7, 17, 19, 26, 29, 36, 44, 46, 48, 51, 53, 61–2, 66, 77, 79, 85, 91, 105–6, 112, 114, 117, 119, 120, 128–9, 137, 154, 163, 173–4, 188, 191, 200, 208, 212, 216, 234, 244, 256, 258, 259
migrant enclaves 19, 26, 134, 157, 162
migrant integration 27
  see also social integration
mikroraion 259
  see also micro-district
Ming Dynasty 58, 68
minimum livelihood guarantee (*dibao*) 97, 203
model communities 70
modernisation 5, 44, 99, 162
moral order 2, 4, 15, 19, 38, 39, 41, 44, 65, 117, 128, 134, 157, 160, 241, 249
  see also morality
morality 3, 135, 170
  see also moral order

Nanchizi, Beijing 18, 77–8
Nanluoguxiang, Beijing, 18, 78–9
native places / the same place of origin (*laoxiang*) 19, 129, 134, 200, 240
nature of cities 20, 219, 226, 231, 245

neighbourhood interaction 7, 33, 43, 72, 108, 160, 162, 166, 212
  see also neighbourly interaction
neighbourhood participation 46, 49, 93–4
  see also social participation.
neighbourhood planners 93
neighbourhood services 52, 94–6, 103, 229
neighbouring 11, 31, 33, 44, 46, 100, 109, 111, 161, 162–3, 166, 171, 189, 225, 238
  see also neighbourly interactions
neighbourly interaction 43, 44, 207
  see also neighbourhood interaction, neighbouring
neo-traditionalism 4, 7, 9, 11–12, 14, 17, 53, 55, 61, 72, 95, 111, 176, 194, 216, 220, 224, 229, 237, 256
neoliberal urbanism, 250, 254, 260
neoliberalisation, 113, 258–9
  see also neoliberalism
neoliberalism 113, 116, 235, 247, 250–1, 252, 254
  see also neoliberalisation
networked society 253
New town 136, 141–2, 144, 150, 169, 189–90, 232, 245, 261
new urbanism 189, 190, 258
Ningde, Fujian province 47

Occidental City 4
Old and Dilapidated Housing Redevelopment, Beijing 75–6
Orange County, Beijing 20, 37, 187–8, 190, 233, 259
organised dependence 9, 33

pandemic 99, 252
Park, Robert 38, 157, 209
parochialism 38, 40, 244
particularism 9, 10, 20, 41, 125, 234–5, 237, 249
Pearl River Delta 54, 131, 170, 255
Peck, Jamie 235, 246, 250
Perry, Clarence 72
place attachment 42, 44–6, 124, 196, 207–9, 225, 233
planetary urbanisation 230, 231, 236–7, 240, 255
planning 7, 8, 36, 64, 70, 72, 81, 93, 140, 149, 217, 251
  socialist planning, 58, 216
  city planning, 12, 106, 118, 167, 128, 175
plot ratio 77, 152, 154, 174, 182, 211, 217
plotting urbanism 178, 210
Polanyi, Karl 21, 171, 238, 250, 252, 261
Polanyian (turn, perspective, argument) 21, 171, 250, 252, 261
political society 237, 250
populism 252
postcolonial 129, 143, 227, 234, 237, 250
preservation 50, 60, 63, 76, 78–80, 82, 84, 87, 89, 90, 110, 156, 259, 263
  see also heritage preservation, conservation
privacy (personal, residential) 7, 19, 20, 44, 46, 51, 52, 65–7, 70, 77, 110, 154, 163, 174, 177, 189, 192, 203, 206–7, 209, 210, 212, 261

INDEX 279

private governance 16, 19, 36, 47, 128, 168, 172–3, 175–6, 193, 194–5, 204, 207, 210, 213, 215, 224, 234, 236, 250, 253, 258, 260
production brigades 118, 127, 224
professionalisation 18, 52, 94, 99, 113, 156, 199, 260
property certificates 144, 151
property disputes 37, 204
property management company / companies 20, 37, 51, 90, 91, 96, 98, 107, 136, 138, 155, 175, 179, 182, 194, 198–9, 200–203, 212–3, 223, 225
property management fees 203, 205–6
property rights 19, 20, 37, 41, 46, 48, 105, 125–8, 131, 132, 144, 152, 155–7, 160, 163, 164, 170–1, 176, 196, 198, 201, 203, 206, 209, 215, 221, 225, 233, 235, 241
property-led redevelopment 48–9, 79, 85–7, 91, 213–5, 233–4, 237, 241
public housing tenants 25, 89, 106, 168, 174
public space 79, 93, 96, 98, 167, 175, 200, 201, 204, 207, 241, 243, 258
public-private partnership 90
Purple Jade Villas, Beijing 184
Putnam, Robert 236

Qing Dynasty, 58 63

reciprocal relations 40, 41, 113, 114, 162–5, 229, 233
regeneration 49–50, 60, 61, 82, 86–7, 90
    culture-led 50
    see also property-led redevelopment
regulation by exception 156
rehabilitation 48, 76–7, 91
relocation 25–6, 28, 48, 74–5, 89–90, 108, 112, 141–2, 151, 215, 249, 257
rental housing 26, 33–5, 42, 44, 60, 63, 89, 106, 117, 120–3, 126, 128, 138–40, 142–4, 147–8, 151, 156, 158–60, 163, 168, 170, 173, 210, 223–4, 238, 255
resettlement housing 142, 144, 153, 183, 199, 213, 225
residential
    differentiation 6, 15, 19, 21, 24–6, 29, 50, 51, 53, 55, 62, 104, 169, 210, 232, 267
    fragmentation 101–2
    landscape 17, 23, 24–6, 195, 231, 259
    mobility 29, 35, 40, 61, 100, 134, 160, 240
    segregation 25–9, 46, 51, 165, 248, 257
residents' committees 10, 26, 30, 52, 72, 96, 97–9, 109, 114, 118, 155–6, 199, 208
retirement estate 180
rightful resistance 225, 233
Robinson, Jennifer 234, 245
Roy, Ananya 156, 227, 234, 238
rural consolidation 222

Schmid, Christian 39, 56, 230–1, 245
Scott, Allen 226, 228–9, 231, 235, 245
security guards 74, 103, 180, 182–3, 205
self-governance 3, 20, 52, 74, 99, 108, 113, 135, 176, 182–3, 193, 202, 212–5, 217, 228–9
self-help 94, 114, 128
    housing 120

self-protection 18, 21, 113, 205, 251
Shanghai nostalgia 62, 66, 83, 228, 231, 259
Shantou 35, 211, 221
Shantytowns 62, 74, 92
Shequ (residential communities) 52, 94, 97, 110, 116, 144, 168, 178, 216
Shikumen 6, 7, 30, 62–4, 80–1, 83–6, 119, 234, 276
Shin, Hyun Bang 78
Simmel, George 38, 240, 246
Skinner, William 2
slums 6, 58, 62, 70, 108, 118–9, 122, 235
small property rights housing 125–6, 131–2, 144
Smith, Neil 48, 258
Smith, Nick 248
social
    capital 42, 44, 46, 165–6, 181, 203, 209, 212, 236
    integration 33, 43, 44–5, 112, 163–6
    mobilisation 49, 108, 153, 198, 202–3, 241
    network / networks 1, 13–14, 43, 102, 110, 160, 240, 244, 249
    participation 42, 44, 93, 108, 124, *see also* neighbourhood participation
Socialised governance 99
socialist city 8, 9, 11–12, 17, 39, 40, 51, 61, 68, 70, 228, 253
socialist man 40, 259
Soho, New York 85
Shanghai (Hongkou) 105
Solidarity 20, 43–6, 110, 134, 194, 196, 201
Song Dynasty 4, 52
spatial fix 39, 228, 259
specificity 230, 236, 256
split households 222, 264
Spring and Autumn Annals of Wu and Yue 226
squatter 117–8, 120, 146, 156
state apparatus 14, 18, 53, 114, 164, 253
state entrepreneurialism 21, 157, 239, 257, 261
Storper, Michael 226, 228–9, 231, 235, 245
subaltern urbanism 235, 250
subdivision 58–9, 70, 104, 107, 118–9, 148, 187, 212
suburban commodity housing estates 45, 100, 223
suburbia / post-suburbia 236, 259
Sun, Liping 9, 112
Szelenyi, Ivan 53

Tang, Beibei 98
Tangjialing, Beijing 19, 124, 129, 136–48, 168–9, 256, 261
tenancy contract 158–60
tenure security 160
    see also tenancy contract
territorial management 98, 164
Thames Town, Shanghai 37, 189, 190, 259
the right to the city 119, 165, 238
third realm 234
three in one (*sanheyi*) 13, 131
three-olds regeneration (*sanjiu gaizao*) 87, 143, 152

Tianjin Road, Shanghai 59, 63, 66
Tiantong Road, Shanghai 59, 65
Tianzhifang, Shanghai 84–6
toilet 122–3, 140, 216, 258
Tokyo 61, 91, 108, 110
Tönnies, Ferdinand 2
totalised society 15, 17, 19, 21, 33, 51, 53, 60, 99, 109, 112–13, 118–19, 128–9, 166, 168, 169, 174, 203, 206, 208, 220, 236, 254
township and village enterprises (TVEs) 13, 126, 247
tragedy of the commons 126
translocal network 131 134, 240
transplanted landscape 186, 190
  see also exotic landscapes
treaty-port cities 5–7, 18, 62, 117
trust / social trust 238, 240

uniformity 257, 258
urban experience 227, 258
urban renewal 47–8, 63, 75–6, 81, 86–8, 90, 102, 106, 112, 116, 120, 149, 183, 223, see also rehabilitation, shantytown renewal
urban revolution 12, 16–17, 19, 20, 169, 221–2, 243, 247, 254–7, 260–1
urban villages (*chengzhongcun*) 3, 15, 18–19, 25, 29, 33–5, 40, 42, 44–7, 53–4, 60, 87, 104, 106–8, 117, 119–24, 128–36, 138, 140, 144, 148, 151, 155–69, 173, 175, 182, 201, 209, 223–4, 231–4, 237–9, 245, 248–9, 255–7
urbanity 18, 186, 190, 225, 228, 238, 241, 245, 248, 255

Vanke 89, 90–1, 142
village corporatism 127, 130, 164
  see also local state corporatism
village shareholding cooperative / company 108, 126, 136, 144, 151–2, 157, 168, 201, 229, 247, 261
voluntary organisation 112, 201
volunteers / volunteering 11, 93, 99, 193

Wacquant, Loïc 165
Walder, Andrew 9, 10–11, 14, 22, 61, 89, 115, 248, 258
Wang, Anyi 65
Weber, Max 4, 5
Weberian sense / idea 1–2, 18, 114
Webster, Chris 125
Wenzhou 133, 136, 181–3
white-collar apartment 140
Wirth, Louis 1, 38, 157
Wissink, Bart 110, 240
work-unit (*danwei*) 6, 8–10, 14, 17–18, 24, 26, 29, 30–4, 37, 38, 48–9, 51–5, 58, 60–2, 68–75, 91–6, 99, 103–4, 106, 108–9, 111–12, 114, 118–19, 134, 172, 176, 197, 200, 210, 216, 252, 254, 274
  see also workplace
workplace, 11, 14, 18–20, 24, 33, 40, 42–3, 45, 51, 58, 60–1, 68–70, 75, 76, 91–2, 99, 100–09, 111–13, 115, 134, 139, 172, 176, 191, 193, 196, 208, 216, 223–5, 231, 233, 234, 242, 248–9, 252, 258
  see also work-unit
workshop of the world 12, 26, 255
Wuxi 232

Xiaba Village, Dongguan 54
Xihu Tiandi, Shanghai 83
Xintiandi, Shanghai 48, 68, 73, 80–5, 91, 220–1, 241, 259

Yamen 3, 5–6, 228
Yeh, Anthony Gar-On 24
Yongqingfang, Guangzhou 16, 88–91, 116
  see also Enning Road, Guangzhou

Zhang, Jun 250, 252
Zhang, Li 136, 174, 197
Zhao, Chunlan 64
Zhejiang village, Beijing 119, 133, 136, 138, 162, 164, 166, 169
Zhou, Yu 252
Zhucun, Guangzhou 34
Zuopu Road, Shanghai 31

Lightning Source UK Ltd.
Milton Keynes UK
UKHW051259151122
412241UK00016B/102